SIGNATURES

SIGNATURES

Literary Encounters of a Lifetime

DAVID PRYCE-JONES

BOOKS

NEW YORK · LONDON

First American edition published in 2020 by Encounter Books,
an activity of Encounter for Culture and Education, Inc.,
a nonprofit, tax exempt corporation.
Encounter Books website address: www.encounterbooks.com

Manufactured in the United States and printed on
acid-free paper. The paper used in this publication meets
the minimum requirements of ANSI/NISO Z39.48—1992
(R 1997) (*Permanence of Paper*).

FIRST AMERICAN EDITION
LIBRARY OF CONGRESS CATALOGING-IN-PUBLICATION DATA

Names: Pryce-Jones, David, 1936– author.
Title: Signatures: literary encounters of a lifetime / David Pryce-Jones.
Other titles: Literary encounters of a lifetime
Description: New York: Encounter Books, 2020. | Includes index. | Summary:
Identifiers: LCCN 2019043396 (print) | LCCN 2019043397 (ebook) |
ISBN 9781641770903 (cloth) | ISBN 9781641770910 (ebook)
Subjects: LCSH: Pryce-Jones, David, 1936– | Pryce-Jones, David, 1936—Friends
and associates. | Authors—20th century—Biography. |
Intellectuals—20th century—Biography. | Literature, Modern—20th century. |
History, Modern—20th century. | Civilization, Modern—20th century.
Classification: LCC PR6066.R88 Z46 2020 (print) |
LCC PR 6066.R88 (ebook) | DDC 828/.91409—dc23
LC record available at https://lccn.loc.gov/2019043396
LC ebook record available at https://lccn.loc.gov/2019043397

CONTENTS

For Alan

1908—2000

WITH LASTING AFFECTION

DIC NOBIS MARIA QUID VIDISTI IN VIA

PREFACE

THE CONVENTION IS that if you happen to meet authors and
have just bought or acquired a book of theirs, you ask them to
sign it. Particularly stuffy authors might refuse but in most cases
they feel flattered and duly inscribe your name and theirs on the
title page or the flyleaf of the book in question. If the mood is right,
they may add "with best wishes" or something of the sort. At a super-
ficial level, of course, such signatures are only the equivalent of an
autograph album. There's more to it than that, however. Added value
perhaps, but association certainly. The human race lives by the stories
we tell ourselves about our identity and our purposes, and that signature helps to make the author's story part of the reader's story.

Signatures is autobiographical in the sense that I'm looking at
the story I tell myself about how I have come to be who I am. The
story that my parents told of themselves is of course the point of
departure. They had started their married life in Meidling, a district
of Vienna, in a house built by Gustav Springer, a successful mag-
nate and grandfather of my mother Poppy. By the time I was born
in Meidling in 1936, my father Alan Pryce-Jones had published five
books. Some who stood round my cradle said, David, that's a lovely
Welsh name, and others said, David, that's a lovely Jewish name.
Alan liked to say that my first spoken word was Gorki, as though I
were already picking up on Russian writers.

My generation in Europe had to deal with the fact that the whole
continent had first almost gone Nazi and then almost gone Soviet
Communist. By 1940, the Gestapo had expropriated Meidling, and
Austria was occupied enemy territory. Nothing was ever again going
to be what it had been. A good many of the authors who signed a

book of theirs for me are survivors from the Age of Dictators, and I wanted to know what they'd been through and how they'd survived.

After the war, Alan became editor of the *Times Literary Supplement*, and in one or two rooms of the house books piled up on the floor waiting to be read. Authors sent him their books for review, quite often writing something relevant and revealing on the title page. He introduced me to people I would never have met otherwise and by now these signed copies seem to me like tickets of admission to the select company attempting to make sense of this world.

SIGNATURES

MAHMUD ABU SHILBAYAH

La salaam

ARABIC, NOT DATED

AFTER THE SIX DAY WAR of June 1967 was over, I spent a lot of time on the West Bank and in Gaza. For the previous twenty years, British Palestine had been divided between Israel, Egypt and Jordan. Now that the parts were re-united under Israeli jurisdiction, my assumption was that the moment was bound to have come for a treaty settling the relationship between Israelis and the Arabs. Moshe Dayan, the Minister of Defence, announced that he was waiting for a telephone call. Flippant though it was, the remark reveals the value system that has been operating for a long time throughout the Western world to give political reality to the conclusions of the battle-field. Victor and vanquished decide how to conduct themselves, the one reacting to the propositions of the other in a process akin to bargaining that is strictly rational and inclining to democracy. Dayan's telephone did not ring because Arabs have a value system that is not just different but totally incompatible, and it too has been in operation a long time. The high and mighty as well as the poor and humble have to gain honor and avoid shame because these values determine what people will think of them. Defeat at the hands of Jews is a shame so absolute that only military success is able to wipe it away. What is at issue here is status, something personal and irrational, not open to measurement or bargaining, and inclining to dictatorship.

Arabs of course have ways of making peace. Harold Ingrams, a British official in the days of empire, describes in his memoir *Arabia and the Isles* his career of treaty-making between warring Arab tribes, a process so delicate and personal that it might well last several generations. Those involved have to be men of experience and authority, ceaselessly attentive to the imperatives of shame and honor for victors and vanquished alike. If they were to conduct themselves according to the Israeli value system, they would have become self-declared losers, disgraced by the shame of it and immediately rejected by their people.

The 1967 war had left the inhabitants of the West Bank and Gaza pretty much in a state of shock. Fearing the worst, more than a hundred thousand of them had fled their homes and were refugees in Jordan. Some houses had been wantonly destroyed in the small town of Qalqilya, but otherwise the war had been almost a formality and there was nothing to fear. It was safe to go anywhere and to talk to anyone.

The formation of public opinion was the business of a few individuals generally referred to as notables. Qadri Tuqan, the el-Masris, Hamdi Kanan, Sheikh Ali Ja'abari from Hebron, Rashad Shawa the mayor of Gaza, were men of experience and authority. They had handsome houses in which a room or two was furnished with seating along every wall. It didn't seem to matter if discussion fell silent and there was nothing for it except another cup of coffee. Friendship and rivalry were hard to distinguish. Some thousands have the surname Barghouti, for example, but which one speaks for the family or is it for the tribe? At the time, all they could do was to insist that the Israelis withdraw unilaterally from the territories that had just been fought over and then they, the Palestinians, would see what to do next.

The values of shame and honor dictated what to the Israelis was simply the demand for an undeserved gift, tantamount to saying that no costs had to be paid either for starting a war or for losing it — something contrary to every Western treaty ever signed. Those same values were evident when, a few months after the end of the war, self-selected Arab representatives met in Khartoum and passed a resolution that there could be no peace, no negotiation, no recognition of Israel. As the issue became one of honor and shame, local notables and their followers no longer had the prerogative to determine their future. A political vacuum was created which the various groups in favor of armed struggle and terror made haste to fill, and continue to do so right up to the present.

At the time, Mahmud Abu Shilbayah was one of the leading Palestinian intellectuals on the West Bank. In person he was a little overweight, his face framed by heavy spectacles and a keffiyeh. His book has a paper cover with the red, white and green of the Palestinian flag on it, giving it the look of a clandestine publication when in fact it is the usual evocation of nationalism as the solution to everything. We sat in a café in East Jerusalem while I tried to explain that in the absence of anything like the social structure of a nation, his nationalism was bound to remain a literary abstraction and nothing could come of it. Nevertheless, on the title page he wrote, "To my friend David Pryce-Jones hoping my people will get a real peace."

HAROLD ACTON

More Memoirs of an Aesthete

1970

DURING THE WAR, I had an initial impression of Harold Acton when he came to stay for quite some time with my parents, Alan and Poppy. Their house had been destroyed in the blitz, and they rented a flat in Athenaeum Court in Piccadilly, conveniently close to the War Office, where Alan was then at work. For fear of being buried alive, Poppy refused to go down to a shelter. In my memoir *Fault Lines* I have described how night after night we sat in the dark with the windows open as a precaution against blast. This was apocalypse worthy of John Martin, the visionary painter. Searchlights fitfully illuminated the room, relieving all of us in silhouette. Against the rolling roar of the bombers and the crash of anti-aircraft guns,

Harold taught us Chinese to help pass the time. He sang Chinese songs learnt in the Thirties when he lived in Peking, as he persisted in calling it. From then until the end of his life, "*nin how*," the Mandarin for "How are you?" was as good as a password.

I was seventeen when I first went to La Pietra, the house on the Via Bolognese in Florence that Harold had inherited from his father, Arthur Acton. Every visit was entertaining, wonderfully operatic. A gnarled old lodge-keeper in rustic clothes and a floppy hat spent a lifetime opening the gate at the entrance. Then as now, cypresses lined the long straight drive, and the heraldic coat of arms of a Renaissance cardinal adorned the imposing façade. A manservant would be waiting at the front door. The house seemed to exist in some timeless sphere of its own, uncompromisingly Italianate.

Harold always received guests in the same cramped corner of one of the reception rooms with a view on to the garden at the back of the house. Spindly uncomfortable chairs formed a tight semi-circle, and Hortense, Harold's mother, used to perch on one of them, a doll-like presence in a black dress set off by a necklace of prodigious pearls. At that first meeting, I knew already that she had given orders to lock up all entrances to the house at nine o'clock at night, so if Harold was not yet home, he would have to climb in through a window as though still an Oxford undergraduate caught by college rules. I also knew that she habitually had one cocktail too many. Supposedly she had once failed to notice a guest committing some frightful social solecism, because, as Harold said in a much-quoted sentence, "Mother was far too far gone on one of her own concoctions."

Harold himself might have stepped straight out of a novel by Ronald Firbank. His upper body swayed and teetered as if the balls of his feet were unbalancing him or he were altogether unaccustomed to walking. Half-closed brown eyes had a gleam of mockery in them, though it was impossible to decide whether this was directed at himself or at you. A permanent twist of a smile and exceptional shiny baldness gave his head the air of a helmet, or in another image, a giant puffball. In a measured sibilant voice, sounding like a foreigner who has learned the English language a bit too perfectly, he might resort to long-lost idiom, for instance saying of someone, "He gives me the pip," or flattering an overweight lady that she was "light as thistle-down." When he told the well-worn story of Brian Howard accosting an exhausted officer returning in 1940 from the collapse in France with the words, "Dun-kerkie didn't work-ie," he was almost singing rather than speaking. A producer in New York once proposed that I interview Harold for the sake of preserving this vocabulary and the extraordinary register of his voice. Harold refused on the grounds that the film's hidden intention was to laugh at him.

I had the impression that in China he had felt himself to be a free spirit, which was why Norman Douglas, another original, had advised him to leave "the frowzy and fidgety little hole called Europe." In the Thirties, my parents-in-law, Harold and Nancy Caccia, had been at the British Embassy in Peking and could describe how at some cultural event this other Harold had once sat on a platform, struck a pose with hand on brow and recited a poem including the line, "I smack the wax hermaphrodite with lilies white and cool." Occasionally he made remarks obscurely implying that in China he had encountered romance. "No, I shall not be visiting Positano," he once said to me, "I might be filled with youthful lust." When Selina Hastings was researching her biography of Nancy Mitford, he had provided her with some material. In the draft she sent him was some remark about Harold "and his bugger friends." Infuriated, he threatened to sue unless this was cut out, saying, "What do these young women know about my private life?"

His style on paper was at least as mannered as his speech. The images in his poems are forced, the words strained and sometimes outlandish. Within a few pages of *The Indian Ass*, his first book of poems, for instance, among many words that dissipate all sense are *vavicel, bakkaris, lappered morphews, ruin-glooms*. No other English writer could have written "Narcissus to His Sponge" (from *This Chaos*, 1930) a poem that begins "This golden sponge, like porous apricot" [porous?] and concludes with the unsurpassable couplet, "Mark this humble square of soap, O poet and abandon hope."

In his view, he had played his part in an aesthetic movement along with the likes of Gertrude Stein, Nancy Cunard, Caresse and Harry Crosby, Countee Cullen and Thornton Wilder. World events have long since overtaken the interwar years and driven the fun of it into oblivion. Published in 1928, Harold's novel *Humdrum* was once a high-water mark of the period, only to become, he confesses, "a book which makes me blush." Reviewing *More Memoirs of an Aesthete*, I risked a phrase about how yesterday's literary experiments become today's hardened arteries. For a long time afterwards he quoted it back to me, with that sly ambiguous smile.

La Pietra imposed the obligations of a great house, a way of life that Harold was determined to live up to. Whatever the weather, he wore a suit with a waistcoat, and I never saw him without a tie. He became a living legend. Tourists would ring up asking which restaurants in Florence he recommended. He held lunch parties in a dining room whose collection of statues, one of them reputedly a Donatello, had the appeal of a museum. John Calmann, my Oxford contemporary and a publisher then negotiating the reprint of Harold's book about the later Medicis, told me that on a visit he had counted no less than eighteen knives and forks, glasses, plates and whatnots, laid at the place on the table where that evening Harold was dining by himself. Violet Trefusis, a grey eminence in Florentine society, one day asked why the statues in the garden were encased in what looked like plastic nappies. A feline Harold took her up, explaining in detail that their private parts were being refigured by experts in Sweden familiar with the proper proportions of gentlemen.

Joan Haslip wrote biographies for the general reader and entertained friends in her house in Bellosguardo as extravagantly as she would have done before the war. A typically feline throwaway of Harold's was, "Joan's books are so fresh because every subject comes fresh to her." When in old age she ran out of money, Harold in an equally typical gesture gave her a picture by Foujita, which she sold for eighteen thousand pounds.

Escorting a very famous film star around the house, Harold spotted that she was a kleptomaniac, slipping whatever she could into her handbag. "And now, my dear," he said inimitably at the conclusion of the tour, "we shall restore the missing trinkets." Every summer, Princess Margaret invited herself to stay. The state bedroom was on the first floor with a Vasari hanging over the bed. A demanding guest, she once said as she was leaving that Harold would now dance and sing for joy. "Oh no, ma'am," he answered, "much too tired." After dining with Anne-Sophie and Michael Grant near Lucca, I was driving Harold home on a minor road with nobody and nothing in sight when the engine suddenly cut out and the car came to a stop. Histrionically he said, "Shall I whistle and clap my hands?" I had only to push in the choke, the flooded engine started, and we drove back in the misty night.

SIDNEY ALEXANDER

Marc Chagall

1988

UNWILLING TO RETURN to her native Vienna after the war, my grandmother, née Mitzi Springer, settled instead in a farmhouse that previous owners had beautified into a villa on the hilltop in Florence known historically as Pian dei Giullari. She died in December 1978. Her heirs, of whom I was one, had generally agreed to sell up. We met there on a day whose silence and sunlight promised perpetual enchantment, and unanimously we took the contrary decision to stay.

Sidney and Frances Alexander were among the first friends we made in Florence. Good hosts and good guests, they lived near the Porta Romana. Large and bulky, Sidney dominated any room, delighting in telling stories with laughter in them. Having served in the war with the American army in Italy, he had stayed in the country ever since, another in the throng of gifted expatriates who have treated Italian literature, music and art as their own. As a side-line and for a fee, he played the flute at weddings. He gave me a copy of his biography of Marc Chagall, recently published at the time. Frances later made it plain that they were both hurt because I then failed to respond to the book. This was partly thoughtlessness and partly because I found something bogus about Chagall's folksiness. They forgave my thoughtlessness.

Sidney was the author of several definitive books about Michelangelo, and one day he took Clarissa and me on a guided tour of the great man's works in Florence. As he spoke in front of statues and tombs, passers-by gathered around to listen to the impromptu seminar. The secret of Michelangelo's greatness, according to Sidney, is that he treated Yes and No as complementary rather than opposites, and he quoted the poem that makes the point. Outside the Accademia he delivered a parting shot, "Modern art is the definition of bogus." In due course he sent me his translations of Guicciardini, the sixteenth-century historian who feared that the Ottoman Turks would invade Italy, and *The Complete Odes and Satires of Horace*. I took my time to write an appreciation of the last admirable book – too much time, as it turned out. Frances let me know that my letter arrived a day or two after Sidney had died.

SVETLANA ALLILUYEVA
Twenty Letters to a Friend
1967

SVETLANA KNEW VERY WELL that she would always be an object of curiosity. What could it be like to be the daughter of Stalin, a world-historical figure who had sent untold millions to their death, including her mother and then her husband? Her defection to the West was a political sensation. In the Eighties and Nineties, she made do in England without family, without home and without money. Some of those in the circles in which I moved got to know her and did what they could for her. Linda and Laurence Kelly, both of them writers with an interest in Russia in its tsarist and its Soviet form, may have begun by feeling pity for her, but this became genuine friendship. Svetlana had been living in an old peoples' home in London before moving to Abbeyfield Home at St Ives in Cornwall, a modern equivalent of the workhouse. When she paid a visit to the Kellys in London, they invited Clarissa and me to meet her. Entering the room, she looked at us with suspicion. There was something secretive but militant about her. She wasn't her father's child for nothing.

Cornwall, Svetlana said with feeling and in her idiomatic English, was the Grand Duchy of Baboons. She was glad to be about to leave the baboons and return to the United States, to Wisconsin, in order to be close to her daughter Olga. However, she regretted that she had not had occasion to go to Wales. Olga had married someone born there. On the spur of the moment, Clarissa offered to show her the country. She refused point-blank. Clarissa had read Svetlana's description of Stalin's death and asked a question about it. "I don't speak about my father" was the angry rejoinder.

Svetlana knew nothing about Clarissa and me except what the

Kellys could tell her. Laurence said, "You've really blown it," but a few weeks later Svetlana decided to stay with us in Wales after all. It was an adventure. I think the three of us were equally surprised to have made a rendezvous at four o'clock one afternoon in the Swan Hotel at Hay-on-Wye. We were late collecting her. In the car, I told her not to expect too high a standard of comfort at Pentwyn, our farmhouse on the edge of Eppynt, which is unspoilt moorland stretching into the distance. She asked, "Does it have running water?" She did not draw curtains; she liked cold bedrooms and warm bathrooms. In the morning she stayed in her room writing, coming down only at lunchtime. After the meal I made sure to write up as closely as possible everything she'd said; her direct speech is quoted from my diary.

Why was I interested in Russia, she wanted to know. The country was gloomy and defeated. Boris Yeltsin, then in the Kremlin, was "a drunken peasant applying a few Communist managerial skills." The Russians now swarming in the West seemed to her "rats and mice leaving a sinking ship." She praised Nikita Khrushchev "for the way he tried to eliminate the KGB but in fact they pulled themselves together and eliminated him." His son-in-law's memoirs make no mention of the Twentieth Congress speech and she didn't read any book based on Soviet archives.

She had heard of the suicide of the author Jerzy Kosiński and thought that if he — and her own mother — could do it, so could she. She went to London Bridge but was wearing a tight skirt that she was hoisting when a red-faced man, perhaps a priest, stopped her and said, "Oh you godless people." The police escorted her home. She came to believe that her mother was sending her a message.

Her mother had decided to divorce Stalin but there had been no arrangements for the children, and so in spite of herself Svetlana reached the permanent black hole of her emotions. Stalin was a monster but she couldn't help loving him and couldn't help talking about him either. He "wasn't the sort of man who'd have parted with his daughter." In her childhood, he'd come hurrying down the Kremlin corridors at the end of a hard day's work, calling for his little princess and making sure she was doing her homework. He insisted that she learn languages. She quoted Lorca and Heine: "Fünfundzwanzig Professoren, Vaterland, du bist verloren."

Those around her father gave him bad advice, she maintained, but it was his personal belief that Hitler would keep his word. Nobody else in Russia trusted Hitler. "When the Nazis invaded on June 22, my father shut himself away for three days. Not till July 2 could he bring himself to talk to the nation on the radio. With my own ears I heard him say afterwards that Russia and Germany ought to stick together as nobody could resist that combination. He always admired the Germans."

Suddenly here she was saying that as her father lay dying, a half-blind old nurse broke an ampoule of glucose into a spoon and was putting some of the glass shards into Stalin's mouth. "Voroshilov took the nurse's arm in horror. Then they insisted on x-raying his lungs when they should have kept him prone. It was chaotic. The only one who kept his head was Beria. Well, he was more cunning than my father. He used to tell him what he wanted, and my father listened, he didn't stop him, he was powerless." (Not an adjective that comes to mind for Stalin. Throughout, she talked of him as small, insecure and nervous about his health; his ears hurt in an aeroplane and he didn't like flying.) What a brute Beria had been, she repeated. Marshal Zhukov had been the instrument for destroying him. She had a friend, General Vishnievsky, who afterwards came and told her, "Imagine, Beria who was so pitiless to others knelt on the floor and pleaded for his life. But they took him out into the yard quickly and shot him."

It was the last week of October, with frost on the ground and mist in the Wye valley. We drove to the tiny village of Rhulen to show Svetlana something of Wales. An early Christian church stands on a pre-historic stone circle, and she sat in one of the church pews as if to pray but a mood overtook her. Perhaps she did not like Clarissa taking a photograph of her; she complained that she felt a "heaviness"; she sneezed, and we rushed her home.

Once we were back, she picked up my copy of her book *Twenty*

Letters to a Friend and annotated a great many pages. On the flyleaf she stuck a photograph of her mother wearing an expression of suffering worthy of a medieval Russian icon. The inscription reads, "To David with admiration from Svetlana Alliluyeva," and she added, signing with her married name, "P.S. Forgive my notes and corrections but those were necessary — L. Peters."

She then read my novel *The Afternoon Sun*, saying that "she didn't think she could be interested in Vienna [the setting] only to find that the writing was 'condensed' and that gave a sense of order." My diary further records that Svetlana and Clarissa spent a morning "making a chicken soup, with fresh coriander, a Turkish recipe with a name something like *chitzima*." Also that we had invited our neighbors Hugo and Felicity Philipps to dinner in spite of — or because of — the fact that his grandfather Lord Milford had been the first and only Communist peer in the House of Lords. Svetlana crept out of the room without a word. Coming down to breakfast the next day, she apologized that she had been too tired to bid goodbye to the guests.

A two-hour drive after nightfall and we said goodbye to her in the Bristol central bus station, seeing her off to Cornwall. One final entry in my diary: "She's a dumpy, grumpy, feisty old thing, *attendrissante*, a natural victim coming up for more and not sure how or why things have turned out so that she is standing in a queue of anorak-clad Baboons on their way to Plymouth and Penzance. 'C'est une Babooness,' she nods towards the girl behind the counter and then at a child kicking her hold-all. What percentage of the world is Baboon? I asked. 'Seventy five.' She smiles and it's warm but at the centre of those blue eyes of hers are black pinpricks, little lasers."

Postscript. Spring Green, Wisconsin, offered Svetlana the company of Olga, welfare benefits, a sympathetic public library and a settled routine until she died. Her pastime was writing letters. Loopy, scrawling handwriting covered untidy sheets of A4 paper made untidier still by marginal comment, interjections, cross-references and second thoughts in or out of context. I never managed to find out the truth or falsehood of her complaints. In her telling of it, lawyers and trusts had deprived her of the money her books had earned; publishers had rejected four autobiographical manuscripts; George Kennan and a slew of American officials had let her down. The tone swung between resignation and rage. She put pressure on me to write to a Swiss lawyer by the name of Peter Hefter to ask where her copyrights now rested and whether they would revert to Olga. At least my letter would make his day unpleasant, she concluded. Mr. Hefter, sounding weary, replied that the necessary explanations had already been done.

Linda Kelly had much the same correspondence; we used to compare notes and planned at one time to make a book out of our boxfuls. Linda gave me several of her books with inscriptions, notably *Holland House*, where radicals with or without private fortunes habitually met and spread each other's ideas in what looks like an early nineteenth-century prototype of the BBC. Laurence inscribed for me *Diplomacy and Murder in Tehran,* his biography of Griboyedov whose dramatic death at the hands of the Persian mob caused an international crisis of a kind that has become all too familiar. He finally summed up the whole tragedy of Svetlana in the two words of the Latin tag, *damnosa hereditas.*

KINGSLEY AMIS

The Folks That Live on the Hill

1990

TAKING A LEAD from pundits and polls, the public pretty much expected Harold Wilson to defeat Edward Heath in the general election of 1970. I had a contract to write for the *Daily Telegraph* Colour

For David

When he goes to Spain

from his ancient friend

W Somerset Maugham

St Jean-Cap Ferrat.
7 april 1953.

Magazine, and so I was invited to the party that Michael Berry, then the owner of the *Telegraph*, made a point of hosting after every election, from the moment the voting closed until the last constituencies declared. The party was in the ballroom of the Savoy Hotel. At the far end of the room, various larger-than-life Snows and Dimblebys dominated a giant television screen. Among those at the table with me was Ken Tynan, elegant in a white tuxedo with a bright red tie and in his buttonhole a matching red carnation. There could be no mistaking his allegiance or his expectation. I had imagined that Ken had to be clever but not very nice, only to discover that he was not at all clever but quite nice, if mostly to those celebrating the political orthodoxies of the hour. Borrowing from Rossini, I took to thinking of him as *un barbier' di qualità*.

Also at that table was Kingsley Amis. The novelist David Lodge had given me (and signed too) a reprint of an essay he had published in the *Critical Quarterly* arguing that Amis might go in for comedy but nonetheless had a "sardonic sense of literary tradition," and therefore was in the company of Henry James and James Joyce, no less. At the same time, he could make a crack like "Change means worse." The results of the voting began to trickle in and suddenly it became apparent that the Conservatives were making gains and might well win. Tynan looked very stony and Kingsley stood up on his chair and then on the table, whereupon he danced a sort of fandango and shouted, "Show the shaggers!" and "Five more years outside barbed wire!"

The opening lines of a poem written to mark a milestone birthday seem true to Kingsley's perception of himself: "Fifty today, old lad? / Well, that's not doing so bad:/ All those years without / Being really buggered about." A private dinner party at which we were guests, and so were Kingsley and his then wife Elizabeth Jane Howard, yielded a similar outburst of his core personality. The lady on his right said that she had just finished reading his new novel and didn't think it was as good as his previous novels. Sitting at a round table with a glass top, we all could see Kingsley's knuckles whitening as he clenched his fists, and then he barked at the top of his voice, "Fuck you!"

On another occasion, at dinner in our house, Kingsley lectured on the importance of not joining the Common Market. My diary notes him saying: "We don't want anything to do with those people. The French are bastards, the Germans are bastards, most of the Italians are too. Two and a half bastards want to get hold of us. As for the little countries, Belgium 'is just a little sod.' He's in thrall to the monosyllables, yet I caught him on the BBC saying what a pleasure it had been to discover the music of Albinoni."

Another diary entry, dated February 1964, describes Kingsley coming to the office of the *Spectator* to organize a letter of protest to the *Times*. (I was then the literary editor, David Watt the foreign affairs correspondent and Joan the telephone operator.) "Flitting from room to room, he borrows a pound off David Watt, off Joan, off the managing director, the fatuous Mr Elliott. 'I've got a girl downstairs, a bit tight, who I'm screwing. . . . At about two thirty he wants to take the boys out to lunch. He is wearing a green fake-Austrian leather jacket with silver buttons and a red leather tie. 'Rather natty.' The boys are David Watt and myself. The girl downstairs is Elizabeth Jane Howard. We go to the Greek restaurant on Whitfield Street. Amis drinks most of a bottle of retsina and then another of Greek brandy. We leave, pulling him out, at four. 'What's the hurry?' he blurts. He insists on paying from a roll of fivers. In the street he asks us if we know how arctic explorers shit. 'It's been bothering me for a long time.' He explains how they have reversible trousers, take them on and off in layers. Incoherent and laughing at himself: 'The turd is frozen hard, you see.'"

My diary continues, "Amis ringing me about the Aldous Huxley book on Science and Literature. 'I had a glance through it this morning on the john, it's no bloody good at all.'"

WILLIAM ANDERSON

Translation of Dante,
La Vita Nuova

PENGUIN CLASSICS, 1964

G OING UP TO OXFORD IN 1956, I expected to meet brilliant
contemporaries. There were a few, and Bill Anderson was
one of them. Another was Dennis Potter, a village Robespierre who
spread throughout the university his hostility to everyone from a
background different to his but who in the end wrote television plays
of reconciliation. In Bill's college, Exeter, was Alan Bennett, whose
natural gift for playing the class system was to redirect him from a
career as a medieval historian into a national treasure, the master
presenter of social grudge as art. Bill's thin features had strain or ner-
vousness in them, but he was tougher than he looked. The slightly
screechy voice could be thought affected, and he let you know that
he was smoking and inhaling deeply. His movements gave the impression that he was late for some important meeting.

Bill was a genuine aesthete. His mother was a choreographer,
and during her pregnancy with Bill she had been working on Bizet's
suite *L'Arlésienne*. To hear this music as an adult, Bill liked to say,
returned him to the snug safety of the womb. His father had been
killed in Normandy towards the end of the war. Bill had no money
but it never seemed to matter. The whole point was to discover
how to approach the civilization created by the great writers and
artists, and then contribute to it oneself. This was a rejection of the
Stalinist and philistine orthodoxies of the university. I'd not previously heard of many of the sources from which Bill took inspiration,
for instance Robert Graves's *The White Goddess* or Owen Barfield who

apparently had theories about literature worth following up. As an undergraduate, Bill was already a complete Dante enthusiast, and his book *Dante the Maker*, published some twenty years later, is one of the best defenses of the high culture of Europe. In a circle of like-minded friends were Robert Symonds, a poet, and John Calmann, who wrote a verse play in five acts about Frederick the Great. When it was time for finals, I crammed Bill and two others into my Morris Minor and we drove to Llanthony, on the Welsh border. Next to the ruined abbey is a pub that then had no electricity. Revision by candlelight was a fitting envoi to Oxford.

Soon after graduating, I had a job as literary editor of *Time and Tide*, a weekly magazine then in the hands of Tim (afterwards a Lord as well as a vicar in the Church of England) Beaumont, descendent of the man billed as the richest commoner in England. The editor, John Thompson, particularly urged me to discover and publish people setting out on a literary career. Bill's poetry had an unfashionable humanist spirit that went against the grain of the times. He was for things beautiful and against things ugly, and the passion of it over the years led him to write about cathedrals, castles, the Green Man, a biography of the artist Cecil Collins, and finally a wide-ranging book about the creative imagination. In order to pay his way, he was employed full-time writing and editing the publications of a major medical charity. He once complained to me of pain between the shoulders, in his words "the stab in the back that all writers have." The last time we met, he knew that he would very soon die from cancer of the lungs brought on by smoking. Following surgery, he had almost completely lost his voice.

The aesthetes were unfortunate. Robert Symonds died young from some inherited genetic flaw, John Calmann was murdered by someone he'd picked up on a motorway in France, and Bill never received the recognition that is his due.

NOEL ANNAN

Our Age

1990

M Y PARENTS' HOUSE in London having been destroyed in
an air raid, they moved to Castle Hill Farm, a couple of miles
outside Tonbridge in Kent. I must have been about eight or nine when
Noel Annan came to stay. In my bed at night and about to fall asleep,
I became aware of his head bald and gleaming as he loomed over me
to give me a goodnight kiss on the forehead. Years were to pass before
I realized how fortunate I had been that he had done nothing more
to me. Devoid of scruples, he several times came sidling up to me at
some gathering and then adopted the confidential and slightly sor-
rowful manner that goes with imparting a nasty little secret, You do
know, don't you, that your father is consumed with jealousy because
you are writing the books he isn't writing. I have never heard another
laugh quite like his, braying and persistent, with no trace of mirth in it.

Writing my book about Cyril Connolly, I had his papers at my
disposal. And in them I found a handwritten letter from Noel
Annan, then Provost of King's College, Cambridge, compliment-
ing Cyril as a writer and critic in really fulsome, not to say exag-
gerated, language. As soon as Cyril died, however, Noel published a
long piece in the *New York Review of Books* rubbishing him as a failure in
life and literature. The toadying and back-to-back the duplicity is all
anyone needs to know about the man. The untranslatable French
expression *faux bonhomme* is an exact fit.

Postscript. Noel Annan's name came up at a meeting of the English
Faculty at Berkeley that I was obliged to attend though I was at
the university for only a summer semester. Thomas Parkinson, a

21

Hemingwayesque character, had tenure and I heard him utter what might serve as the definitive mixed metaphor. "Noel Annan? I never knew such bullshit from a horse's ass."

———

W. H. AUDEN
Collected Shorter Poems, 1927–1957
1966

THE NEWDIGATE PRIZE for poetry is awarded every year at Oxford. Those who enter for it have to write a poem to a title set by the judges, and in 1957 it was "Earthly Paradise." I was in my second term reading history at Magdalen College. My rooms were in the handsome New Building, famously misnamed because it dates from the eighteenth century. From my desk I had a view of the deer in the park. Images from childhood worked into the poem that I wrote and submitted.

One morning, there was a knock on the door and W. H. Auden entered and sat down heavily on the sofa. Professor of Poetry at the time, he was one of three judges of the Newdigate. I had never met him. Yours is much the best poem, he said, and I want you to know that I voted for it, but I couldn't persuade the other judges so I'm afraid you are only the runner-up.

In his lifetime, Auden became perhaps the best-known practicing poet in the English language, and John Anstey, editor of the *Daily Telegraph* Colour Magazine, commissioned me to write a profile of him. Auden lived in New York but spent summers in Kirchstetten, a village not far from St. Pölten in Lower Austria. "I should like to become, if possible, a minor Atlantic Goethe," was how he had come to speak of himself. In his speech, the American letter *a*, short where

Oxford would have it long, was a sign of his dual identity. His was a face like nobody else's, wrinkled and deeply furrowed all over like some animal's hide, possibly due to age but more likely to inner distress. "A wedding cake left out in the rain" was Dom Moraes's image for the devastated appearance. There was something awkward about him, nonplussed. Even out of doors, Auden could be seen shuffling about in carpet-slippers.

Receiving me at the house in Kirchstetten, Chester Kallman launched into a critique, evidently well prepared, of the village and its inhabitants. He had lived with Auden since before the war. To judge by his air of condescending superiority, he thought highly of himself. A smile stretched across his face making a disturbing feature of his teeth. Also in the house was a Greek teenager.

Auden was at work in what had been the loft of a farm building tacked on to one side of the house and converted into his study. The sole approach was up an external staircase of rickety wooden posts and planks that creaked when anyone trod on them and which led up to a retreat where he surely would not be disturbed. There on the desk were drafts of poems and sheets of paper with word games, acrostics and aphorisms. On a table lay the twelve massive volumes of the *Oxford English Dictionary*, one or two of them left open where presumably he had been engaged in his favorite sport of chasing rare usages and meanings. I also copied down a line of rhymes: blot, dot, jot, got, what. He gossiped about friends and contemporaries: Cyril Connolly, John Betjeman, John Sparrow the Warden of All Souls, and Hugh Gaitskell. Guy Burgess had been coming to stay with him when the scandal of his defection to Moscow broke. "Arthur Koestler, me no like-ee," he said, imitating the pidgin English supposedly spoken in the Orient. Why? I asked. "Underdog!" he said in a normal voice, as if that settled it.

At the end of the afternoon, Auden wobbled his way down the staircase and Chester Kallman gave him a martini, and ten minutes later another, and ten minutes after that a third. By the time Kallman and the Greek teenager had got him to bed, it was about half past seven and he was past making sense. They gave him a flask of Chianti, and he lay on his side sucking at it like a baby with a bottle, gurgling, splashing red wine now and again onto the sheets and over himself.

Next day, I gave them a lift to Vienna. Kallman was making up to the Greek teenager, with much laughter between them as they directed me to the gay bar where I was to drop them. Uninvited, left sitting by himself on a red plush sofa in Sacher's Hotel, Auden was a picture of distress.

BERYL BAINBRIDGE

Injury Time

1977

THE PUBLICATION OF *Young Adolf* brought Beryl Bainbridge into my life. For whatever reason, I failed to have her sign my copy, but she did sign two of her previous novels. That Hitler had spent some months before the First World War in Liverpool with his elder brother Alois was a fantasy that powerfully confused fact and fiction. Born and brought up in Formby, just outside Liverpool, she interpreted all experience as desolation stretching away into immeasurable distance.

She lived by herself in a part of London colonized by men and women much like her, talented in one or another of the arts. A creeper cloaked her house, and inside it was a junkyard. Stuffed animals in glass cases or under bell jars cluttered every space. Out of one wall jutted a plaster cast of a chorus girl's leg, from the Locarno Ballroom in Liverpool. A crucifix had been remodeled as a candlestick.

Her father, the youngest of nine children, had left school at the age of nine. "The general impression my mother gave was that he had married above himself." When she was eleven, she joined the Young Communists and later was briefly a Catholic. "I was terribly wanting my mother's approval but doing everything not to gain it." In 1954 she married, but her husband soon emigrated to New Zealand. His mother broke in and fired a revolver. On the stairs was the bullet hole, none too well replastered.

More often than not, a Bainbridge novel reaches its climax with a grotesquely contrived death. My copy of *Injury Time* contains a bundle of notes from our conversation, and one of them reads, "To have a sense of well-being destroys your personality." I coined a word for her: murderee.

ELLIOTT BAKER

The Penny Wars

1968

IN THE SUMMER OF 1968 and again in 1970, I taught creative writing at the California State College at Hayward, a wonderfully tidy suburb of San Francisco. Bob Williams, a member of the faculty, had arranged my invitation to Hayward. In 1964 he had spent a sabbatical year teaching at the Writers Workshop of the University of Iowa, where I was. We first met at a getting-to-know-you faculty party where he gave me a disquisition on the Yiddish word *putz*. Tequila was his drink because it had "no waste motion." Free spirits, he and his wife Hatch, more properly Harriet, had decided not to have children. Bob had published a couple of novels under his full name of R. V. Williams. He had come up the hard way. His father, a railway guard, had been a bigamist. In the war Bob had driven a landing craft at Salerno on D-Day, which entitled him to a college education paid for by the Fulbright program. If only he could have written as vividly as he talked about his experiences of battle.

Somehow, maybe through Bob Williams, Herb Caen, the gossip writer of the *San Francisco Chronicle,* heard that I was at Hayward and I believe it was through him that I was asked to do some reviewing for the paper. Elliot Baker's *The Penny Wars* was one of the novels I was sent. His first novel, *A Fine Madness,* had set him up as a writer from whom masterpieces could be expected. *The Penny Wars* apparently tells a tight story of relationships gone wrong, but much more profoundly is about America and Europe discovering one another in the shadow of Hitler. Baker, I wrote, allows his characters "to speak and laugh and cry for themselves," and that was something that "went out with the classics." Still, it might win him the honorific title to which he aspired, of Great American Writer.

Back in London, several years later, a letter arrived from Elliott. It turned out that he and Helen, his wife, had settled here and we lived only a few hundred yards apart. We took to meeting in a favorite café on Kensington High Street. The blueness of his eyes, the energy of his person, was telling. One day, he let drop that his real surname was Sukenik, though he was no relation of Yigael Yadin, the famous Israeli soldier and archaeologist, originally born Sukenik. And he also let drop that in 1945 he'd been in an infantry battalion engaged in the Battle of the Ardennes. Afterwards they'd all volunteered for a mission behind the German lines, killing SS concentration camp guards before they could kill their prisoners.

Elliott's conversation was like his books – you didn't know whether to laugh or cry. An obsessive gambler, at home in the lurid world of clubs and croupiers, Mafiosi, blackjack, odds and debts and threats, he committed himself to hackwork to pay for his losses.

Elliott had made a huge sum of money writing the script for *Lace,* a popular television series. Due to the time change with Hollywood, it was the middle of the night when the producer telephoned to commission the script of *Lace Two.* Elliott refused. Every twenty-four hours for several consecutive nights, the producer woke him up again, each time offering a million more. Finally he said, "Name what you'll do it for and that's positively my last offer." So Elliott became the best-paid scriptwriter in the United States. A very well-known lady romancer had a three-book contract for ten million dollars but didn't actually feel like writing the stuff. For a token ten thousand dollars Elliott ghosted one of her books in six weeks. And still his own books were written, mostly in his tragi-comic style, though *Klynt's Law* is slapstick that had me laughing aloud. A second obsession, more restricted than gambling but equally deranging, was the insoluble riddle of Shakespeare's identity.

In the end, he and Helen returned to the United States. We used to correspond. Modestly he made no claims, but I sensed his regret that time was running out and he wouldn't ever know whether or not he was accepted as a Great American Writer.

ARTURO AND ILSA BAREA

The Forging of a Rebel

1972

STRICTLY SPEAKING, I'm stretching a point, since the copy I have of this book is a French edition published by Gallimard in 1948, and he and Ilsa both signed it for my mother, "For Poppy with our love." They had married in 1938 when Arturo was press officer and censor for the Republicans in Madrid under attack from General Franco and the Falangists. Both of them were socialists but never Communists. John Dos Passos, one of the writers Arturo handled, described him in the siege as "underslept and underfed." Arturo also knew Hemingway well and had the integrity to say in a review of *For Whom the Bell Tolls* that, "as a novel about Spaniards and their war, it is unreal and, in the last analysis, deeply untruthful."

Arturo and Ilsa escaped to England and lived as freelance writers. She translated his books. In a review in September 1941 George Orwell paid him a compliment, for once rather awkwardly phrased: "One of the most valuable of the literary acquisitions that England has made as a result of Fascist persecution."

In the Sixties when I came to know Ilsa, I was a literary editor and she was a publisher scouting for manuscripts. She had survived too much hardship to be sentimental, and it showed in the tough set of her face. Poppy was already dead by then, yet Ilsa used to make something of the fact that she, Poppy and I had all three been born in Vienna. Her own book baldly titled *Vienna* and subtitled *Legend and Reality* is the last word on the history and inhabitants of that equivocal city. At the age of sixteen, in 1918, she took part in a political demonstration just as the Habsburg monarchy was falling. Troops opened fire, some students in the front line fell and the young man marching next to her immediately ran away down a side street, continuing to run until at last he reached the safety of New Zealand, and he would have run still farther if he could have. That was Karl Popper, she said, who'd been so traumatized by this ordeal that his great book *The Open Society* was intended to ensure there'd be no repeat.

SYBILLE BEDFORD

A Legacy

1973 REPRINT

"THE LITERARY SCENE ought to glow with bright mysterious personalities like Sybille Bedford," I once wrote, "but rarely does so." Her father, a German count, had the aristocratic virtue of keeping himself to himself. Grandfather Herz was eminent, cosmopolitan and Jewish. For the sake of the fiction, she changed the family name to Merz. There was a trace of a foreign accent in the way she rolled the letter *r* in her speech. The characters she writes about call each other Mammina, Caro, Herr Baron and Principessa, and it is taken for granted that civilized people speak the major European languages. "La bêtise n'est pas mon fort," is a saying of hers: stupidity is not my strong point.

Evelyn Waugh was the first to point out that she was neither nostalgic nor apologetic. Continuing to give primacy to personal feelings and fates, she brought the past into the present. Her fiction has an afterglow, like Lampedusa's *The Leopard*. She's been in love with Aldous and Maria Huxley and other famous men and women, but it was difficult to extract from her anything about them. No name-dropping.

She took pride in her knowledge of wine, paying her way by buying twenty or thirty cases *en primeur*, and waiting for the right moment to open one case and sell the rest. When she came to the house, I consulted a friend who was in the trade and he recommended Château Verdignan. Sybille had not heard of it, she sniffed and tasted and said, Never mind, there are ten thousand vineyards, you can't know them all.

SAUL BELLOW

Humboldt's Gift

1975

Humboldt's Gift is Saul Bellow's tenth work of fiction, and Barley Alison, its London publisher, was highly anxious about it. I imagine she had paid more money for it than was sensible. Saul was known to say that people bought his books not to read but to leave them lying on coffee tables as evidence that they were highbrows. Barley intended to have this book sold, read and talked about. I was to write it up in the Colour Magazine of the *Telegraph*.

Preparing to come to London for the publicity, Saul set Barley's nerves jangling. Her recent letters, he wrote, had been "charming and impossible, heavenly and hellish." She was underestimating his fatigue and overestimating his strength. He had no objection to meeting me and dining together, for some reason thinking the meal would be Provençale. But the BBC was after him, and his last experience with them had been dreadful. He spelled it out to her: on a sweltering day in Chicago ten men had come into his house, turned off the air conditioning, blown the fuses, asked ignorant and clumsy questions, and he was never again going to spend four hours under the cameras, with artistic picture editors all the more pleased the grimmer and queerer they made their subjects look.

In the event, Saul proved easygoing. It happened to be another sweltering day, and we sat it out in the shade of a tree at the center of one of the Kensington squares. He was in a mood to tell stories, reminiscing about the state school that had taught him Latin, and about his childhood friend, the son of Italian Mafiosi bootleggers in the years of Prohibition. In 1968 there were student riots here, there and everywhere, including Chicago. A member of the conservative-minded Committee on Social Thought at the University of Chicago, Saul had been greatly distressed by the violence. By chance in the street he encountered his childhood friend, now a *capo famiglia*, and told him what was happening. The question then was, How many are there? About two thousand. Right, give the word and we'll have them out by two o'clock.

I told him how as a small boy I had been in France in the blitzkrieg of 1940, taken by my aunt Helene (always known as Bubbles) and her husband Eduardo Propper de Callejon, a secretary at the Spanish Embassy in Paris, to Cannes in the Vichy zone and then to safety in Spain and Morocco. Saul said, You went through something close to the Jewish experience. He felt that he had never quite done justice to his experience of being Jewish. Anti-Communism for him was a straightforward matter, but fear of what critics would say compelled him to hold back on unfashionable semi-mystical beliefs that he held about human nature, and he regretted what he could only stigmatize as cowardice.

Over the years, Saul read and generously endorsed several of my books. Passing through London, he would come to kitchen suppers in the house, sometimes alone and sometimes with Alexandra, his Romanian wife and a mathematician. He was a first-person writer whose fictional protagonists one and all are projections of himself. So much so that Joseph Epstein, who knew him well and is himself a writer with style and imagination, raises the possibility in an essay that Saul couldn't construct convincing plots because he "wasn't truly a novelist." A master of language, though, without a doubt. His letters are second only to Byron's for their immediacy and vivacity. I find myself quoting him quite often, for instance his Socratic view that the unexamined life is not worth living, that death is good for some people, and the analogy that Israel is a moral resort area, what Switzerland is to winter holidays.

BERNARD BERENSON

The Italian Painters of the Renaissance

1952 EDITION

AFTER THE DEATH OF POPPY in February 1953, an immediate question for Alan, my father, was what to do about me. The obvious solution was to send me for the entire school holidays to stay with Poppy's mother, my grandmother, called Mitzi by some and Mary by others. Exploiting every form of theft from legal chicanery to strong-arm Gestapo squads carrying the loot off in armored cars, the Nazis had dispossessed her wherever she had property. Having spent the war in Canada, she was unsure where to live in Europe outside German-speaking countries. In the lobby of the Hotel Excelsior in Florence she overheard a conversation about a desirable property for sale in Arcetri, a cluster of old houses that is virtually a suburb of Florence but whose olive orchards and cultivated strips have the look of traditional countryside. San Martino was a farmhouse, a *casa colonica* done up as a villa between the wars. The seller, a baroness, judged it prudent to return to her native Germany. No sooner had Mitzi moved in than hopeful Communists painted a hammer and sickle on the portal. Poppy did not live long enough to visit San Martino, but she imagined the Communists dispossessing Mitzi, just as the Nazis had done, and maybe even slitting her throat. "I'd like to see them try" was Mitzi's response to this warning.

Alan was extremely attentive to Mitzi. His letters to her were regular bulletins, and he addressed her on the first page invariably as "Darling." In a characteristic gesture of largesse, he had bought a second-hand Bentley, and proposed that we drive it to San Martino. On the way there, we could take in the Pont du Gard or the Roman remains at Nimes and Orange, but in the years to come, he said, I would surely have plenty of opportunities for classical sightseeing. Part of his task as editor of the *Times Literary Supplement* was to be in touch with famous old writers, and with them it was a case of now or never. Architectural monuments would always be there, human monuments would not. He arranged that we were to call in on Somerset Maugham in the South of France, Max Beerbohm in Rapallo and Percy Lubbock near Lerici, where Shelley had drowned.

The fourth famous old person was Bernard Berenson. Some years before, my grandmother had invited me to accompany her to Bruges and I could recall museums with some of Memling's dough-faced portraits. My housemaster at Eton had taken several of us around the National Gallery. Otherwise I knew little or nothing about art or art history and had no special feeling for either. Until I was in Florence, I had never heard of Berenson though he was then at the height of his fame. Every door was open to him. He had identified great artists, authenticated their works and been involved in the selling of masterpieces to the best collections, in the process building his own fortune. His library was one of the finest in Europe, and according to rumor he had read all the books in it. Mitzi and BB were two of a kind, both assuming that their reputation and social success put them on an equal footing with the men and women in the brilliant aristocratic and literary circles in which they moved. After her first husband's death, Mitzi married an Englishman and through him acquired the new name and identity of Mary Wooster. BB had been born in Lithuania as Bernhard Valvrojenski, but made his way in New York and Paris and Berlin with a measure of assimilation as Bernard Berenson. Mitzi and BB both converted to Christianity. I was then seventeen, and could not have had any realistic idea of the psychological pressures or the experiences that drove people like these to be so fearful about their Jewish origins.

Even a teenager like me was invited to lunch with Berenson and expected to refer to him as BB. We drove across the Arno to Settignano. At the top of a wooded hill, I Tatti seemed an imposing country house. BB was in a wheelchair in the garden. Small, neat and very tidily dressed, he had the sharply defined features of someone accustomed to command. A trim white beard added a touch of informality. Courtiers came to pay homage, the guests, ourselves included, fussed around him. We sat down to lunch about twenty strong.

BB had put me on his left, and early in the meal he asked what I was doing at school. I had just been admitted to the Eton College Literary Society, and I explained to him that the members met once a week in one of the headmaster's rooms and took it in turns to read something they'd mugged up and written, usually on some safely conventional subject. And what will you be writing about? BB asked. The Norman Kings of Sicily had been my first choice but they were confusing, and the Dreyfus affair was simpler. I had read one book about it, and I also was aware that Mitzi's husband and my grandfather, Eugène Fould, had been cut out of the social life of Paris on the grounds that all Jews couldn't help having treason in their nature and were guilty like Dreyfus. The name of the Marquis de Jaucourt had come down to me as the one and only person in high society who had crossed the Place Vendôme to shake my grandfather's hand. BB turned red with anger. He raised his voice. Everyone else was silent. A passage in his diaries *Sunset and Twilight* gives an impression of the passion in his voice at that lunch. "I lived through the *affaire*, and was in Paris off and on through most of it. Anti-Semitism was rampant. Paris was reeking and drenched and soaked with it, and most Academicians and other writers were anti.... High society rabidly anti-Jewish. Never have I encountered such expressions of hatred, of loathing, as I used to hear against Jews from the mouths of Parisians." From the far end of the table, someone whom I've always and perhaps mistakenly thought was Hugh Trevor-Roper, broke in with some distracting question.

Unintentionally, I had said something about the condition of Jews in general, and him in particular. Jews were rounded up and deported in September 1943 when Italy dropped out of the war, and German Nazism became the order of the day. Although Berenson was among the best-known Jewish personalities anywhere in the world at that time, he was at the mercy of murderous thugs. Friends spirited him away from I Tatti to safety in the house of the Marchese Filippo Serlupi, who had diplomatic immunity as Ambassador of San Marino to the Holy See. At the end of the war, BB was able to pick up life at I Tatti at the point where Italian Fascists and German Nazis had compelled him to abandon it. The air of normality was deceptive. Next to him was this schoolboy who didn't grasp that a dining room full of guests with silver on the table and old masters on the walls was all very well but was the symptom of an unhappiness too deep to cure.

In the course of my career, several publishers and friends have suggested that I write a life of BB. His conflicts of interest and the ambiguities of his character are beyond resolution. It's trivial but still indicative that after that lunch he gave me a copy of *The Italian Painters of the Renaissance*, the book that made him famous, and whose dust jacket spells his name Bernhard, although he signed the title page "with the best wishes of Bernard." Of course it was now out of the question to write a school essay about the Dreyfus affair. Alan came up with the suggestion that I should give an account of the great men I'd been introduced to on our journey. He proposed the working title of "Four Human Monuments."

Back at Eton, I spent my spare time writing up these encounters. An uncomfortable silence fell over the room when I finished reading this first attempt of mine at journalism. Nobody had a comment. Robert Birley, then the headmaster and a kindly man with a lot of abstruse knowledge at his fingertips, at last said that it wasn't done to write about one's friends, and besides, if they were famous it was snobbish.

ISAIAH BERLIN

Translation of Ivan Turgenev,

First Love

1956 AND 1982 EDITIONS

As a child, my mother lived in one of the apartments of 54 Avenue d'Iéna, a handsome house close to the Arc de Triomphe in Paris, and Aline de Gunzburg lived in another. First as girls, then as adults, the two were the closest of friends. By the time I came up to Oxford in 1956, my mother had died, Aline had married Isaiah Berlin, and the two of them were as good as family to me. I was always welcome at their house in Headington, a typical English gentleman's residence built in stone in a setting of lawns and old trees. A manservant, usually Portuguese, opened the front door. The ground floor rooms were spacious, and Aline's classical good taste and beautiful possessions made the most of them.

To the right of the hall was a study for Isaiah, a room of organized untidiness in which he sat for hours dictating letters that kept selected friends up to date with his news and views, his anxieties and hopes, and since his death they have been edited and published in four hefty volumes. He was generally supposed to be working on a book, even a series of books, about the political and philosophical ideas that have made the world what it is. That huge and self-perpetuating correspondence exhausted his time and his energy, and excused the missing masterpiece.

Isaiah wore heavy old-fashioned suits, and out of doors an old hat of brown felt, giving him a conventional appearance. The expression on his face was one of amusement and curiosity. I couldn't help thinking he looked like the hero of a cartoon by H. M. Bateman and something quizzical or funny in every sense of the word was about to happen to him. His rapid-fire conversation suggested that he couldn't quite keep up with his thoughts. Fluent in Russian, Hebrew and German, he held his own in French and Italian.

Up to Headington came André Malraux, Edmund Wilson, Teddy Kollek, Shostakovich, Stravinsky, the great and the good visiting one of their number. I once asked him if he attributed greatness to anyone he'd met, and after a moment's hesitation he came up with Virginia Woolf (who hadn't reciprocated). Anyone with intellectual aspirations would certainly be familiar with his characterization of people as either Hedgehogs or Foxes, and they will also have understood from him that desirable ends are often incompatible. It used to puzzle me that he accepted social recognition such as knighthood, the role of first and foundational President of Wolfson College, the Order of Merit, and yet spoke lightly and even dismissively about these achievements. This might look like false modesty, but the real driving force, I think, was the timidity inherent in his Jewish identity. An inner spirit warned him that it was all too good to be true, that critics were disguised Cossacks and that clever Jews like him had to pay the price. Backing carefully into the dangerous limelight, he could hope to be all things to all men, and get away with it.

Hitler and the Holocaust were issues that he left to specialists. Several times I heard him say that, all things considered, Stalin was worse than Hitler. He might have been a Sovietologist as influential as Leonard Schapiro or Robert Conquest, but limited himself to anecdotes, for instance about his meeting in Leningrad with Anna Akhmatova or his trip out to Peredelkino to spend a day talking to Boris Pasternak about *Doctor Zhivago*. Zionism was the one and only firm commitment in his life, and every year around Christmas he and Aline would escape to Israel.

Even so, he kept to his standards as well as his compromises. When he found himself in a hotel lift with Menachem Begin, he refused to talk to a man who had resorted to terror in the cause of Zionism. In London, he lunched regularly with Eric Hobsbawm, who not only remained an apologist for Stalinist mass murder to the very end but held that the state of Israel ought to be liquidated. Isaiah also practiced the same double standards with Richard Wollheim, a professor of aesthetics who so dreaded being identified as Jewish that he denied there was any such thing as anti-Semitism and meanwhile refused to leave a long-distance flight that had landed at Tel Aviv for fear that his feet touch "imperialist" soil. I also heard him say quite often, perhaps out of unacknowledged competition, that Hannah Arendt's *The Origins of Totalitarianism* was a bad book whose opening sentence contained two mistakes. Had he used his gifts and his experience to write a comparable post-mortem of contemporary ideology, he might have exercised the kind of definitive moral and political influence in British national life that Raymond Aron enjoyed in France.

All allowances made, it was entertaining and often a surprise to be in Isaiah's company. Once when I was staying with the Berlins in their flat in Paris, the three of us went with Nicholas Nabokov, the musician and cousin of the novelist, to a cinema in the Champs-Élysées. The tough hero of the film was supposedly an Oxford don. The whole audience was then obliged to listen to Isaiah and Nicholas discussing at full blast which Oxford don could be the model for the lead in this film. The manager loomed up to ask for silence. The film's theme music, the two of them went on to speculate, had been lifted from some other composition, and they started singing to identify the original, whereupon the manager threw us all out into the street.

"Liberty, efficiency and democracy, three beautiful but incompatible ideals. Discuss" was a question that candidates for an All Souls Fellowship one year were invited to answer. Jeremy Wolfenden, a contemporary of mine at Eton and Magdalen College, had written a paper consisting of a brief series of aphorisms, so brilliant that Isaiah was keeping it in his room. We read them. At least I knew before everyone else that Jeremy would have the Fellowship. On another occasion, I had lunch at Headington with Isaiah and Roy Jenkins, then the university's Vice-Chancellor. They discussed who should become Provost of Worcester College, a position vacant at that moment. The name of the historian Hugh Thomas was in the air. Basing themselves on personal stories nothing to do with scholarship or proficiency, those two establishment fixers agreed that Hugh "really would not do." On the other hand, when two friends of mine, William Miller and Paul Thompson, published an article in an undergraduate magazine about eavesdropping on Soviet radio traffic during their national service, I told Isaiah that they were to be tried at the Old Bailey for breaching the Official Secrets Act, and he immediately contributed ten pounds to their defense fund.

Isaiah sponsored me for a Harkness Fellowship and for entry into the Foreign Service, both times in vain. He argued against any involvement in the Hungarian revolution of 1956 or its aftermath, because the harm I might do to myself was greater than any possible reward. He also argued that I shouldn't write *Next Generation*, a book about Israel, because I was a public schoolboy educated to think that Israel's qualities are mistaken and its mistakes are intentional. One day in February 1974, when Aleksandr Solzhenitsyn had just been expelled from the Soviet Union, I happened to be the guest of Aline and Isaiah in the royal box at Covent Garden, where he was a director. The *Times* had published an article by a professor with the thesis that this expulsion had nothing to do with Communism but was another episode in the historic debate in Russia between Westerners and Slavophiles. Isaiah had better qualifications than anyone to expose this pernicious nonsense but refused to do so because, he kept saying, the professor had his credentials, and I couldn't get him past this evasion. A couple of years later, my book about Unity Mitford and other English fans of Hitler met with some residual pre-war fascism and anti-Semitism from Oswald Mosley and his supporters. A few telephone calls from Isaiah, and perhaps an article, would have been enough to stop the scandal. By chance, I was invited at the time once again to the royal box. Isaiah offered to lean out and make a speech to the opera-goers in the stalls below spelling out how badly I'd been treated. Such an exhibition of himself was inconceivable. This was his way of ducking out.

On a Saturday in June 1989, I opened the *Times* and discovered that Roger Scruton had written an article about Isaiah on the occasion of his eightieth birthday. Publication of this piece was in itself quite enough to rattle Isaiah, but there was much more. Apart from one paragraph of incomprehensible speculation about Isaiah's personality, Scruton's line was clear, his tone regretful: thanks to the Cold War, Britain and its democratic values were under sustained assault and Isaiah had not taken his due place as champion *honoris causa* of right-thinking people. That Sunday, I dined with friends in London and one of them must have denounced me for saying that, alas, I did think that Isaiah lacked civil courage and therefore didn't do justice to himself or his convictions. On the Monday, Isaiah telephoned to say that he had heard I agreed with Scruton, and could this be true? A long typewritten letter followed. In his words, the article was absolutely odious, deeply offensive, loathsome, making false accusations, reminiscent of the kind of accusation right-wing liberals in pre-1914 Russia had to put up with from the Black Hundreds, also Goebbels-like. My response was upsetting, he said, because he had known me for so long and held me in such affection. I felt obliged to point out to him that Goebbels would have stopped him writing and excluded him completely from public life, while Scruton wished him to write more and be more active in public life. One must carry on as before, he concluded in his letter to me, adding in ink, "so be it" – and so it was. He made sure that I knew I had done wrong. Noel Malcolm, later a fellow of All Souls and therefore a colleague of Isaiah's, reviewed *The War That Never Was*, the book I wrote about the implosion of the Soviet Union. I happened to run into Isaiah at the time and he said, "If Noel Malcolm finds that you have written a good book, then you have written a good book. I shall not be reading it."

One evening Isaiah was one of ten guests at a dinner given by Mary and Sir Nicholas Henderson, generally called Nico, a public figure after a career as British ambassador in Warsaw and Bonn, Paris and Washington. Another guest was Lady Falkender, who had been Harold Wilson's private and political secretary in Downing Street throughout his time as Prime Minister. When Isaiah was put on her left at the table, he said to Nico, I can't possibly sit next to Lady Falkender, you'll have to change the *placement*. The room was small, we could not help overhearing him, and then we had to shuffle around the table, elbow to elbow. During the meal, Lady Falkender hardly spoke and then left as soon as she could. What was that about? asked Nico. It turned out that the *Times* had serialized Lady Falkender's diary, and in one passage she described an interview with Radji Parviz, the Shah of Iran's ambassador in London from 1976 to 1979. Entering his study, she had found him reading something Isaiah had written. According to her diary, Lady Falkender had reacted, perhaps broken the ice, by saying, Isn't Berlin some sort of charlatan? You see, Isaiah concluded, there could be no question of sitting next to someone who thinks me a charlatan.

Surviving Isaiah by many years, Aline sold Headington and moved to London. From time to time, I called on her. She liked to recall old days in the Avenue d'Iéna, and how my mother had been like a sister to her. Aline had spent the war in New York, and gave me copies of evocative letters my mother had written to her from London in those years. She might mention Isaiah anecdotally, but in my hearing never referred to the way I had upset him.

ADRIAN BERRY

The Next 500 Years

1995

IT WAS DIFFICULT TO KNOW quite where one was with Adrian. Good-natured, he would be welcoming and seemingly diffident, only to say something extravagantly wild, giving away that one had no idea what was going on his head. Quite possibly this was a protective strategy that he had developed to keep his parents at arm's length and remain himself. His father, Michael Berry, owned and edited the *Daily Telegraph*, a position so demanding that he had not much energy or emotion for anything else. As the eldest son, Adrian was brought up expecting to inherit a great paper and the editorial responsibility that went with it. Adrian's mother, Lady Pamela, monosyllabic Pam, was the daughter of F. E. Smith, Lord Chancellor and Earl of Birkenhead. Her social energy was unlimited and she used it to influence government and the arts. Her lunch and dinner parties were the talk of everyone who mattered, or who might one day matter, in Westminster, Mayfair and Fleet Street. Humor, reluctant or sardonic, crept into Adrian's voice when he spoke of his mother herding the guests into the family home in Lord North Street.

One of those guests was Alan, my father, and Lady Pam invited him for a cruise on the *Virginia*, the Berry yacht, bringing me as a friend and companion for Adrian. Weighing over a thousand tons, the *Virginia* was a miniature liner, complete with an ex-Royal Navy captain in a uniform and a large crew. The drawing room had still-life flower pictures in the style of Matthew Smith, perhaps even by him. I must have been just eighteen, a year or so older than Adrian. My mother had not been long dead, and on board was Lady Elizabeth Cavendish, whom Alan was wondering whether to marry, as I was to discover later.

The *Virginia* first put in to Antibes. Alongside was a ship of similar size. There appeared to be nobody aboard. Adrian and I decided to explore. In a moment we were having to explain ourselves to Sir Bernard and Lady Docker, whose yacht this was. Snobbish England mocked him for making a fortune and mocked her for spending it with nouveau riche vulgarity. The Dockers were amused by our trespassing. They suggested inviting Adrian's parents and then asked a steward to mix a cocktail that sent us dizzily back to the *Virginia*. Next day, we sailed past Corsica to reach La Maddalena, an Italian naval base on Sardinia. For security reasons, the authorities made everyone fill in a form that among other details asked for the names of father and grandfather. Hoping to pass themselves off anonymously, Lady Elizabeth wrote tenth Duke of Devonshire and ninth Duke of Devonshire, while Lady Pam wrote Gypsy Smith and Gypsy Smith.

Like me, Adrian went up to Oxford in September 1956 — in his case to Christ Church. The Suez crisis was upon us. British forces were invading Egypt. Undergraduates were going to the station to catch one or another train that would get them to London in time to join a mass demonstration. A life-long high Tory, Adrian telephoned the Oxford station master, introduced himself as the Proctor and asked for a loudspeaker announcement that undergraduates were forbidden from demonstrating and would be sent down if they disobeyed. The station master fell for it and so did most undergraduates. In much the same have-a-go mood, Adrian financed and edited *Parsons' Pleasure*, a magazine so scurrilous that its life was short.

Leaving a party at Christ Church late one evening, I was walking through the cloisters when I saw W. H. Auden approaching from the opposite direction. While we were chatting, Adrian came by. I introduced him to Auden and he invited us up to his room on the floor above the cloisters. Adrian had been at the same party as me and I knew he had drunk too much, but it seemed churlish to refuse. We reached the room but there wasn't time to sit down. Suddenly Adrian was violently sick all over the papers and notebooks on Auden's central table. None of the work on that desk could have been salvaged. To his great credit, Auden took it in good part. No reproach. Abandoning Auden to the task of cleaning up, Adrian and I hurried away.

Whenever we met, Adrian was likely to want to tell me about the latest report by some astronomer on the conquest of space or some new theory about the colonization of the planets. My recollection is that he had no formal education in any branch of science but was displaying the passionate enthusiasm of the autodidact. Science fiction has never caught my imagination, but Adrian's futuristic world was a model of creativity and adventure with the odd brickbat thrown at any experts with contrary opinions. The mix of conventionality and mischief-making was his special element.

Silently he mourned that his father had been obliged for financial reasons to sell the *Daily Telegraph*. The promise of editorship vanished. The *Virginia* was sold to President Tubman of Liberia, who had a heavy cannon mounted on the deck, and this so unbalanced the ship that she capsized and lies on the sea bed somewhere off the coast of Africa.

JOHN BETJEMAN

Summoned by Bells

1960

M Y FATHER WENT UP TO Magdalen College, Oxford, in October 1927. Immediately and brazenly, he ignored the university and college rules and regulations and was sent down in his second term. That was time enough to begin a lasting friendship with John Betjeman, then in his third year in the same college. They had a lot in common. Literature was a good thing in itself but they also saw that it was the way to get themselves talked about and invited by people whose invitations they wanted to have. Being amusing was much the same as being shocking for up-and-coming *Vile Bodies*, to borrow the title of the novel in which Evelyn Waugh sketched the bright young things of that generation. A particularly skittish passage in *Summoned by Bells* depicts Alan arriving for a drink on a Sunday wearing just a bathing costume and sitting at a harmonium to play a hymn whose verses have been re-written as lampoon, including the line, "and the pansies all sing flat."

Betch (as I choose to render Betj, the usual spelling) inhabited a private land of his own, and the nicknames of his friends were a kind of passport for entry into that land. For obvious reasons Alan was Big Nose, which soon became a single word and then due to a typing mistake Bognose, or variously Bog and Boggins, and finally Captain Bog on the grounds that war-time rank was bound to be comic. A letter on February 18, 1933 headed "Darling Bog" congratulated him on becoming engaged to Joan Eyres-Monsell, but had advice: "You must explain that you were once inverted. She won't mind at all." Moving to Vienna ostensibly to write, Alan forsook Joan when he fell in love with Poppy Fould-Springer. Twenty years old, she had lived an extraordinarily sheltered life. On October 6, 1934 Betch wrote that he had been "staggered" to read in the *Times* the announcement of Alan and Poppy's engagement. "Oh Bog, Bog, how I miss you and how I envy your success. Don't marry without a long period of probation. . . . My God, Bog, have a care."

In 1937, just over a year after I'd been born, Betch was describing me as a baby with "rabbit's ears on his dress" and hoping that I'd grow up fit to sing treble in some surpliced choir. I have a photograph of him sitting at a table, pen in hand and notebook open. "Ici je suis dans Auxerre," he wrote along the lower margin, and to one side, "Truly yours Jean Paul Sartre Betjhomme." Sartre's novel *La Nausée* was published in 1938, a clue to this photograph's date.

Anglicanism in all its manifestations, liturgical and architectural, was sanctified in Betch's private land, and he made no secret of it. The conversion to Catholicism of Penelope, his wife, lovingly nicknamed Filth or Philth, kept them apart for the rest of their lives. Betch precipitated a similar crisis in Alan's marriage when he telephoned Poppy to tell her that earlier in the day he had entered Westminster Cathedral and caught sight of Alan face down on the floor with arms extended in the form of a cross, all in the ritual of conversion to the Catholic faith. Poppy had known nothing about this, and took it that changing his spiritual persona without telling her compromised their mutual trust. Forced to choose between her and Catholicism, he chose her.

In February 1953, Poppy died of cancer in Paris. She was 37. Three weeks previously, we had been together in Seefeld, then an undeveloped village in Tyrol, and one morning she had put on skis. Everyone in the family had thought it better not to tell me that she was seriously ill. My housemaster at Eton gave me the news and drove me to Heathrow so that I could be at the funeral in the Père Lachaise cemetery. To this day, I have no idea if Alan had listened to Betch and told her that he was an invert, and if not, then whether she had discovered it for herself. What I do know is that Alan took me back to school, and we found Betch waiting for us at the door of the house; he had spent the afternoon there. Years later, he told me, "I knew

COLLECTED POEMS
1975

David Price Jones —

— 1976 —

— Robert Graves —

Deyá

the Captain would be sad so I wanted to meet him on his return."

Paul, his own son, was a year or two younger than me, but happened to be in the same house. After Poppy's death, or in the next term, the two fathers took their boys out to tea a couple of times in The Cockpit, an ancient and picturesque restaurant in Eton High Street. I was old enough to understand that my nickname of Baby Bog signified admission to his private land. Betch spoke of and to Paul as The Powlie, or more simply It. None of us quite knew what to do for the best or where to put ourselves when he would say things like, I can't be too sure but I think It is about to speak. As if he hadn't heard, Paul remained self-contained and silent.

Poppy had not long been dead when Alan took me to Ireland. He did not disclose that the purpose of the trip was for me to meet Elizabeth Cavendish, then staying at Lismore Castle with her brother, the Duke of Devonshire. One morning when we were alone visiting the garden of another show-place, Alan sprang the surprise that he proposed to marry Elizabeth. I felt he was betraying Poppy and said so, my emotions running away with me. The consequence was that Alan spent the rest of his life in the United States, sometimes settled, sometimes unsettled. My stepmother manqué, Elizabeth was to complete a triangle by devoting herself to looking after Betch to the end of his life.

Betch didn't seem to notice that he had become a national treasure. Pathos was his medium. We went on one or two expeditions in London in search of friends or sights, and he was embarrassed to be recognized in the street. Every Thursday morning, he was in the habit of entertaining the children in one of the wards in St. Bartholomew's Hospital. I took my daughters to meet him and he told them that even if they peeled their grandfather Alan as they might peel an onion, they still wouldn't know him. Now and then, postcards would arrive addressed to Baby Bog.

The title page of my copy of *Summoned by Bells* reads, "Inscribed for David P-J by John Betjeman ARTISTE & CALLIGRAPHER," the two descriptive but imaginary nouns in capitals.

PRINCESS MARTHE BIBESCO
Le Perroquet Vert
1950 EDITION

IT WAS 1959 when I met Marthe Bibesco in her small apartment on the Quai Bourbon in Paris. By then, she was a wizened old lady, huddled in her shawl and her memories. We had tea. She talked French and English as though they were interchangeable languages. Her father, Ioan Lahovary, had been the Romanian Minister of Foreign Affairs. Her husband, George Bibesco, had a forebear who had been *Hospodar* of Wallachia, a title with more than a touch of Ruritania. Marthe was the last one still alive who could talk from personal experience about Marcel Proust and the aristocratic circle which he fictionalized. She had known pretty well everyone who had graced a Paris salon in the first fifty years of the twentieth century. Evoking the almost ghost-like cultural scene of long ago, her memoirs and essays mostly came out in limited editions, octavo, with expensive paper and bindings aimed at bibliophiles.

A novel, *Le Perroquet Vert* dates from 1923, and she was giving me a reprint as a wedding present. The inscription reads, "Il savait se taire en souriant sur un secret délicieux." In a literal translation: he knew how to keep silent and smile about a delicious secret. Clarissa and I had been married for a few months and that explains "delicious" but there was nothing secret about it.

In 1967, Clarissa and I went to Romania. Having experienced the Iron Curtain in Hungary and Czechoslovakia, I prepared for this journey by getting introductions from Miron Grindea. Born in the provincial Romanian town of Onesti, he had reached Britain and safety on the eve of the war. As a refugee, his extraordinary feat was to launch, edit and fund *Adam*, a literary magazine every bit as respectful of high culture as Marthe Bibesco. Nicolae Ceauşescu and his wife Elena were already set on their egomaniacal course. On Miron's recommendation, Nina Cassian, the poet, not only received Clarissa and me but somehow had scrounged an orange, usually an unobtainable delicacy which politeness obliged us to eat with ceremony and a sense of guilt. Another of Miron's contacts was a Professor of literature at Bucharest University. I rented a car and we drove with him to a large and low house in dark stone about a dozen miles beyond Bucharest. This was Mogosoaia. Here Marthe had received the good and the great from all over Europe. Expropriated from the Bibescos, the place now belonged to the Writers Union. That afternoon, a lone guardian let us into damp abandoned rooms containing plastic chairs already dingy, and Socialist realist posters on the walls. The Communist fantasy that the happiness of some depends on the unhappiness of others was exposed in the ruination of this once great palace. Out of doors we sat on a bench at the edge of a lake. In or around the water, innumerable masses of frogs were keeping up an unbelievably deafening chorus of croaking, a dismal unvarying altogetherness that served as a metaphor for Communism.

PAUL BOWLES

Two Years Beside the Strait

Tangier Journal, 1987–9

1990

SOME PEOPLE HAVE all the luck and Paul Bowles seemed to be one of them. 1910 was a pretty good time for him to be born, and New York City a pretty good place to be born in. There was quite enough money in the family for a private income, the young Bowles was already writing prose and poetry and composing music, and on top of all this he was conspicuously handsome. Here was a natural recruit to the ranks of those in the public eye. His first visit to Tangier was in 1931, and from 1947 onwards he was to live there till the end of his life in 1999, not exactly an expatriate or a drop-out, rather a visitor on an extended stay in a place that in his hands might as well have been a suburb of Sodom and Gomorrah.

Just before the war, he married Jane Auer, also an American, seven years younger than him. Both of them gay, they were pioneers of anything-goes, apparently free from inhibitions of any kind, perhaps pioneers in the modern syndrome of being happy to be unhappy. Besides, Jane had had a tubercular knee and was an alcoholic. Their unusual personalities and equally unusual writings have given rise to an extensive and growing literature that praises in academic prose the withdrawal into unreason of this couple. *Two Serious Women*, Jane Bowles's one and only novel, is set in Central America, in a hotel that proves to be a chamber of horrors more or less unrelated to reality.

American characters in Paul Bowles's fiction are too naïve to understand the complexities either of Morocco or of Islamic culture. Clinging single-mindedly to their view of the world and its ways, they become victims of themselves. As for Arabs in his fiction, they have customs and codes which they do not share but still expect strangers to observe, and they will punish disrespect and disobedience. Few writers have ever written with such affinity as Bowles about the sense that easily afflicts Westerners in Muslim countries, that there is a cultural compass somewhere to guide them but they cannot find it. That is how complexes of superiority and inferiority very soon sprout into racism and a vision of supremacy. *The Sheltering Sky* and *Let It Come Down* are works of genuine cultural discovery. Less well known, *The Spider's House* is an evocation, full of unspoken menace, of the war of national liberation the Moroccans waged to gain independence from France.

I had not been back to Tangier since childhood. Looking at the past with hindsight, I had been one of the lucky people. At the time of the German blitzkrieg in May 1940, my parents were in England, having left me in France in the care of my aunt and uncle, Bubbles and Eduardo Propper. I have described in *Fault Lines* our flight from the Germans, first to Vichy France and from there to Spain and Morocco. Tangier meant safety, food, blue sky and permanent sunshine. In 1968 I returned with Clarissa and could show her the house I'd lived in; the bench on which I'd sat to watch the British fleet steaming out of Gibraltar in the pale grey dawn; the Marshan where I had played football with Arab boys my age; the casbah and the Petit Socco, the busy heart of Tangier.

The city had since become a sort of open-air nightclub for drugs and sex tourism of every kind. In an old file I had preserved the address of Paul Bowles – Apartment 20, Immeuble Itesa, telephone number 17883. It was an uninhabitable dump of cheap stained cement blocks, without even a minimum concession to domesticity. Here he lived with the solemn, not to say surly, Muhammad Mrabet. Introduced as a writer with whom Bowles went gathering traditional tribal tales that he published under his own name, Mrabet was in fact functionally illiterate. They spent the day smoking kif, the cannabis grown in Morocco. The smell of it impregnated not just the dark and shuttered room but the entire building. Draped around him in various stages of trance was a troop of beachcombers and free-loaders, pimps and prostitutes of both sexes, dreamers, worshippers of the Jane Bowles cult, and somewhere in the mix a published poet or two.

Quite why the brilliant and privileged Paul Bowles had chosen to model himself on the kind of character the deranged William Burroughs or the solipsistic Allen Ginsberg might have invented is a mystery. The Zeitgeist seemed to be working overtime. Impassive, he allowed this life of kif and stupor to wash over him. Toward the end of a boring morning, one of the hangers-on wanted to buy something and Bowles handed his wallet over without comment. The more unconventional his life had grown, the duller he became in himself and in his writing. It was not a case of old age or failing powers but more simply that he had progressively lost all idea of who he really was. He seemed not to realize the lengths to which he had gone in order to prevent himself from becoming the great writer he might have been.

ARNO BREKER

Bildnisse unserer Epoche

NO DATE

THE LIFE AND TIMES of Arno Breker is a warning that bad art has the power to do great damage. Born in 1900 near Schwerin in northern Germany, he had a studio for his sculpture in Paris during the mid-Twenties, and he liked to present himself as the successor to Rodin. His French was fluent. Returning to Germany in 1934, he was a skilled self-promoter, soon accepted in the highest Nazi circles where he was habitually described as "Hitler's favorite sculptor." His busts, usually in bronze, highlighted prominent Nazis, including at least two of Hitler. He cast statues a little larger than life, many of them warrior figures in the nude striking heroic poses, for example brandishing a drawn sword regardless that the statue's prominent penis was a ridiculous contrast, a sort of prop; or muscle-bound males also in the nude raising high in the air a blazing torch or a Laocoön-like serpent. At the entrance of the new Reich Chancellery built for Hitler by Albert Speer were two Breker reliefs representing with labored symbolism The Party and The Army. Hitler himself initiated and led the campaign against what he called "degenerate art," and Breker played a star role in what was effectively totalitarian control of aesthetics and artists who were potential opponents.

Extolling power, conquest and will, Breker praised and promoted the spirit of Nazism through his sculpture in the way that Leni Riefenstahl did in the medium of film or Carl Orff in the music of *Carmina Burana*.

In the summer of 1940, the French showed themselves unwilling and unable to fight for their country, and it looked as if France could never recover from a comprehensive defeat. An armistice was signed on June 18, 1940, and five days later Hitler made his one and only visit to Paris, a somewhat cursory tour that lasted from dawn to noon. Photographs of the occasion make him out to be lost in his own thoughts, with the Eiffel Tower in the background as though certifying that he is indeed a man of destiny. Breker appears in some of these photographs. Hitler had specially invited him, having him stay in his headquarters and flown with him to Paris in his private aircraft. At one point they were five minutes away from Breker's Paris studio, but apparently there was not enough time for a detour to it.

A Wehrmacht General was appointed Military Governor of German-occupied France, and this immediately posed the moral question: How was one to behave? Was a Frenchman to buckle under and obey Hitler's bidding evermore, or on the contrary resist, and if so, by what means? Should a German relax and enjoy superiority over all the French or take care not to offend French sensibilities? Invited to conduct a star-studded *Tristan und Isolde* at the Opera, Furtwängler refused on the grounds that he would not conduct "on the back of German tanks." Herbert von Karajan, an honorary Colonel in the SS, felt no such scruple, and immediately took Furtwängler's place.

Breker similarly exploited the position of supremacy that the Wehrmacht had won. In May 1942, under German auspices, an exhibition of his work was staged in the prestigious Orangerie. Artists and critics who had made Paris the world's center of pre-war contemporary painting attended the opening. Endlessly talked about and publicized, this was perhaps the peak of collaboration in the four years of occupation. One measure of this general corruption was the compliment that Aristide Maillol, then the most eminent of French sculptors, paid to Breker when he called him "Germany's Michelangelo." Breker's moment of triumph signified that the old moral and political values were no longer applicable and it was in order, unquestionably normal and even respectable, to fall in with the new Nazi masters. France today is still paying the price.

It so happens that in 1955, I had been stationed for a year of national service in Krefeld, a smallish industrial town in the Rhineland. The regiment was quartered in a magnificent no-costs-spared barracks built for the Wehrmacht in the Hitler period. When I arrived there, the rubble of Allied bombing raids was still piled high in the town center. The ruin was worse in Düsseldorf, the nearest big city. Some of us now and again went into the Park Hotel on the Königsallee, a handsome boulevard with what appeared to be shops but were only the front walls of bombed-out buildings.

None of the men in that barracks knew or cared what the local Germans thought of them. Speaking German, I could not help noting that the locals were outwardly polite, not to say deferential, but among themselves they were full of resentment. Trivial incidents such as a waiter accused by one of our corporals of overcharging in some Gasthaus, or a policeman prevented by law from enforcing traffic regulations, could lead to an unpleasant confrontation. At the time, it seemed to me, such people believed that history had come out wrong. The spoken word and body language conveyed a sense that they should not have to see themselves as victims. They handled themselves differently; there was some lingering element of collective purpose and duty. My novel *Safe Houses* has a scene taken from real life when dozens of old men gather in a restaurant and sing forbidden Nazi Party songs.

Holt Rinehart had published my books in New York, and the day came when the editors there had a suggestion for me. They had bought the archive of a photojournalist by the name of Roger Schall. Somehow he had managed to obtain an *Ausweis* from the German Military Governor, giving him permission to go where he chose and photograph whatever he fancied in occupied Paris. My aim in *Paris in the Third Reich,* the book I published in 1981, was to provide historical context to his snapshots.

The book's final section consists of interviews I had with Germans or Frenchmen whose particular experiences were worth recording. The German reactions were mixed. Albrecht Krause, a senior member of the Military Governor's staff, rather exceptionally held that Germans would have to live with sackcloth and ashes for the next five hundred years to atone for what they had done. Gerhard Heller, the censor and therefore responsible ultimately to Josef Goebbels and the Propaganda Staffel, described the numerous writers beseeching him to put on their manuscripts his stamp of approval, complete with swastika, without which they could not be published. Jean-Paul Sartre was one of the most persistent, spending hours in Heller's office.

The Düsseldorf in which Breker had come to settle in old age was very different from the city I had once been in. He himself was much like the type veering between boastfulness and resentment that I had encountered during national service. Museums and collectors fell over themselves to have one of his pieces, but "they," whoever they were, boycotted him. More than thirty years had passed since he had accompanied Hitler in Paris, but the memory of that occasion still touched him because he saw it as the greatest compliment to his artistic gift as a sculptor. That same day, Hitler invited him to dine and awarded him the Nazi Party's Golden Badge, its highest decoration.

We crossed a bit of garden to reach his studio, where busts and statues were assembled in some disorder. Hideous as ever, Nazi kitsch was on a support system in that studio. *Bildnisse unserer Epoche,* the book he pressed on me, is a collection of photographs of men and women, usually public figures who sat for him mostly in the 1950s and 1960s. Their features express admiration of power, conquest and will. Not just Germany but the whole of Europe has to pay the price for that.

CHRISTOPHER BURNEY
The Dungeon Democracy
1946

THE TWENTIETH CENTURY gave rise to the literature of the concentration camp, and it will be remembered for this special branch of historiography, perhaps for little else. The mindset of anyone with claims to be human is already conditioned by the century's central political experience as recorded for example by Aleksandr Solzhenitsyn, Varlam Shalamov, Hanns Mayer (writing as Jean Améry), David Rousset, Tadeusz Borowski, Etty Hillesum, Emanuel Ringelblum, and Primo Levi. Christopher Burney has his place in that select company. From August 1944 till the end of the war, he was in Buchenwald. How the British would have behaved under Soviet or Nazi dictatorship is an unspoken question about the identity of the nation. Only a hundred pages long, Christopher Burney's *The Dungeon Democracy* is about staying true to oneself and surviving. Like Primo Levi's *If This Is a Man*, it was written in the immediate aftermath of the war and published in 1946 when the world was not yet ready to come to terms with atrocity on the modern scale.

Burney's story begins conventionally enough. Born in 1917, he was the direct descendent of Dr. Charles Burney (1726–1814), the composer and leading musicologist of his day. Charles's daughter Fanny was a popular novelist who in the revolutionary year of 1794 married the French General Alexandre D'Arblay, and went to live in France. (London's Soho still boasts its D'Arblay Street.) Pentwyn is our family farmhouse twenty minutes from Hay-on-Wye, and every time I drive to that bibliophile town I pass Oakfield, the handsome red-brick house that used to be the Burney home. At the age of seventeen, Christopher Burney ran away from Wellington in the hope of becoming a soldier rather than the classical scholar that the headmaster intended him to be. Rolling stone, laborer, mechanic, exile in Paris most of the time, he was undergoing just the right preparation for joining the wartime Special Operations Executive, whose purpose, as Churchill himself put it, was to set German-occupied Europe ablaze.

In 1942 Burney parachuted into France. He was 25. One or another instance of carelessness had allowed the Abwehr, German counter-intelligence, to round up all those with whom he had been due to cooperate. After he had been on the run for eleven weeks, the Gestapo succeeded in capturing him. To be in their hands, he found, was "absolutely terrifying." They were within their rights to sentence him to death by a firing squad. Condemned, he was sent to Fresnes prison in Paris, where he spent more than 500 days alone in a cell. Spared from execution probably because the Germans hoped to trap other SOE agents through interrogation, he then had to endure deportation in a cattle truck and the ordeal of Buchenwald. "I could have told accurately what it is like to walk the last few steps on this earth," he wrote in *Solitary Confinement*, his second and final book, as much of a masterpiece as his first.

His writing is lit with glimpses of the inner self that enabled him to confront Buchenwald. Sunday churchgoing in lost Herefordshire summers had formed his character, along with Shakespeare and *The Wind in the Willows* and roast beef. "I had been left free to scan the horizon of existence," is how he saw himself. As for the concentration camp, "The most striking characteristic of the S.S. was their crass stupidity. They were all men who had seen in Hitler a man who offered them the means of living by the only gift they had – brute force." To nickname them the Toad, Bat-ears or the Kindly One was to mock their stupid brutality. The Commandant SS Sturmbannführer Koch was a sadist with a side-line in embezzling Party funds. Frau Koch was the pervert whose lampshades had to be made of tattooed human skin. The SS doctor, Hoven by name, was "a small dark man with shifty eyes . . . a murderer of no mean talent." Among the prisoners were some fifty British pilots who had been shot down and as the war was coming to its end the Commandant started to hang two of them every day. With extraordinary altruistic courage, Burney went into hiding under the floor of one of the camp's huts and through intermediaries he offered the Commandant a bargain. When the camp was in British hands, the Commandant would have to answer for his crimes. If he stopped these executions, Burney promised to speak for him in court. In horrific circumstances, he had done the right thing and it worked. Burney's testimony was duly heard and judged not to be enough to spare Koch from the gallows. "If we follow only our emotions and our appetites, it will mean Back to Buchenwald for me and a maiden trip for most of you," are the closing words of *The Dungeon Democracy*.

Liberated, he was skeletal thin. In due course he made a life for himself, with a wife and children and various jobs, at one point in a bank and at another point writing a report for the United Nations. Friends had lent him a house with the pleasing name of La Car-rotière in a small town in Normandy, about an hour by car from Paris. In the summer of 1973 I visited him there. He looked fit. Over a meal, I drew out of him things he had left unsaid in his books but which recurred in his dreams. He had carried corpses from the transports and laid them in piles. Once he was sent for punishment to the Buchenwald stone quarry and would have died there if an elderly Viennese socialist had not used his influence and rescued him. One morning four Russians in his block suspected a fifth of informing, and they bounced him to death.

To ask him why he now lived alone, as it were in self-induced solitary confinement, seemed to put me on a level with Toad or Bat-ears; besides, I couldn't help noticing that his car had a yellow GIG badge, the initials standing for *grand invalide de guerre*. The French Government paid him a full pension as a former officer with the Resistance. A less grateful government awarded him the MBE, of all inopportune medals.

Back in London and angered by the indifference of officialdom to Burney, I took his case up with a ministerial pen-pusher. Mightily pleased with himself and hardly able to button his trousers over his belly, this oaf held that Burney had been on active service, and nothing need be done for him, certainly not in respect of a pension. I found I was talking to someone unable to imagine the Buchenwald ordeal or ask himself if he could have survived it. "Don't incite the hornets" was his way of telling me in a letter that he had no expectations.

RAYMOND CARR
English Fox Hunting
1976

MY SPECIAL SUBJECT as an undergraduate was the French Revolution. I took it in part because Raymond Carr was teaching it. He was different from other Oxford dons. He assumed that you were as clever as him and talked as though to an equal. There was something of Groucho Marx about him, though he was taller and much more elegant. Perhaps it was his way of seeing the funny side of things, or his laugh at the folly of those with opinions opposed to his. The register of his voice moved between counter-tenor and baritone, with an intermittent sort of guffaw.

The lecture was at nine o'clock in the morning, in hangover time, not that that affected what Raymond might be saying. On one occasion his opening sentence was, "My God, Robespierre was a shit." Charlotte Corday finished off Marat in the bath, the subject of a clearly improvised discourse from Raymond on what sets female murderers apart from male murderers. Unable or unwilling to draw a line between curiosity and mischief, he had called on Sir Oswald and Lady Mosley at Crux Easton, where they were living after their release from prison. He was there on the day that Julius Streicher, the most vicious and public of Nazi anti-Semites, was hanged. Raymond walked out once and for all when he heard Lady Mosley saying, "Let's stand and drink a toast to a gallant Christian gentleman."

Raymond and his wife Sara had a house at Great Milton, a few miles from Oxford. I owned a Morris Minor and could drop in there uninvited, along with the jeunesse dorée of the moment. The atmosphere of permanent partying led Evelyn Waugh to write Raymond off as a "tipsy buffoon," a phrase surely with an echo of envy. After I told A. J. P. Taylor that I was not prepared to have tutorials with someone as biased as him, I asked Raymond to be my tutor. It was against the rules to be taught by a fellow in some other college than yours, but Raymond paid no attention to trivialities of that sort. He once told me that he would admit to the college anyone with an *x* in their name, because they were likely to be foreign and exotic.

Original and inspiring, Raymond brought the past alive. When he was about fourteen, his mother caught him reading as usual and had asked, "Don't you have any ideas of your own?" María Jesús González wrote a massive biography that treats him as the greatest contemporary historian of Spain. In the years when she was at work on it, he would keep muttering, "God, how I wish the woman would go away."

The Jerusalem Committee was the brainchild of the ebullient Teddy Kollek; its purpose was to help him have his own way as Mayor of that city. Members of the Committee, Raymond and I were summoned to Jerusalem to discuss how to celebrate the three thousandth anniversary of the rule of King David. Professors and clergymen bombinated for much of the morning, until Raymond interrupted, "If I hear another German talking about his *Geist* [soul, spirit, spirituality] I won't be responsible for the consequences."

The birth of one of his children had tested his own *Geist*. There were complications. The gynecologists asked him if they should save Sara or the child, as they could not save both. Sara, of course. When the moment came, the child was not breathing. Already summoned in case he had to give Sara the last rites, a distraught priest spilled holy water over the child who then came to life with a scream. Even a hard-bitten atheist like Raymond could speak of a miracle.

I never saw him out on the hunting field but others would say his courage was alarming. He survived horrifying falls. The usual spoilsports criticized his book on hunting, whose final sentence is a quote from Trotsky of all people, and a typically brilliant tease: "The attraction in hunting is that it acts on the mind as a poultice does on a sore."

JUDY CASSAB

Diaries

1995

THESE DIARIES BEGIN in April 1944, when Judy Cassab (née Judith Kaszab) had unpinned the yellow star from her clothing and was living under cover in Budapest, then in the hands of the Gestapo and the Arrow Cross, the Hungarian Nazis. Back from two years of forced labor in a Soviet camp, her husband Jansci turns up occasionally, still wearing his yellow star. Sheltering during the siege of Budapest, fifty of the most savage days in the war, Judy could nevertheless write, "I am still longing for my painting." She and Jansci emigrated in 1951 to Australia and in no time at all Judy was exhibiting and receiving commissions to paint the portraits of eminent men and women. The diaries develop into a cheerful social almanac.

Agi Yoeli (née Agnes Izak), an internationally recognized ceramicist and sculptress, put me in touch with Judy when I was in Australia. Both of them had grown up in a town in Slovakia known as

Beregszasz to Hungarians and Berehovo to everyone else. Judy's father ran a brick factory; Agi's father ran a shoe-making business. In Agi's apartment in Tel Aviv hangs a portrait in pencil and charcoal of her mother. Done by Judy at the age of sixteen, it is as beautiful and finished as an old master drawing. Except for this one drawing, everything they had possessed at Berehovo had been stolen or smashed.

In 1944, Agi and her family were among thousands from Bere-hovo mustered in the yard of the Kaszab brick factory and then deported to Auschwitz. Agi was put to assembling fuses in the Birkenau factory within the camp. Her father and mother, her husband Laczy and her newborn child were murdered. At a station waiting for a train in the aftermath of the war, Agi recognized the SS woman who had killed this baby and was now passing herself off as a victim. Instead of having the woman arrested, Agi picked a bunch of flowers in the station master's garden.

NIRAD C. CHAUDHURI

Thy Hand, Great Anarch!

India 1921–1952

1988

NIRAD CHAUDHURI lived in a cosy North Oxford house with a front garden full of flower-beds. I'd come on the wrong day, he was expecting me tomorrow but his face showed only pleasure: no sense of discomposure or misuse of his time. The ground-floor sitting room had large speakers for playing music, and a word processor. Until now, he explained, he'd used a typewriter. Compact, he couldn't have been more than five feet, if that. In his early nineties, he was wizened but energetic, well able to spring up unaided from his armchair. He moved about at a run with now and then a wobble in it, and his laugh was an appealing high cackle.

When he was one hundred years old he published *Three Horsemen of the New Apocalypse*, remarking in the preface of this lament on the decline of civilization that he had never read or heard of any author producing a book at that age. *Self-Destruction* is a book he'd written in Bengali about the last hundred years in Bengal. On erotica, he'd penned a footnote in Greek, and he turns the page up in the middle of the book, commenting, "That's mischief-making." Indians, he says, began to display fossilized minds about fifty years ago. Concluding this must have a physiological basis, he has since then eaten only English food. He refers to himself as coming from the Bengali aristocracy. Now there's nobody like him.

Wordlessly, Mrs. Chaudhuri carried in cups of tea, but otherwise was invisible all afternoon, leaving us two men to get on with it. Theirs was an arranged marriage. European music, he says in *Thy Hand, Great Anarch!* has been his main recreation, and in his anxiety that she might not understand or sympathize, the first time they were alone together he asked if she had heard of Beethoven, and was reassured that she could spell the name correctly.

Thy Hand, Great Anarch! is a resounding rebuke to the many tub-thumpers who accuse the British Empire of being a conspiracy to enrich a lot of murderers and thieves at the expense of innocent natives. Here is a fresh and contrary assessment of some of the current political and historical clichés about India and Britain and the relationship between them; it goes against the grain with an intellectual lordliness all its own for 972 astonishing pages, and it is without doubt one of the most original books published in the English language since the war. Already on page 20, Nirad Chaudhuri is thinking the unthinkable as he describes a strike in the Calcutta of 1921. English soldiers with rifles and fixed bayonets were standing by for violence. "I looked with admiration at their bearing," he writes, "those alien soldiers, belonging to the army of our foreign rulers, seemed to me, who had always resented political subjection, to be the sole defenders of civilisation."

Kishorganj, the small Bengali town where he was born in 1897 and where he grew up, is a place he recollects with grace and hardly a touch of nostalgia. His father, a lawyer as well as a merchant, introduced him to the world's high culture. Shakespeare, Napoleon, Raphael and Edmund Burke were household names. For the sake of the literature, Chaudhuri taught himself French and German. Immemorially settled in their ways, Hindus and Muslims were defenseless when in the twentieth century the hitherto unknown ideology of nationalism would pit one community against the other, culminating in irreparable exchanges of population, partition and massacre over the whole sub-continent.

By the 1920s, Chaudhuri was a journalist publishing articles in English and Bengali, and later a commentator on All India Radio. "I stopped writing in Bengali in 1937," he lets drop in *Thy Hand, Great Anarch!* "when I came to lose faith in the future of the Bengali people." Eighteenth-century India had been stagnant. Hinduism and Islam had decayed to mere forms. Far from abusing or exploiting India, the British had vitalized it. In all Indian history, there had been no better government. Adapted from the British and transferred to Indians, nationalism in his perspective had proved to be nothing more than the mutual hate of Hindus and Muslims, and the hate of both for the British. The real shock, though, is that at the very moment when high-minded Indians were busy transplanting the British model of power and civilization, the British people had lost faith in themselves. Indians were acquiring a beautiful but empty shell. What was on offer was not worth having, it was "mindless aping of the lowest things in the Western democratic culture." Abandoning India to this fate, the British were betraying it and that was their real fault. Looking very directly at me, Chaudhuri asked, "Why did the British rat on India?"

Subjects of conversation swung from wine, books, roses, food and history to English customs and today's lack of continuity. He had gone into print in the *Sunday Telegraph* with a defiant stance: "Today, I find St Augustine with his two great books to be more relevant to our existence than any book by a contemporary author." He saw a series of social enigmas in Jane Austen. He backed up quotations from Mérimée's *Columba* and delved out of a cupboard new recordings of Handel's *Messiah* and *Le Nozze di Figaro* with the best contralto he'd ever heard. Then he played several recordings of "Vissi d'arte" in order to decide if the Tosca of choice was Lisa Della Casa, Tebaldi or Callas. Perhaps Welitsch?

On the title page of my copy of *Thy Hand, Great Anarch!* he wrote, "My books have [intended word "made" accidently omitted] new friends for me out of strangers – and today I have had another experience of the same kind. Nirad C. Chaudhuri, Oxford, 12 May 1989."

Postscript. In an article I mentioned an error that Chaudhuri had made writing about the disaster of December 1941 when Japanese aircraft sank at sea the *Prince of Wales* and the *Repulse*, misnaming it the *Renown*. Soon I received from him the kind of letter written by someone apologizing for an unforgivable wrong.

ALASDAIR CLAYRE

A Fire by the Sea

1965, ENLARGED EDITION 1973

THE OLD EATON HALL in Cheshire was the place where Officer-Cadets doing their National Service were prepared for commission. Arrival there was something of a shock. The sheer mass of the building was unbelievable. Alfred Waterhouse, the architect, had designed a monument that represented the thrust and achievement of the Victorian age, and in particular the wealth of the owner, the 1st Duke of Westminster. In keeping with the post-1945 emphasis on equality, a later Duke had handed Eaton Hall over to the army. We lived in grandiose rooms adapted to dormitories. It never felt right to be clattering in studded boots down huge marble stairs or racing to a lecture past a majestic old master painting.

Early one half-dark morning, we assembled for drill. Taking the parade was the Senior Officer-Cadet, identified by his shoulder flashes and cap badge as a Grenadier. Recruits from all five regiments of the Brigade of Guards did their basic training at the same barracks, Caterham in Surrey. I didn't recognize him, but it was understood that guardsmen, like birds of a feather, flocked together. Instead he started to shout at me, "Stamp your feet, you idle Coldstreamer!" and the next thing I knew, this officious fellow was handing out extra drills as punishment.

Some time later, and by then a second lieutenant, I had to take my platoon to Pickering in Yorkshire, where the army had a range for rehearsing with live ammunition the infantry tactic designated as Fire and Movement. It was winter and the ground was white. The camp was a cheap affair of Nissen huts left over from the war, with a mural that Rex Whistler had painted on his way through its sole redeeming feature. As I was crossing from one of these huts to another, I heard someone playing a flute. Opening the door, I was face to face with the Grenadier who had thought me idle. This was Alasdair Clayre. The music was Schubert, and he was reading Immanuel Kant. He had been Head of School at Winchester. We both had scholarships to Oxford and he would be going up to Christ Church and I to Magdalen at the beginning of the coming academic year. Meanwhile in the course of the military exercises at Pickering, he and his platoon won some sort of competition, and then had to give a demonstration to the rest of us.

Several generations of Alasdair's family had been doctors and lay missionaries, one of them his father. His mother was to tell me that the father had died when Alasdair was 19 and the loss was so testing that Alasdair could hardly get over it. However that may be, he had the confident good looks and manner of someone on the highway to eminence: a large head with strong features, brown eyes bright with intelligence, a laugh that was almost a shout. Those in contact with him soon recognized his exceptional intellectual energy. We made a point of attending the lectures of Edgar Wind and Isaiah Berlin, and on one particular occasion my attention wandered and I failed to follow the discussion. What was that about, I asked Alasdair afterwards. "Three things have been said today," and he summarized them in unforgettably lucid language. (At a conference I once attended, Margaret Thatcher chose to speak last: she had the same power of synthesis and by coincidence also began by saying, "Three things have been said today.")

One afternoon I happened to meet Alasdair walking across Christ Church Meadows. No doubt we soon engaged in undergraduate chatter about the meaning of this and that. The profound but unapproachable part of his character suddenly took over and right there and then, ankle-deep in long grass, he sang Schumann's great lament for the human condition, *Ich grolle nicht, und wenn das Herz auch bricht* (I bear no grudge even though my heart is breaking).

For the summer vacation of 1957, friends of Alasdair's proposed to charter a yacht that accommodated twelve people – each paying their share – and would sail down the Italian coast from Naples. He arranged for me to be one of this gang. We were still on the train chugging through southern France when he announced that his life's purpose was to reconcile Wittgenstein and Christianity, something too far above my head to have any meaning. The train pulled into the station in Naples. I was lifting a suitcase down from the rack overhead when an arm came through the open window and our hand luggage was gone.

The money in our pockets was all we now had. We decided it would have to do and we would board the yacht as planned. A few days later we were on a beach discussing how to get home. An elderly English lady approached and apologized for eavesdropping, but was sorry for us and offered to lend whatever money we needed. Behind her back stood her son and his wife grimacing, as much as to say, Mother's letting herself be exploited again. By the time the yacht was back in the Naples marina, I had just enough money for a ticket to Rome and the *gettone* with which to call the only Italian I knew, Princess Letitia Boncompagni, a friend of my parents. She was in. It was a hot day when I found my way on foot from Rome station to the Villa Aurora. Unprepossessing as I must have been, the Princess greeted me with the realistic question, How much do you want? and invited me to the lunch party she was about to give. So I met Ignazio Silone and Gian Carlo Menotti.

When it came to Finals, the whole university seemed to have heard that the Chairman of Alasdair's Examiners, the forbidding philosopher Professor J. L. Austin, had said that it had been a real pleasure to read his papers and congratulated him. Such a compliment was virtually unknown. It seemed in the natural order of things that Alasdair went on to win a Prize Fellowship at All Souls, the last word in academic prestige. The world was open to him. I joked that he would end up as His Grace Field Marshal Professor Lord Clayre.

Clarissa and I were married in July 1959 and we saw a lot of Alasdair. At weekends we had the run of a cottage at Somerhill, the great Jacobean house with an estate on the edge of Tonbridge. The owners, Sir Henry and Lady d'Avigdor-Goldsmid, otherwise Harry and Rosie, and their two daughters Sarah and Chloe, used to invite house parties of the old and famous and the up-and-coming young. Alasdair was a perfect fit. After dinner, he might play his guitar and sing his own compositions, perhaps the melancholic "There's a Cold Wind Blowing," or the rather ludicrous "The Invisible Backward-facing Grocer." The Goldsmids nicknamed him The Clarifier.

In 1961, he and I published our first novels, mine entitled *Owls and Satyrs*, his *The Window*, both the kind of book that reviewers damn with faint praise about awaiting with interest to see what this author will do next. That same year, like any right-thinking intellectual at that moment, Alasdair went to Israel. An envelope addressed with Byronic spelling to Childe Pryce-Jones and postmarked Tiberias contained the words of a song for Clarissa. The opening lines are, "I heard a baby cry / And saw a mother lean her golden head / Across the cradle with a lullaby," leading to the final couplet, "And then a winter darkness, still and long / Closed over child, and golden hair, and song." The intimation of the child's death is unmistakeable, though I made nothing of it at the time. Isaiah Berlin happened to be in Israel, and he was more perceptive. In a letter to his Oxford colleague Stuart Hampshire in October 1961, he described an encounter with Alasdair and their discussion about which kibbutz might provide solitude and a private life. "I do not know quite what is wrong, but something certainly is," Isaiah concluded. "There really is a screw loose somewhere – rattling audibly."

Together Alasdair and I visited Wormwoods Scrubs and Pentonville for articles about the prison system. Alasdair took up architecture and in the course of qualifying won the profession's major award, the Leverhulme Gold Medal. *A Fire by the Sea* is his one book of poetry, and he reworked and extended the contents for a subsequent, more presentable edition. "Pope Kept Awake at Limehouse" reflects his own experience of living in a studio near the Commercial Dock.

Ten times the bray of "Bye bye baby" stuns the waking day,
still as great ships glide by with silent lights
loud "Bye bye baby" rocks the sleepless nights.

He also collected folk songs, composing, performing and recording some of his own. Broadcasting, work and play, the cooperative principle, political economy, were subjects that fully engaged him one after the other until they were exhausted. Friends bandied about various theories to explain why he didn't find a cause or a task or an office that would hold him and allow him to do the good for the whole society that he so evidently wanted to do. Perhaps he found everything too easy and was searching for something he wouldn't be able to do.

Although at first fully engaged emotionally with his numerous girlfriends, he dropped them without ceremony when the affair was exhausted. Over the years, one after another had come to sit weeping in our kitchen and they seemed to get younger the older he grew. In 1974 he married Felicity Duncan, a leading literary agent. Since her father was a Member of Parliament, the ceremony took place in a chapel in Westminster. The marriage lasted six years. Subsequently living on his own, borrowing a good many thousand pounds from his mother for a flat, he was evidently searching out new people in his life, or so we thought.

A breaking point for Clarissa and me was Alasdair's sudden and total conversion to The Process. This was an offshoot of Scientology operated by a couple who called themselves Mr. and Mrs. de Grimston, quite likely a pseudonym. The purpose of The Process was obscure. What was clear, however, was that everyone associated with it was obliged to make their money over to the de Grimstons. Like many others, Clarissa's brother, David Caccia, admired and trusted Alasdair. A relation had left him a substantial fortune that he was ready to give the de Grimstons on Alasdair's say-so. I had it out with the de Grimstons. I could not help noticing that in one corner of their office was a pile of books promoting Nazism and Fascism. Then I had to tell Alasdair that the whole point of being an Oxford philosopher and fellow of All Souls was to promote reason, not rubbish. It was inexplicable. Eventually he apologized, David Caccia did not beggar himself but the damage had been done.

A few days into January 1984, I was walking towards the BBC when I spotted Alasdair coming out. Distress was visible on his face. For the past three years he had been researching and writing *The Heart of the Dragon*, a book about China from which a thirteen-part television series had been made. The book was now out and he'd just been interviewed about it on the BBC. He said it had been a fiasco, he couldn't answer the questions, he'd dried up, he had to confess he didn't read Mandarin Chinese but was restricted to secondary sources, he couldn't be a serious historian. I tried to reassure him and said it didn't matter anyhow, audiences wouldn't remember if he'd performed well or badly.

A few days later, Felicity telephoned with the news that he had thrown himself under a train. He was 48. A psychiatrist who had had sessions with him said that usually people on the borderline of genius and madness kill themselves much younger, when they are around 20. We had been granted these extra years with Alasdair and should be grateful for that. Have nothing to do with genius, the psychiatrist summed up, it creates and it destroys.

LUCIEN COMBELLE

Péché d'Orgueil

1978

ONE OF MY EARLIEST MEMORIES dates from June 1940. A four-year-old, I was at Royaumont, our family house near Chantilly. Woken up in the middle of the night I understood that the Germans might arrive at any minute. I dressed in the dark. The grown-ups were in a panic. All day long, we drove south. At some point we slowed down amid desperate people from all levels of the population clogging the road in a *sauve-qui-peut* already being compared to the biblical Exodus. The face of a woman staring through the car window has stayed with me.

A good number of politicians and writers, with Irène Nemirovsky at their head, have come up against the fact that the absence of moral structure committed the French to save themselves at all costs, putting paid to any idea of sacrifice and resistance on behalf of the nation. As the German army was marching unopposed into Paris, to give one example of degradation, a solitary colonel tried to set up a machine-gun position at the Porte d'Orléans, only to be prevented by a police inspector. Or again, Otto Abetz, the German Ambassador, accompanied the troops in a civilian car flying a swastika. To his amazemernt, crowds in notionally Communist working-class districts turned out to applaud him.

The decision not to defend the historic capital city of France led irrevocably to surrender and humiliation. Under enemy occupation life of course must go on. The relationship between victor and vanquished is decidedly ambiguous because it has to take into account all sorts of obligations. Disregarding a century's experience of hostility and harm at the hands of Germans, a majority of the French became willing collaborators. Intellectuals, some of them very public figures, in particular miscalculated the costs and benefits of Nazi collaboration, compromising themselves and leaving a lasting stain on the national character.

By general consent, André Gide was the leading French writer of the day. The armistice had hardly been signed when he was noting in his *Journal*, destined for publication: "To come to terms with yesterday's enemy is not cowardice but wisdom; as well as accepting what is inevitable." Each and every collaborator would have subscribed happily to that pronouncement. Gide retired to Tunis, where he lived out the rest of the war apparently unconcerned with events in his own country. Compare and contrast this self-indulgence to the campaign against Hitler led by Thomas Mann, by general consent the leading German writer of the day.

Commissioned to write *Paris in the Third Reich,* I had assumed that former fascists and collaborators would not be willing to speak to me. Literary etiquette made me introduce myself first of all to Henri Amouroux. His history of the German occupation runs to ten monumental volumes, pulling off the exceptional feat of writing objectively with a patriotic bias. Enthusiastically, he opened his

INSIDE
THE THIRD
REICH

*To David Pryce — Jones
with best wishes and
thanks for our interesting conversation*

MEMOIRS
BY
ALBERT SPEER

*Albert Speer
Heidelberg, 25-VI-76*

Translated from the German by
RICHARD and CLARA WINSTON

Introduction by
EUGENE DAVIDSON

WEIDENFELD AND NICOLSON
5 Winsley Street London W1

files, providing names and addresses and vouching for me. A dark underworld emerged.

Jacques Benoist-Méchin still believed that it was rational for a defeated France to side with a Germany out for conquest. Morality did not come into it. "I was pushed by events," was his excuse. He had been to Germany with his good friend Ambassador Otto Abetz, and he had accompanied Admiral Darlan to Berchtesgaden in 1941 to negotiate with Hitler over Syria. It had been impressive to meet Hitler, this "very extraordinary man" who had so much power. After the war he was sentenced to death and *indignité nationale*, but his presidential reprieve after a few years gave away that this was more for the sake of appearances than justice. Alfred Fabre-Luce, another influential intellectual, had taken greater care to cover his tracks. Henry Coston, himself a born conspirator, specialized in the accusation that Jews and Freemasons were conspiring to remake the world in their image, and the whole purpose of his career, implicitly murderous, was to denounce them to the authorities. In 1948 he was sentenced to life imprisonment with forced labor. Listening to him, I discovered that in the three years he actually served, he had forgotten nothing and learnt nothing.

In this rogues' gallery, Lucien Combelle stood out. A young man from a modest background, he had come a long way. Undoubtedly intelligent, he had literary ambitions and by the end of the Thirties he had become the secretary of André Gide. The writers he hoped to emulate valued achievement above equality. Pride in himself was the source of his Fascism. A key sentence, "I went and listened to the sound of the drums," allows *Péché d'Orgueil* to be both confession and excuse. Condemned to fifteen years of hard labor, he benefited from the amnesty granted to French fascists of all sorts. For several decades now, the European Union has been doing its utmost to reduce the concepts of occupation and collaboration to anachronisms in order to spare the feelings of French intellectuals of Combelle's generation. The inscription here nonetheless conveys residual memories of shame and guilt. "Cette insolite histoire franco-allemande pour un historien anglais, une façon comme une autre d'être européen, en profonde *entente cordiale.*" I translate: "This exceptional Franco-German story which for an English historian is one among other ways of being European, with the deepest Entente Cordiale."

Postscript. Pierre Belfonds, a go-ahead publisher, bought the French rights to my book. A wretched first translation had to be scrapped. I was due to talk about the book on "Cinq Colonnes à la Une," then the leading television program covering the arts. Four weeks before publication, Belfonds telephoned. Someone very important was objecting to my book but he could not divulge who this was, nor what the grounds for suppression were. All he could say was that he was not prepared to put the future of his firm at risk for my sake.

CYRIL CONNOLLY
Previous Convictions
1963

A S THE AUTHOR OF A BOOK about Cyril Connolly, I am sometimes asked why anyone should read him. Well, the case for the defense might open with a plea that he's a pretty good representative of the 1930s intellectuals who took opinions from the Left and dined on the Right. At that time in the wake of James Joyce and Marcel Proust, it was an item of faith for would-be writers that a successful novel was the only literary success worth having. In Cyril's opinion, a shelf life of ten years was enough to qualify a book as a masterpiece. "If it was any good once," according to an aphorism of his that took account of changing taste, "it isn't any good now." Published by the hole-in-a-corner Obelisk Press in Paris in 1936, Cyril's novel *The Rock Pool* was the kind of standard tribute to bohemian life that a good many of his contemporaries were also paying. In the course of researching in Cyril's papers, I found notebooks of varying sizes in which he'd written a page or two of fiction and left the rest blank; so many false starts for that absent masterpiece.

A stronger line of defense is the tone of his language as it ranges naturally all the way from humor to despair, sometimes combining both extremes. "Imprisoned in every fat man a thin one is wildly signalling to be let out" is a phrase of his that has become more or less common stock, and another is "It is closing time in the gardens of the West." His humor was sudden and unexpected, for example describing being alone in the country with nothing to do and nobody to see as "practicing death," or saying of the sexually charged Vita Sackville-West that she was Lady Chatterley above the waist and Mellors below.

Finally the work speaks for itself. From 1940 right through the war and up to 1950, Cyril edited *Horizon*, a magazine of such a high literary standard that it has hardly dated at all. Week after week from 1954 and then for over twenty of the following years, he was to write the lead book review for the *Sunday Times*. Committing himself to be a regular critic, he made fun of it too, in the context of reviewing fiction: "Brave and agile, the reviewer enters the ring.... He disembowels a few old hacks. But his onsets eventually grow futile, his weapons are blunted, his words are stale ... eventually the jungle claims him."

"At Eton with Orwell,/at Oxford with Waugh,/He was nobody after,/and nothing before." Cyril's much-quoted deflation of himself, written apparently impromptu in the visitors' book of a friend. Born within six weeks of each other in the summer of 1903, the three of them were engaged in unacknowledged competition, very different personalities though they were. Orwell is on record saying, "Without Connolly's help I don't think I would have got started as a writer when I came back from Burma." Only a few months separate the publication of *Animal Farm, Brideshead Revisited* and *The Unquiet Grave*. Orwell and Waugh both had their conception of the way the world should turn out; Cyril was lamenting the way he had turned out. In the manner of someone said to be drowning, Cyril in *The Unquiet Grave* sees his whole life pass before him, his loves, his travels, his faults, his admiration for the great predecessors who had left masterpieces for posterity. Proust had once written that human beings would always be dissatisfied because they want something other than what they already have. Cyril liked to apply this existential truth to himself in the original and elegant French, "Le plus grand amour c'est l'amour d'autre chose." It was singular of him to make failure out actually to be achievement.

Among books lying about in the house as I was growing up was *The Condemned Playground*. And there, in "Where Engels Fears To Tread" (whose sophistication and brilliance I only understood years later) a sentence suddenly stood out: "It was no coincidence, Pryce-Jones, that you have lived near three royal palaces." The family name on the printed page!

In the summer of 1953, my father took me to the Bayreuth Festival. Cyril Connolly was there, and so was George Weidenfeld, who had just published *Ideas and Places*, a book edited by Cyril and the first of his to appear on the Weidenfeld list. Both these men were on their own. A generous American lady, Jane Panzer (not necessarily a surname to flaunt in Bavaria at the time) had a huge car and a chauffeur. We were all driven to Pommersfelden, where Countess Schoenborn explained how an American General had tried to requisition the house, but she had turned him away on the grounds that it was too grand and its collections too important to be treated this way. On a sideboard in the dining room were rows of double eggcups in ornate eighteenth-century silver. One egg is never enough, Cyril said, but three is too many. Cyril also complained about his wife, Barbara Skelton. George was afterwards to maintain that Cyril had been licensing him to have an affair with her. I couldn't have known it then, but this was the beginning of a drama that generated gossip still current years later.

Barbara was beautiful and demanding. In Cyril's papers is an enlarged photograph of her stark naked somewhere on a beach in a classic femme fatale pose. When she and Cyril divorced, George was cited as co-respondent. She then married George, and when she divorced him Cyril was cited as co-respondent. The symmetry was damaging for all concerned. *Tears Before Bedtime* and *Weep No More*, Barbara Skelton's two memoirs, portray Cyril as a figure of fun, either to be laughed at or sneered at, in any case to be taken at his own valuation as a failure.

Also in these papers is Cyril's lengthy account, mostly in the form of handwritten letters, of an equally fraught amorous passage. He had then been married for ten years or so to Jean Bakewell, a freethinking American who nevertheless was tiring of Cyril's wayward self-indulgence and had gone by herself in the summer of 1939 to stay with friends on the French Riviera. In London and far from feeling abandoned, Cyril was having an affair with Diana Witherby and had just learnt that she was expecting his child. (She was to publish poems in *Horizon* and collect them in a very slim volume; the unborn child would grow up to become a judge.) Cyril persuaded the seventeen-year-old Janetta Woolley (first Janetta Kee, later Janetta Jackson, later still Janetta Parladé) to drive with him across France and somehow help him explain to Jean about Diana. When they stopped for the night in the town of Tulle, Cyril was arrested by the local gendarmerie for *détention de mineur*. When I invited her to the house and we went over the burlesque documentation, she said she would sue if I put any of this in print. As soon as my book was out, however, friends and enemies were writing or telephoning that Janetta was going around accusing me of suppressing one of the most important episodes in the history of Cyril's libido and my book was therefore no good at all. One unexpected critic on these lines was the war hero Paddy Leigh Fermor, who sought me out to say, "The trouble with you is that you belong to the wrong team." I answered that I hadn't known a match was being played.

"David with love from Cyril — Somerhill Sept 1965 in gratitude for so many pleasant meetings," Cyril wrote in my copy of *Previous Con-*

victions, a selection of his literary articles and reviews. Bibliophile that he was, he especially valued copies of books with inscriptions and associations. He asked me to correct the proofs of *The Modern Movement,* and repeated his previous "David with love from Cyril," adding, rather ungrammatically, "who spotted everything but 'exercises' for 'exercases' but left wee Blakmur – gratefully, Cyril," with the date December 1, 1965. By then, Cyril had married Deirdre, and they lived first in a house on the estate of Lord Gage at Firle, then in Eastbourne. At one point, we were a ticket short for a performance of *Don Giovanni* at Glyndebourne. Staying behind, a dishevelled Cyril came out of the house barefoot and wearing a bathrobe, and as he waved the black-tie party off to the opera, he started grimacing and mouthing, "In Italia mille tre."

Rosie d'Avigdor-Goldsmid refused even to greet George Weidenfeld, much less to acknowledge that some things might be in his favor. In the same spirit of solidarity, Rosie and Harry made a point of inviting the Connollys to Somerhill for the weekend or at least for Sunday lunch. In spite of a very full meal, we went one day to the tea-shop in the Pantiles in Tunbridge Wells. Waiting for his order of poached eggs, Cyril suddenly improvised in a voice loud enough for people at other tables to look round, "This is the start of a new literary movement, it's a revolution. Down with Koestler! Down with Spender!" (I have D. H. Lawrence's *Pansies* inscribed, "Stephen from Cyril with gratitude for benefit received and in the hope of benefits to come," which puts Spender in his place without seeming to do so.) The Pantiles also had a very good second-hand bookshop. Cyril had first pick of books that had been delivered from the library of a poet who had just died, and he bought an armful. I found *Indian Ass,* Harold Acton's early volume of poems. Cyril asked to have a look at it, and I only saw it again years later in Tulsa, Oklahoma, along with the rest of the archive he had sold to the university there.

"Connolly's being funny again," he said of himself in *Enemies of Promise,* though the line between giving pleasure and giving offence couldn't ever be very clear. He couldn't resist being funny, even about friends as loyal as Rosie. She would sign off a telephone call by blowing three make-believe kisses into the receiver, *mwah mwah mwah*. Cyril imagined her offering him a birthday present, he could have whatever he had set his heart on. A tree, Rosie, that's what I'd really like. A tree, Cyril darling, of course you shall have a tree, order it and send me the bill. But Cyril darling, what's this, a thousand pounds for a tree? Yes Rosie, it's a very rare tree that's come all the way from China, *mwah, mwah, mwah*.

We were living in Kensington in 1971, in a house big enough to give a party to launch my novel *Running Away*. It was a fine summer evening. The guests met on the lawn, among them not only Cyril but also, quite naturally, George Weidenfeld, the publisher of this book. When Cyril came out at the back door we suddenly realized that we had unconsciously committed the faux pas of inviting two men who everyone there knew were not on speaking terms.

At the far end of the garden was a medium-size bench. George and Cyril were not shaped to squeeze up there for any length of time, but they did, uncomfortable and bulbous but out of earshot. They were almost the last to leave. On several occasions later on, one or the other would tell me how glad they were to have been reconciled in my garden.

Breakfasting at Somerhill, one of the guests told Cyril that the character Everard Spruce in Evelyn Waugh's *Sword of Honour* was obviously an unflattering caricature of him. A furious Cyril pulled from his pocket a letter from Waugh denying in strong language that Spruce was based on him, and using even stronger language to blast anyone and everyone who thought he was — surely the kind of face-saving lie to which novelists can be driven. The sparring match between the two had opened with Cyril's generous review in the *New Statesman* of Waugh's first novel *Decline and Fall*. Several Waugh books have insupportable characters, clowns really, the name Connolly fixing their lowly or buffoonish status. It is never clear if Waugh is being malicious or giving way to his idea of a private joke.

The *Tablet*, the weekly edited by and for Catholic intellectuals, sent

Waugh a review copy of *The Unquiet Grave*. "Twaddle" was his instant reaction on reading the book, and in red ink he jotted bad-tempered or scornful remarks. He cannot have imagined that Connolly would ever read them. Waugh was pleased to note in his diary that his review had caused consternation. In the aftermath, Cyril nonetheless spent a weekend with Waugh and devoted a whole issue of *Horizon* to *The Loved One*, Waugh's American extravaganza. In 1971 a series of unlikely events put Waugh's review copy of *The Unquiet Grave* into Cyril's hands. Offended, he took those red ink jottings at face value. Waugh himself was already dead. Cyril's only redress was to sell the books that Waugh had presented him, special editions with inscriptions though they were. Writing about Waugh one last time he didn't try to get even, being more thoughtful than rude: "A genuine ill-doer and not merely an ill-wisher to the human race, is an object of fascination." There's competition in it, maybe even admiration. It comes to mind that when George Orwell was dying, Cyril arranged for Waugh to visit him in hospital. Orwell had intended to write about Waugh but he was too close to death to finish the essay. In his judgment, "Waugh is about as good a novelist as one can be while holding untenable opinions." These three writers disagreed but their opinion of each other is the literary centerpiece of the age.

ROBERT CONQUEST

The Great Terror

1968

THE QUESTION WITH BOB is whether he was a poet who happened to be a Sovietologist or a Sovietologist who happened to be a poet. I tend to think the former, because poetry answered to his view of making whatever there is to be made out of emotions, colors, life itself. Published in 2009 when he was in his nineties, *Penultimata*, contains about a hundred new poems. One of them, "Last Hours," best expresses the let's-get-on-with-it Bob that I knew and liked.

> Dead in the water, the day is done.
> There's nothing new under the sun,
> Still less when it's gone down.

He and his two closest friends, Kingsley Amis and Philip Larkin, proved their vocation by playing the games with language and perception that poets play, three Musketeers at a time when not much else was disturbing the quiet little cemetery of English literature.

My friendship with Bob goes back to 1963 when he was foreign editor of the *Spectator*, and I was its literary editor. At the time, the Soviet Union appeared to be gaining the upper hand in the Cold War, and its criminality at home and abroad was a regular subject for discussion with others on the staff, for instance Tony Hartley and Iain Hamilton. It was amazing that so clear-minded a chap (he liked the word) as Bob should ever have joined the Communist Party, what's more in 1937, which thanks to Stalin was one of the most frightening years in Russian and indeed European history. In 1944 he was posted to Bulgaria as a liaison officer to Bulgarian units fighting under Soviet orders, or to put it bluntly, preparing for a Communist take-over under cover of driving the German army out. After this formative experience, he joined a department of the Foreign Office set up to research the Soviet Union.

Communism was to the twentieth century what sorcery had been to the Middle Ages. The claim of the foundational doctrine of Marxism to be a science was pure witchcraft. Something known as the dialectic was said to be the key to progress, and everybody had to make sense of this figment. The state was supposed to wither away, leaving us all to look after ourselves as though back in the Garden of Eden, yet in the starkest of contradictions the Communist state granted itself ever more total power over the individual in every aspect of daily life. The organizing principle of class became a sentence of death, exile or dispossession for tens of millions of men and women defined as bourgeois, capitalist, kulak or whatever could be profitably exploited.

Bob had spent the Sixties studying Soviet demographic statistics and census returns in order to measure as accurately as possible the drastic fall in population brought about by Stalin's criminal policies. *The Great Terror*, published in 1968, was straightforward in language, firm in tone and careful in depicting the ruthlessness with which Stalin had sent to their death millions of Party members, soldiers from the rank of Field Marshal downwards, princes and peasants and anyone else whom he judged fit to distrust. Eight years later, on the eve of the Gorbachev era, Bob's *The Harvest of Sorrow* was the first fully documented account of the Soviet collectivization of agriculture and the famine deliberately induced in the Ukraine which also cost millions of people their lives. Only when the Soviet Union was reincarnated as Russia did he go there and meet the people whose fate he had brought to the world's attention.

A mystery of the age is the eagerness with which so many people in the democracies took at face value whatever the Soviet Union said about itself. Suspending their critical faculties, Western Communists and fellow-travelers had no trouble justifying mass murder, subversion, treason and mendacity. The sophisticated and the unsophisticated alike, the rich and the poor, seemed in a trance, spellbound. It was phenomenal that intellectuals (with old Etonians such as Perry Anderson or Neal Ascherson foremost among them) should be deceiving themselves as much as they were deceiving others.

Two versions emerged of everything that had occurred concerning the Soviet Union. On the one hand, Bob was the leading historian telling the truth about atrocious events, and on the other hand, Eric Hobsbawm was the leading propagandist falsifying these same events. For him, Communism was bound to triumph because the Soviet Union could do no wrong, whether it was invading other countries or oppressing the defenseless. He was skilled at misrepresentation, for instance whitewashing Communism as "a formidable innovation" in social engineering; and simply omitting everything that told against him, for instance the massacre of Polish officers at Katyn or the concentration camps of the Gulag. Bob pointed out that Hobsbawm suffered from a "massive denial of reality" and added very characteristically, "If he chooses to write rubbish, then good luck to him." David Caute, a friend of mine since Oxford and himself influenced by Marxism, put the issue once and for all in a review: "One keeps asking of Hobsbawm: didn't you know what Deutscher and Orwell knew? Didn't you know about the induced famine, the horrors of collectivisation, the false confessions, the terror within the Party, the massive forced labour of the Gulag?" Another Oxford contemporary, however, once asked me how I could bear the company of the well-known fascist Conquest. (Constantine Fitzgibbon, a colleague with a career very similar in war and peace to Bob's, gave his Sixties collection of anti-Communist essays the ironic title *Random Thoughts of a Fascist Hyena*.)

In an interview in 1994, Hobsbawm gave away that his high hopes for Communism still had a total hold on him. The astonished interviewer picked him up: "What that comes down to is saying that had the radiant tomorrow actually been created, the loss of fifteen, twenty million people might have been justified?" To which the response was "Yes." Proven morally corrupt by his own words, and wrong by the course of events, Hobsbawm nonetheless had at least ten honorary doctorates from well-known universities, and received the prestigious Companion of Honour from Prime Minister Blair. Bob had just two honorary doctorates and no civic awards in Britain, though a grateful George W. Bush in the United States did give him the Medal of Freedom.

Towards the end of his life, Bob required the help of Liddie, his solicitous wife. His voice became almost inaudible, his handwriting almost illegible. We would have to gather round closely in the effort to catch what he was saying. Among other things, he felt that the limerick was a literary form with unexplored potential, especially suited for taking pretentious persons down a peg or two, and he protected himself from the libel laws by circulating some of the cleverest of them anonymously. The most-quoted of his limericks is a masterpiece of Sovietology:

> There was an old Marxist called Lenin
> Who did two or three million men in.
> That's a lot to have done in,
> But where he did one in,
> That grand Marxist Stalin did ten in.

A Garden of Erses is a collection that came out in 2010, and from the inventive rhyming, humor and raunchiness it was easy to deduce that Jeff Chaucer, the ostensible author, was really Bob. When eventually all his limericks can be published unexpurgated, they will help to qualify Bob for immortality.

ANTHONY DANIELS
ALIAS THEODORE DALRYMPLE

The Proper Procedure

2017

EIGHT OF TONY'S BOOKS are on my shelves, most of them credited to Theodore Dalrymple, his favorite nom de plume. All are marvelously idiosyncratic, the work of someone closely observing the human comedy while himself standing apart from it. A prolific journalist as well, his articles are usually about behavior consistent with the doctrine of original sin. The prose has two registers, one of which is controlled mockery of the many who ought to know better; and the other is the warning that things are awful and we have yet to see how much more awful they will become. In many respects he is the Charles Dickens of the modern age.

A doctor by profession and resolutely curious by instinct, Tony has made himself familiar with all the ills to which everybody is heir. Work or foreign travel familiarized him with every sort of pain and failure. In Liberia at a time of anarchy, he happened to see thugs saw-ing the legs off a grand piano, an example of cultural barbarism so extreme that nothing could ever be done except report it. By the time he was employed as doctor and psychiatrist, first in Birming-ham's City Hospital and then in its Winson Green Prison, he had every reason to subscribe to the credo of the genuine conservative, namely that the veneer of civilization is frighteningly thin, hard to create but easy to destroy.

In the early 1990s, Tony made his mark with a short pithy col-umn for the *Spectator*, afterwards collecting the whole lot into a book, *If Symptoms Persist*. "For David and Clarissa, in praise of the modern world, Theodore" is what he wrote with typical gamesmanship on the title page of my copy, following up in the foreword on the very next page with what he really thought: "I am convinced that the poverty of spirit to be found in an English slum is the worst to be found anywhere ... for sheer apathy, for spiritual, emotional, educa-tional and cultural nihilism and vacuity, you must go to an English slum. Nowhere in the world — at least in my experience — are peo-ple to be found who have so little control over, or responsibility for, their own lives and behaviour." Worse still, they are under the illu-sion that others, "the Social, the doctor, the Housing, the Council" will come to the rescue and "make them whole" as he puts it.

A good twenty years later, he went over this ground once more in *The Proper Procedure*, a collection of short stories. The opening pas-sage of the opening story goes, "Life in Percy Bysshe Shelley House, a concrete tower opposite its identical twin, Harold Laski House, was growing more and more intolerable." Note the compressed suggestion of the multiple horrors of town planning, bureaucracy, contemporary architecture, cultural pretension and elitist patronizing of the uneducated masses. What a wonderful satirical effect the juxtaposed names of Shelley and Laski have! The very next paragraph gathers speed: "What a country! The people couldn't even speak or spell their own language properly, and hardly knew that any other languages existed. They knew nothing of their own literature and cared even less; their pleasures were coarse and brutish, their food revolting, their manners, if such you could call them, appalling. It was not so much that they lacked refinement, these people; rather they hated refinement and persecuted it wherever they found or even suspected it." No wonder Tony wrote for me on the fly-leaf above his signature, "Something to quell your optimism, if ever you feel any."

Several generations of intellectuals have succeeded in imposing their belief that the collective is superior to the individual. They have encouraged inspectors, social workers, administrators, planners, civil servants and indeed virtually all employees of the state to re-design our culture, what's left of it, to adapt the title of one of Tony's books. The unrefined men and women whose sad fate so upsets Tony are victims of theories developed in libraries and now being tested to destruction. Who would have thought, Tony put the question in one of his articles, that within a few years of the conclusion of the Cold War Britain would have undergone so much creeping Sovietization. Intellectuals come standardized these days, they have much the same education, much the same friends, much the same experience from which to draw much the same conclusions, with the witless togetherness of herd animals. And who could conceivably have imagined that someone defending old civilized ways of living would necessarily be compelled to go against the grain.

PHILIPPE DAUDY

Les Anglais

1989

L IKE A BULL, Philippe Daudy charged through life. Born in 1925, he had an energy that seemed to be powering ideas, and what's more, ideas that rapidly evolved into projects.

Eight formative years of his childhood were spent in Ethiopia, where his father, Bernard, was a doctor. Researching for the Pasteur Institute, Bernard died from a snake-bite. Back in France, Philippe was still a schoolboy when the Germans overran the country. His teacher was dismissed because he was Jewish. Philippe's reaction was characteristic. Mouvement Ouvrier International, the resistance movement he joined, was on the Left, quite likely a Communist front, consisting mostly of Yiddish-speaking Jews and Spanish Republican exiles. When they attacked the German transport depot at Villeurbanne in Lyon, Philippe was hit by a bullet that passed close to vital organs. For fear of being denounced, he could not be treated in a hospital. Never extracted, the bullet was to give him permanent trouble. At the end of the war, many members of this resistance movement proposed first of all to shoot collaborators and then to become Communists. Philippe, still only twenty, was one of those who argued them out of both courses of action.

Joining Agence France-Presse, the news agency, Philippe covered the post-1945 fighting in Greece and Korea, and he was a foreign correspondent reporting from Tito's Yugoslavia — rather too favorably, he came to think. In 1968 he married Marie-Christine Gouin, a childhood friend of mine since we had been neighbors at Royaumont. Once the commission to write a book about Britain was signed, they moved to London and bought a house in deepest Chelsea. I was able to introduce Philippe to some of the people he wanted to interview. The first draft of *Les Anglais* was too conventional he decided, so he rewrote it. The sympathy he revealed to all things British in his final version contrasts with the condescension that came naturally to Anthony Sampson, whose *Anatomy of Britain* was a sort of competitor.

One day Philippe said to me that the ancient Greeks believed in *daimon*, an untranslatable word which he took to mean being possessed by a spirit stronger than oneself. Supposedly thanks to my *daimon* my books were so many judgements about the rights and wrongs of this world, so many attacks and defenses. And this from a man who had been in a fire-fight with the Gestapo and stood on a platform in a crowded hall to tell the truth about the Soviet Union.

MILOVAN DJILAS

Conversations with Stalin

1962

ONE OF JOHN ANSTEY's editorial suggestions was that I should write about the Balkans for the *Telegraph* Colour Magazine. So in the spring of 1967, I found myself in Zagreb, the capital of Croatia, which at the time was just one of the seven different entities of the Yugoslav federation. I had an introduction to Vlado Gotovac, a Croatian nationalist and open advocate of reform, all of which the Communist regime would find intolerably provocative. The look on his face made it immediately obvious that he believed my visit was bound to be recorded and held against him. Leading me to the window, he pointed out numerous policemen in plain clothes standing by shiny black cars, evidently a team keeping him under surveillance. In due course he was arrested, tried and sentenced to four years in prison.

In Belgrade, the poet Miodrag Pavlović took me to a bookshop. The man I glimpsed browsing before we hastily backed out was Alexander Rankovic, until lately chief of the secret police that had maintained Josip Broz, alias Marshal Tito, in power as head of the Yugoslav Communist Party and President of the country. Tito had lived in Moscow for five years, astute enough to survive Stalin's Great Terror. "Tito is a smart fellow!" Stalin said approvingly, "He has no problems with enemies – he has got rid of them all."

During the war, Tito had two equally important but incompatible objectives, to drive the German army of occupation out of the country and to prepare for the post-war Communist take-over of power. Milovan Djilas, his deputy and a hard-line Communist with the blood of so-called class enemies on his hands, had accompanied him on missions to Moscow. Tito then broke with Stalin in the first assertion of the very same nationalism that eventually would destroy the Yugoslav federation. Stalin famously boasted that he had only to shake his little finger and Tito would fall. Tito's immediate transformation from Party hero to Party villain was the manipulation of opinion that George Orwell unforgettably defined as a Two Minutes Hate. James Klugmann, for instance, a member of the Central Committee of the British Communist Party, had worked clandestinely through British Intelligence to put Tito in power, but now wrote to order *From Trotsky to Tito*, a polemic designed to trace a straight line of treason between the two.

In a similar transformation from Party hero into villain, Djilas became Tito's arch-critic, as Ian Kershaw expressed it in the second volume of his comprehensive history of twentieth century Europe. For Djilas, Communism in practice was a social system that enriched and privileged the unscrupulous few and impoverished everyone else. To the world at large, Soviet Communism was evidently a cover for Russian imperialism. Tito had him sent to prison for nine years. While serving the sentence, Djilas wrote *Conversations with Stalin*. Posterity will always have to take into consideration this unique and frankly devastating memoir of Stalin in the crisis of war.

Out of the blue, I telephoned him. He invited me to his house. Only a few months earlier, he had served out his sentence, and still had what he called "the look of a convict." A Montenegrin, he had grown up amid banditry, feuding and rebellion. First and foremost he was a dissident, willing and able to tell the truth as he saw it, no matter what the cost. "I know nothing about you," Djilas said to me, "you may be a spy or provocateur. But if you have any influence, use it to tell the Americans that they must win the war in Vietnam." The United States alone had the strength to stand between the Soviet Union and China. If it were to withdraw, he feared, countries including his and mine would be compelled to take sides in a merciless battle of the great powers for supremacy.

Hearing this point of view, Mark Schorer, an eminent biographer and chairman of the English literature faculty at Berkeley, arranged for me to speak about Djilas on the university campus. There were even promotional posters. Djilas had credentials. Nevertheless, those who came to listen to the talk were in favor of withdrawing in order to lose the war, and they were noisy about it too. In common with dissidents, I failed to convince.

LAWRENCE DURRELL

Constance

1982

A NOVELIST IS SUPPOSED to create his or her own world, fictional but believable, and word of mouth in the Oxford of my day kept on promising that this was what Lawrence Durrell had done. And so he had. *The Alexandria Quartet* fixed in my head a whole carnival of characters suave yet exotic, with names like Mountolive and

Pursewarden, who expressed themselves in aphorisms, quotations and generally playful literary language. Latter-day Cleopatras, the womenfolk — Clea, Justine, Melissa — were working their passages through the cultural mix-up of the Middle East complete with Copts and Muslims. At home, the British were living in the darkness of *Look Back in Anger*, the void of *The Birthday Party*, the morbid paintings of John Bratby, and Durrell was a light to lighten them. Nobody else was writing like that.

The Suez campaign of 1956 for a few days looked likely to provide my introduction to Egypt. My national service had not much longer to run, but my regiment was on stand-by, busily camouflaging whatever they could with paint supposedly as yellow as the desert. Many of the men had previously been stationed along the Canal. *Shufti* and *bint* and *baksheesh* were familiar terms in their vocabulary. A ditty that went, "King Farook, hang his bollocks on a 'ook" told you what the guardsmen were thinking. At the last minute, we were stood down and I went up to Oxford as planned. More than ten years were to pass before I was in a position to match the extravagant world of *The Alexandria Quartet* against the grime of Egypt.

Gamal Abdel Nasser, the Egyptian strongman, had used his 1956 victory to militarize the country. The kind of Levantine characters who had caught Durrell's imagination had no means to defend themselves. Dispossessed, their businesses and fortunes sequestrated, Alexandrian Greeks, Italians, Jews, Armenians, fled to the United States and Canada, lucky to escape with their lives. Victor Simaica Bey was one particular family friend whose estate was confiscated. Waguih Ghali's novel *Beer in the Snooker Club* has a scene in which a rich lady is obliged to hand out to expectant but shame-faced fellahin the legal right of each to a miniscule strip of her land. Worse was to come as Nasser lent himself to the Soviet Union, opened concentration camps for those who might disagree with him, and squandered the country's future in wars that led nowhere.

By the time the *Daily Telegraph* Colour Magazine sent me to interview Durrell in 1982 to coincide with the publication of *Constance*, he had settled down in Sommières, a historic fortified village in Provence. The foundations of the bridge across the river Vidourle had been laid in the reign of the emperor Tiberius. "Monsieur du Rèle," the locals called him. The house he lived in had been built around 1900, a provincial villa with the only slate roof in this region of semi-circular terracotta tiles. The rooms were sparse, impersonal except for some Chinese lacquered boards and a framed sheet of manuscript that Stendhal had written. The verandah room in which he lived and did his writing had pastel-shaded stained glass and a table with a green plastic cloth. Impervious to his surroundings, he evidently had no interest in what money can buy. "I'm terribly flush" was one of the first things he said, as though that was that.

Durrell was a homunculus, a sprite, one of the company of Pan, stocky, his shoulders broad and his legs bandy. A bulbous nose made his head seem disproportionately large and strong. He was wearing a blue shirt and white shorts so ill-fitting that his private parts were exposed. He lived with a much-younger woman and presumably she might have told him to arrange himself but he had sent her out of the house and we never met. Accompanying me, Clarissa and our son Adam, then nine, said nothing at the time, but down the years couldn't help remembering this give-away sight.

Bored to be questioned, bored to be famous yet proud of it too, Durrell laughed at the literary hoo-ha of publishers and agents. His papers have long been in the University of Southern Illinois, and he joked about a couple of American academics "who know more about me than I know about myself." In the same tone of delighted disdain he said, "I'm in the Michelin Guide as one of the tourist attractions here. Couples ring the bell to shake my hand when I'm probably naked in the swimming pool. Partly it's my fault because I made the mistake of appearing on French television."

At about ten o'clock in the morning he started in on the red wine. The old soak, the smoker, the bar-room story-teller, the fabulator, the poet, the colonial, the stag, he could even play the part of the colonel frowning at the young of today who go in for what he called "squirty couplings" and think that's all there is to life. Which reminded him that he'd been employed to rescue a film script set in ancient Egypt, so he had eunuchs parading with *papier-mâché* phalluses sixty foot high: "That's not box-office," the producer had said.

The moment I was back home, I received a letter hotfoot from Durrell with a request not to mention one or two things from our conversation. I wasn't aware that he'd been filling me in with what he described as his "yogic theories about fucking." Whatever these theories might be, he was afraid that they would "hamper the free-selling run of the book and raise blushes and irritation" on the part of *Telegraph* readers. Within a few volatile years, a change of taste had turned his fiction first into a requiem, and then without warning it vanished out of sight down one of the twentieth century's literary rabbit-holes.

AMOS ELON

The Israelis: Founders and Sons

1971

FOR MOST OF 1962 I was living in Haifa or Tel Aviv gathering impressions for *Next Generation: Travels in Israel*, which was published a couple of years later. Some of those I met and even wrote about became lifelong friends and one of them was Amos Elon, whose reporting for *Haaretz*, the daily newspaper of record, had already made him an internationally known journalist. Born in Vienna in 1926, he was seven when his parents brought him and his sister to what was then the British Mandate of Palestine. His Hebrew, German and English were fluent. Immensely well read, he had a sardonic sense of humor and excelled in pointing out ignorance, inconsistency and stupidity. Once upon a time, a great many Jewish intellectuals wrote and talked their way to fame in the cafés of Vienna, and that was the course Amos's life would naturally have taken. It is hardly an exaggeration to think of him in the same frame as Joseph Roth or Stefan Zweig.

On behalf of *Haaretz* Amos was in Hungary at the time of the anti-Communist revolution of 1956, then their correspondent in Washington, finally travelling extensively in order to write his first book, a suitably ambiguous portrait of post-Hitler Germany with the title *Journey Through a Haunted Land*. Establishing himself, he married Beth, an open-minded American prepared to make her life in Israel. Tel Aviv was then a city whose inhabitants rose early in the morning and went to bed early in the evening. The Elons were different. Their house was a sort of unofficial media center for anyone on some reporting assignment. Karl Meyer of the *New York Times*, the *Magnum* photographer Erich Lessing, Herbert Pundik editor of the Danish paper *Politiken*, were among those who liked to think there was a secret self-selected network known as the Friends of Amos Elon. When Amos pushed his spectacles high on the bridge of his nose or took them off altogether and started describing reality in the Middle East, it was time to listen. He had an undoubted streak of melancholy, which at first I thought was an individual trait, until I realized that everyone in the country had the same deep-down but unspoken regret that they could no longer live wherever they had once lived.

What now looks like Israel's Golden Age of enforced isolation came to an abrupt end in May 1967 when Gamal Abdel Nasser ordered Egyptian units to take up positions in the Sinai Desert. The watching world wondered whether Nasser might make good his threat to eliminate Israel. John Anstey, editor of the *Daily Telegraph* Colour Magazine, sent me to cover what became known as the Six Day War. On the day when I caught up with Amos, he was back home in his house on Hazayit Street in Tel Aviv, too exhausted to talk except to say that he had been at the front somewhere in Sinai in a jeep with General Avraham Yoffe, a man larger than life in more ways than one. The General was standing up and surveying the battle through field glasses when Amos heard him groan, "My God, war is boring!" (At that time, the novelist Mordecai Richler remarked just as memorably that if planes were overhead he'd rather they were ours.)

Nobody that I know of had anticipated that the Palestinians on the West Bank of Jordan and in Gaza would ever come under Israeli rule. Writing in the *New York Review of Books* and the *New Yorker*, Amos was among the very first to propose unilateral Israeli withdrawal from all Palestinian territory, in effect arguing that victory in the Six Day War had given Israel unwanted responsibility for other people and that was no victory at all. Put another way, the Arabs were to pay no price either for going to war or for losing it. No Israeli had previously written a book like Amos's *Flight Into Egypt*, published in 1980. An official guest in the country, he met and admired the then President Anwar Sadat, Mrs. Jihan Sadat and other Egyptians whom he took to be genuine peacemakers. The repeated attempts to restart a peace process seemed to me fanciful; I tend to believe that on the evidence available a Palestinian state is bound to be an Arab tyranny like all the others, and not worth having. Those in the know often expected Amos to reject my opinions lock, stock and barrel, but he never did. In spite of our differences, he even gladly endorsed my book *The Closed Circle: An Interpretation of the Arabs*.

Touring in Tuscany, Beth had visited Buggiano, a small but beautiful town on top of a steep hill about an hour from Florence. On impulse, Amos and Beth bought a house in a secluded spot at the end of a lane. The more time they spent there, the more their critics accused them of turning their backs on Israel and nationalism, so making a bad situation worse. We saw the Elons so regularly that I am pretty sure their retreat to Buggiano was motivated as much by aesthetics as by politics. Here was an ideal setting for reading and writing, for growing fruit and making wine.

We had inherited a family house high up at Arcetri on the southern side of Florence, and together with Beth we prepared a surprise fiesta in the courtyard to celebrate Amos's sixtieth birthday. Guests were to come from six countries. Karl Meyer edited a Festschrift of some twenty contributors whose columns made and unmade reputations, while he himself observed that what distinguishes Amos's writing "is its passionate and humanizing sense of fairness; he deals justly with friend and adversary, despising the wretched little orthodoxies that unworthily divide them." I still see the look on Amos's face as he entered the courtyard and the assembled guests sang for him.

I hear Amos telling stories, for instance how President Johnson had summoned Abba Eban, the Israeli Foreign Minister, to Washington and opened conversation by saying, "I was a-sitting here scratching my ass and thinking about Is-ra-el." In one session at a conference, the egregious South African novelist Nadine Gordimer said that if Amos was sincere about the Palestinians he would go to a barricade and get himself shot dead on their behalf, and I hear him reply, "Did you get yourself shot on behalf of Mandela?" A woman by the name of Dina Vierney sued me for describing her as the teen-age model and mistress of the sculptor Maillol. I hear Amos immediately quoting from memory a passage from the diaries of Count Keyserling, social busybody par excellence, recording that Vierney had indeed been the mistress of Maillol. I hear him describing how he had come to Vienna to be interviewed on television in the aftermath of the first invasion of Iraq, when an old man in front of a shop displaying books about the Middle East turned to him and said that he hoped Saddam Hussein would throw the Jews into the sea. Why is that? Amos asked. Because some of them might come here, was the unexpected answer, and life would then become bearable again. Beth wrote comprehensive books about Italian cuisine, practicing it herself at the highest level, and one day just before lunch I hear Amos warding off his diet by saying to her, "I don't want any of your Third World food."

The Pity of It All (2002), his last and most powerful book, is the master-work of a lifetime, a heart-felt and fully researched account of the Jewish experience in Germany from nineteenth-century emancipation to the Third Reich. As Amos had found for himself, it is wishful to believe in happy endings, and Jews should always have in mind where else they can live. On a visit to Buggiano I saw him one last time rising up the stone stairs of his house on the chair lift chanting some dog-Latin and giving a very good imitation of a papal blessing.

JOHN FULLER

Collected Poems

1996

AT THE LAUNCH PARTY, John, a friend since we were undergraduates, unscrewed a pen and wrote impromptu, "From a Georgian to an Edwardian."

NICHOLAS GAGE

Eleni

1983

THIS BOOK IS ABOUT EVIL, specifically an act of evil particular to Greece in the twentieth century. The relating of what happened further raises the more general and indeed abiding question of how the individual to whom evil is done should rightly and properly respond. There are ambiguities. To do nothing might be to follow the biblical injunction to turn the other cheek, but it might also leave the victim to internalize the evil and blame himself for what another did. Vengeance is mine, saith the Lord, but the avenger will almost certainly have to be as morally defective as the evil-doer.

At first glance, Nicholas Gage looked like a Brooks Brothers type of American. He was reputed to be one of the best investigative journalists on the *New York Times*, specializing in stories about cops and robbers. In person, he was soft-spoken, self-effacing. It seemed all of a piece to learn that his name was an anglicized form of Nikola Gatzo-yiannis. Investigating in professional style the life and death of his mother, Eleni, however, he is not dealing with identity but touching the heights and depths of human emotions.

Eleni lived in Lia, a village in the Grammos Mountains just on the Greek side of the frontier with Albania. According to a very summary sentence in the book, she was "an ordinary peasant woman, subject to all her doubts, fears and prejudices planted by her up-bringing and her primitive world." A day came when fifteen heavily armed men turned up in the village. Communists were taking over the region. The world war was giving rise to a civil war on the issue of who would rule peacetime Greece. At the Yalta conference, the great powers decided which countries were to be in the Soviet bloc and Greece was not one of them. Preparing for a long-term militant future, the Greek Communist Party then organized the unprece-dented atrocity known as the Paidomazoma. This was the effective kidnapping of as many as 28,000 children between the ages of three and thirteen and their transfer to the Soviet Union or to the new People's Democracies in Eastern Europe. Eleni could not submit to such an affront to her instincts and beliefs. She enabled her children to escape without her and rejoin their father already in the United States since before the war. The Communists accused her of treachery, tortured her, held a kangaroo trial and finally put her before a firing squad. "My children!" the unfortunate Eleni screamed as she died.

Safe in the United States, Nicholas Gage was tormented by the in-justice of it all. Out of fear for themselves, some in Lia had denounced Eleni and some had borne false witness. Communist ideology shut out morality. With a bit of luck and a lot of detective work he tracked down the Communist judge, one Achilleas Lykas, who had presided over Eleni's judicial murder. Nicholas had a hand-gun tucked in his waistband and knew "absolutely" that he wanted to kill Lykas because, he says, it would give him relief from the pain that had filled him for so many years. When the opportunity at last came, "I couldn't do it." So complex is human fate that retribution repeats and extends the evil it was supposed to redress. All Nicholas can do in the face of this reality is spit all over Lykas. The murderer pays a small price, the victim is not freed from suffering. *Eleni* has as much insight into tragedy as the ancient Greek classics.

Postscript. In 1980 the trial took place in Cologne of the so-called Paris Gestapo, three SS officers guilty of deporting Jews from France during the German occupation. Day after day, I found myself sitting next to Michel Goldberg, a Frenchman. His father had been arrested in Lyon, tortured, deported and finally murdered in Auschwitz. The head of the Lyon Gestapo was the infamous Klaus Barbie, and Michel held him responsible for his father's death. He told me (and repeats in his memoir *Namesake*, published in 1982) how posing as a journalist he had traced Barbie, a fugitive in Bolivia, and contrived to have a rendezvous with him. "All I need is the will," he observed, but in the event, like Nicholas Gage, he too could not bring himself to press the trigger of the revolver he had brought.

MARTHA GELLHORN

The Honeyed Peace

A Collection of Stories

PENGUIN, 1983

THE SIX DAY WAR IN 1967 began on a Monday. The very next day, the Arab Legion was already pulling out of the West Bank. A rumor went round that King Hussein of Jordan had ordered these troops to take up positions defending his palace in Amman. An Israeli officer with a jeep offered to drive me to the rapidly changing front line. It was about nine o'clock in the morning, and the famous correspondent James Cameron was already in the jeep swigging whisky out of the bottle. Quite soon, he passed out and the empty bottled rattled on the floor. A shell had smashed through the roof of the Church of the Holy Nativity in Bethlehem. A Greek Orthodox Archbishop and some Israeli paratroopers stood about in swirling smoke and dust.

King Solomon's Pool is near Bethlehem, and across an expanse of grass there strolled the even more famous war correspondent Martha Gellhorn. An apparition, she was in a khaki outfit, tailored and immaculate, for all I know fitted out by Balmain or Givenchy. She might have come straight from the hairdresser. Among other places, she had reported from the Spanish civil war, Hitler's Germany, Chiang Kai-shek's China and Ho Chi Minh's Vietnam. My impression was that war served an imperative psychological purpose of providing more evidence of mankind's persistent folly, and by extension, evidence of her superiority. (That day she did not file, I believe, unlike James Cameron, who made up what he'd failed to see. "Not one of your best pieces, Mr. Cameron," was the memorable comment of the military censor, a thoughtful young lieutenant.)

On the way to Pentwyn, our house in Breconshire, we used to drive past, and once or twice stop at Catscradle, Martha's bolt-hole at Kilgwrrwg, a village near Chepstow. Her inscription of *The Honeyed Peace* reads, "For David, splendid lunch company." A tour manager by occupation, Clarissa took me to China in 1982. Martha wrote, "I cannot wait to hear your China report. Note (for me) flies, spitting, overall smell of human manure. If now gone, I'd say huge success. Also water (at all safe?), visible disease like lepers. I think China may be the rare improved state."

Early in 1983, the *Tatler* commissioned a profile of her. I would understand, wouldn't I, that she refused to speak about Hemingway and her time as his wife. She seemed not to notice how in fact she did tell stories about him. At the beginning of the war, he took delivery at La Finca Vigia of a new-model Lincoln, so new that it was the only one in Cuba. Showing it off, he drove Martha to his favorite bar in Havana. He wanted to stay there but she had had enough of his cronies and their talk. At the wheel on the way home, he made a gesture of annoyance that she had obliged him to leave. The back of his hand caught her cheek. Grabbing the wheel, she steered the car into a roadside tree and wrecked it. "I told him, Ernest, if you ever hit me again I'll shoot you." The marriage was finally over when Hemingway was refused permission to cover the landing on D-Day but Martha disguised herself as a nurse, slipped on to a hospital ship and reported the invasion from Omaha Beach.

MARTIN GILBERT
The Second World War
A Complete History
1989

M ARTIN AND I ARRIVED on the same day in the autumn of 1956 at Magdalen College, Oxford, where we were to read history. Two years of national service was obligatory at the time. Martin had been in the Intelligence Service, learning Russian, a junior conscript in the Cold War. Knowledge of the language and the geopolitical background were undoubted assets. My grandfather Harry Pryce-Jones, a career soldier, saw to it that I did my service in his old regiment, the Coldstream Guards. Stationed in Germany, at least I practiced my German.

The Oxford history syllabus began with the Anglo-Saxons and stopped well short of the present. In charge of taking us through the first thousand or so years, K. B. McFarlane (Bruce, not that any undergraduate would dare to call him by a first name) was one of the country's most formidable medievalists. He looked the part, a large ungainly man with a crabby expression, wearing a brown tweed suit and sitting almost sideways in an uncomfortable chair, stroking the tabby cat in his lap. Whether out of perfectionism or sterility, he could hardly bring himself to publish anything. A few days after arriving, I was writing about the Romano-British system of communication. He'd given me some thirty sources and wanted to know why I hadn't used them. In the time available I had been able to read only one book and half of another. My method was faulty, he explained; the right way to read was to turn to the book's index and look up anything you needed.

Another historian and Fellow of Magdalen College was John Stoye, of Yugoslav origins, author of a lively book about the 1683 Ottoman siege of Vienna. On the same staircase as mine in college were the rooms of Karl Leyser. A refugee from Germany, in spirit he was still gripped by emperors and bishops in the Dark Ages of the German past. So good-natured was he that he didn't mind my exploiting Brahms's song for a pun on his name, "Immer leiser wird mein Schlummer."

By the beginning of our second year, it was obvious that Martin was a born historian. Wasting no time, he already showed that he could find his way through archives and primary sources. A. J. P. Taylor was also a fellow of Magdalen. He was then a national figure on account of his television lectures on modern history. Delivering them apparently impromptu and without hesitation, he had in fact written out and learned by heart what he would say. He consented to have as pupils only the eight handpicked undergraduates who were thought to have the best prospects for a good degree and success in their careers, preferably in the academy or the media. For Taylor, the objective of historiography was to get your point across even if this was only prejudice dressed up in assertive prose. He expected Martin to be his protégé, but Martin instead came to the McFarlaneite view that the historian owes it to his subject to be completely knowledgeable and impersonal.

After graduating, I soon found myself literary editor of *Time and Tide*, a weekly magazine. The editor, John Thompson, hoped I'd discover new talent. The reviews Martin wrote for *Time and Tide* were his first appearances in print. In one of them, dated July 27, 1961, he laid out the ground rules as he had learnt them at Oxford, with a split infinitive thrown in too: "It is necessary for the historian to continuously cross known ground, sift published materials, and search out new evidence." *The Appeasers* (1965), his first book, co-authored with Richard Gott, established what has become received opinion that the background of Prime Minister Neville Chamberlain and his supporters left them unfit to understand anyone from a background

To

MY MOTHER

For David
with admiration
from Svetlana Allilueva.

October - 97
Wales.

P.S. Forgive my notes & corrections of
the translation — but those
were necessary.
L. Peters

as different as Hitler's. (Gott had a similarly privileged background, with a Field Marshal in the family. The Soviet defector Oleg Gordievsky exposed the fact that Gott had accepted money from the KGB, which put him in the same bind as the pre-war appeasers, unable to understand the real nature of those with whom he was dealing.) Martin then wrote biographies of Lord Allen of Hurtwood and Sir Horace Rumbold, two very different characters who nonetheless typify on the one hand the willing dupe of the period and on the other hand the realist.

In Oxford days, Martin was not the proud Jew he later became. Nobody could know, he once said confidentially, that behind the name Pryce-Jones were Jewish origins. Three years old at the outbreak of war, he had been sent on his own to Canada. Though not Jewish, the woman who had him in charge took the trouble to learn to cook kosher for him, and wrote a weekly letter that she pretended came from his mother, who did not communicate. In the family background was his uncle Leo Trepper. Born in Poland, he emigrated to Mandated Palestine and became a Communist, only to return to Brussels at the outbreak of war in order to run the outstanding Soviet spy network known as Rote Kapelle. Stalin trusted his pact with Hitler and disbelieved the network's warning in June 1941 that the German army was about to invade. Many of Trepper's agents were liquidated either by the Gestapo or the NKVD, then the acronym of the Soviet secret police, but Trepper himself was to survive years in the Lubyanka. He returned to Israel and is buried there.

Marriage to Susie Sacher brought Martin's Jewish identity out into the open. She was as thorough a researcher in the archives as he, and was to write a book about the English National Opera. Members of the Sacher family were major shareholders and directors of the Marks and Spencer chain of supermarkets and also lifelong Zionists. Susie's parents, Audrey and Michael, owned a house in Jerusalem. Martin was to take every opportunity to travel to Israel and stay there for long periods of research. There's a tight circle of Israeli academics, writers and diplomats with the historical knowledge, the intellect and the will to defend Zionism in times of peace as well as war, and Martin took his place in it.

The preface of *Exile and Return* (1978) opens with a statement that he is answering questions frequently asked about "the nature, the evolution, and the aims of Zionism." Martin particularly documented the persecution of Jews by Germans turned Nazi and Russians turned Soviet, all making Zionism a default ideology for survival assembled from the mass of evidence left by victims and victimizers. Published in 1978, *Auschwitz and the Allies* shows that the Allies were fully informed of the program of mass murder but bureaucratic indifference and obstruction put paid to plans to bomb the railheads from which Jews were deported to their death. When I was in Vienna in 1984 writing a book for the Time-Life series "The Great Cities," out of the blue Martin sent me a summary of the deportation of 50,000 Viennese Jews between March 1938 and the end of 1943.

In an unusual concession, Soviet Jews in principle during the 1970s had permission to emigrate to Israel. In practice, the Soviet authorities withheld exit visas for a number of handpicked Jews, refuseniks as they were known. Here was a cause readymade for Martin, the Zionist and Russian speaker. *The Jews of Hope* (1984) is a journalistic account of the cat-and-mouse game the KGB was obliging some Jews to play. A couple of years later, *Shcharansky. Hero of Our Time* was the biography of someone internationally celebrated for refusing to compromise even during his years in the Gulag. At some point, in a familiar tactic, the KGB detained Martin at Moscow airport, stripped him to his underwear, and photographed him.

Martin was in the habit of sending postcards to his friends from forsaken Russian towns where he was pursuing refuseniks. Here is one, half covered with colorful postage stamps. "I bought you this card in Tbilisi but as the Georgian government had only just decided on its new currency (the Lada) there were as yet no stamps. So I flew to Moscow and bought these – in Communist days £2,300 worth – but now not 50p – about a quarter of a cup of coffee. I am in St Petersburg now, having visited Jews greeting me today in remote villages where the temperature was *minus* 29 — and my face is burnt, lips cracked, and fingers being thawed by the radiator they specially brought into my room in the Asturia Hotel. Hope to see you soon — much to tell!"

The American president, Ronald Reagan himself, wanted Martin to brief him on the subject of refuseniks. The president's Boeing flew Martin by himself to Washington and an aide conveyed him to the White House. A session of thirty minutes was due to start at half past twelve. At five minutes to one, Reagan entered the room, complaining loudly about dissatisfied Congressmen who were making trouble for him. Martin had not got a word in before another aide hurried Reagan away to greet his lunch guests. Once again the sole passenger, Martin was then flown home.

Winston Churchill's son, Randolph, had been under contract to write his father's official biography. Finding that the necessary research was beyond his capacity, he advertised for a qualified assistant. A fledgling Oxford don at the time, Martin responded, and Randolph had the sense or the good fortune to take him on. Randolph's name is given as the author of the first two of the eight volumes of the official biography, but rumor was already putting it about that Martin was his ghost. The remaining six volumes are anyhow exclusively his. Each is between a thousand and fifteen hundred pages long, weighing so many pounds that they are awkward to handle. All have two and sometimes three companion volumes of similar bulk containing supporting documentation from all possible sources. Martin must have felt unqualified admiration for Churchill and unqualified hostility for Communism and Nazism, but he is the only historian I can think of who accumulated facts for their own sake, not for commentary or the formation of opinion. Martin's eighty-odd books are free from value judgments. The man himself is missing from the monument.

PHILIP GLAZEBROOK

Byzantine Honeymoon

A Tale of the Bosphorus

1979

A T ETON IN the early 1950s, Philip Glazebrook already appeared
to be an onlooker, not a participant. Thanks to his red hair,
pale eyes and a certain gravity, I knew who he was but we never
exchanged a word. A joker in the Eton pack at that moment was
David Winn, who could be seen slipping away with Philip to play
golf, the opposite of team sport. Both were writers in the making.
In 1963, David drowned in a sailing accident. In one of his letters to
me, Philip observes that one has to overcome self-esteem and accept
writing something less good than the writing of one's most brilliant
contemporary. "Not to have grown out of that dilemma is the real
tragedy. I often wonder if David W. would have progressed beyond
that point." Thanks to other Glazebrooks successful in their fields, a
conventional education and some private money, Philip was often
dismissed as a dilettante, an oddball who was either too serious or
not serious enough. The opening sentence of the obituary that the
Times published in 2007 is an impressive example of the sneering
he was up against. "Philip Glazebrook was one of the last of a near-
extinct breed, the genteel man of letters."

Four years as an honorary attaché at the British Embassy in Rome
provided material for fiction, especially *Try Pleasure*, Philip's sophisticated first novel. Here he makes fun of a dislikeable true-to-type
member of the Foreign Office, clearly a personal enemy. I believe
Philip and I met more or less by chance in Florence when I was staying with my grandmother. "All that may be said for identifying Italy

so inextricably with Youth is that I am conscious of no regret for lost youth, but only for lost Italy.... Instead of a pensione in Vallombrosa I clocked in at the Reigate House of Correction for my autumn shot at getting a novel off the ground. Do you know about Mount Pleasant at Reigate, a glum mansion put at the disposal of 'artists' by the munificence of a starch millionaire."

The Eye of the Beholder moves easily from Cheshire and Scotland to Mexico City and Antigua. In a review I wrote, "If it had been free of the structure of a novel this would have been a wonderful travel book." Philip picked up this recommendation, telling me, "Ever obedient, I did at last write a kind of book of travels (a mixture of my own outing to Kars with my interest in nineteenth-century travellers to those parts)." Revealing the inner self, he also noted, "I was more pleased to have my Travels accepted as publishable than any novel since my first. Perhaps because of my admiration for real travellers, perhaps because of the sensation of peeling off the green spectacles and false nose of novel-writing (where you masquerade your own views as the views of your characters) I have more the feeling of 'being published' in this case than in others. Also, consequently, more the feeling of being a fraud whose pretensions will be uncovered by merciless pens."

Journey to Khiva was published in 1992, and I think my comment on it prompted Philip to return the compliment, "accepting as gospel truth the favorable line taken by so elegant and perspicacious a pen as your own ... twenty-five years of rather intermittent production has taught me that all but a tiny pinch of reviews are nothing but further irritation. I cannot help looking in the papers in hopes of one of those reviews that (whether favourable or not) comes from an intelligence which has twigged what you are up to and why you wrote the book."

Philip lived in a handsome Regency house in Dorset, very much a gentleman's residence. Once when I was staying there, he invited Fred Warner to dinner. A member of the Foreign Office, he had been a friend of the Soviet agents Guy Burgess and Donald Maclean and had accompanied Kim Philby on some motorbike trip in Europe, bringing on himself the nickname of Red Fred as well as numerous interrogations with the security services. He had been posted to Burma, and in an encounter that had entertained a small circle, David Winn had advised Fred to learn Burmese so that he could earn a living translating Burmese poetry when the going became really rough. Reminded of this tease, Fred hit the table so hard that he brought down the delicate candlesticks. Philip followed it up with another invitation to Fred, keeping me in the picture. "I will tweak and probe till candles once more leap from sconces as Diplomat's Shoe Strikes Table." Fred was selling his Dorset estate, "so may well regret yet his inadequate grasp of Tamil, or whatever language it was David Winn advised him to master against a destitute old age."

Philip would have wished to be a successor to Layard, Kinglake, Burkhardt, Mungo Park, Richard Burton, Speke, the adventurous men who opened paths all over the world and whose books, preferably first editions, he collected single-mindedly. Surely one of the most surprising novels in English literature is Philip's *Captain Vinegar's Commission*, a pastiche of this Victorian genre with its military and imperial undertones.

For lengthy periods he abandoned home and civilized life, and on returning he was in the habit of isolating himself again in some bleak place where he could write up the latest experiences without distraction. He did not feel justified in "making the house miserable whilst I worked, a place of whispers and tiptoes and dying fires and silent meals." In his heartfelt words about the self-discipline imposed by blank paper, "I behave like a savage, speak to no one, act furtively, kick the dog, have always taken cottages before (where, like Baudelaire, I can be self-catering and fais bouillir et mange mon cœur)."

Some colorful idea, some recapitulation of the past, in the case of Kars and Khiva the romance of distant inaccessible places, had a grip on his imagination. He and I had a joke correspondence using paper and envelopes that bore no relation to where we actually were but spun a misleading story. Letterheads I received from him include the Venice-Simplon Orient Express, M.V. Innisfallen of the City of Cork Steam Packet, the Gellert Hotel in Budapest, the Hotel Bulevard in Bucharest, the British Embassy in Rome (dated long after his service as honorary attaché) and the Turban Amasya Oteli. Also postcards variously postmarked from Tallinn, Urfa, Prague, the Algonquin in New York and Hawthornden Castle where writers are supposed to stay in and write, that is to say another House of Correction.

Always cadaverous, losing most of his red hair as he aged, he was not the weakling that he might have appeared to be. He was resting on the bed in a Moscow hotel when a man came into the room carrying a knife and demanded money. Philip immediately grappled with him, and eventually managed to hold him down on the bed and wrest the knife away. The man then fled. Philip had suffered several cuts. The woman receptionist on that floor of the hotel must have heard the scuffle but refused to respond. The blood on Philip's arms was not enough for the police in the local station to register the assault.

Here is a letter ostensibly from Celik Palas Oteli in Bursa, written after what he calls a ramble in the Levant. Unusual as others may have judged him to be, Philip evidently had come to terms with himself. "I found I had manufactured for myself a Hero-Narrator . . . an attitude not wholly in accordance with my real one when confronted with the ups and downs of solitary travel. You leave things out – the dull bits – and after re-writing a time or two, you have clean forgotten them. By dull bits I mean trying to find somewhere to have breakfast in a shabby dusty Turkish town, after sharing your bedroom with two stout Turks, when every eating shop seems to be selling only corba iskembe. Still, there's nothing like Travel: I had, I suppose, six days out of the month which I will never forget, and what other recreation could claim so high a proportion of bulls-eyes? Only when crossing the Syrian border from Urfa to Aleppo (which took eight hours at the mercy of some very reckless young urban guerrillas) did I think that a 47-year-old father of four with a comfortable home was possibly in the wrong place. Syria is in the hands of the successors of those bashibazuks and Arnauts and Nizam deserters who terrorised the Ottoman Empire. But an hour or two at Baron's Hotel of course restored me to absolute trust in the flatness of the earth under an Englishman's feet."

HERBERT GOLD

Biafra Goodbye

1972

IN THE SUMMER OF 1972, I moved from Hayward to the far larger and more important California State University at Berkeley. Besides creative writing, I also had to teach a class in English literature. At the first of these classes, a man my age introduced himself as my Vietnam instructor. And what might that be? I asked. The class will only want to talk about Vietnam, he answered, you don't have the right information, I'll deal with the questions. There won't be any, I told him, because I'd send such questioners to the South East Asia department. You won't get away with that, my instructor promised.

Early in the morning, I would walk across a beautifully tended grass lawn with water sprinklers adding to the freshness. Rioters had smashed the big plate-glass window of my classroom. Fearful that refitted glass was bound to attract more of the same violence, the authorities had boarded up the window. Entering that darkened room, I was invariably taken aback by the message daubed in huge black letters on the board: "Go fuck yourself teacher pig." On one typical occasion, my assistant threw her copy of *Nostromo* across the room, asserting tearfully to one and all, "I'm not going to read this shit." She had become a radical feminist, it turned out, because her father did not have the money to pay for the violin lessons she'd set her heart on. On another occasion amid a lot of laughter I had to admit that I didn't know what the word "roach" meant to druggies. One fine day Allen Ginsberg and three thousand innocents sat cross-legged outside on the campus grass and kept up for hours their chant of *Om Mani Padme Hum*. To generalize, most of those who had anything to do with the university appeared to believe that if they didn't know something it wasn't worth knowing.

Those were strange times in a strange place. There was a sense that the past was giving way to a future that declined to be born. Everybody around seemed to be busy filling their lives with nothing. At Berkeley, someone tried to set fire to the rare books section of the library, where Sir Francis Drake's navigational map was on display. Professors in their angry hundreds crowded in to the auditorium intending to wreck a speech that Ronald Reagan, then Governor of the State, was to give. Such was his charm that almost instantly they showed they couldn't applaud loud enough or long enough. Flower children drifted from Haight-Ashbury to take part in demonstrations against the Vietnam war. Many were barefoot but the police and the National Guard wore boots. One of my students, Mark, was bright and at the sight of him in the front line chanting "Ho Ho Ho Chi Minh" I asked him to name the countries clockwise adjoining Vietnam. The anger in his face showed that I had broken a spell. Huey Newton and Eldridge Cleaver led the Black Panthers from fortified headquarters in the city. Posed photographs showed them cradling rifles. "Off the pigs" was their call to arms.

Herb Gold took me in hand. Other writers were recognized locally, for example the poet Louis Zukovsky or Sol Stern, editor of the magazine *Ramparts*, but Herb was the only one with a national reputation. So famous was he that whoever scribbled graffiti on the walls of public lavatories had come up with "Herb Gold has exceeded his ecological quota" and he could only have thought that his joke rested on common knowledge about Herb's numerous wives and children. More graffiti in the same hand read, "Donald Duck is a Jew." *Salt, Fathers* and other novels of his dealt with love and death, origins and family life, in short the great themes of classic fiction. His essays appeared in *Commentary*, *Harper's* and even *Playboy*. I told him I could never be an American writer, the country was too big and diffuse for storytelling. We all have our patch, he answered. The essays and articles collected in *The Magic Will* and *My Last Two Thousand Years* make sense of the life he is living: no flower child he. He took me to one quite smart party of friends. He and I were the only ones to leave when they passed around what I then knew was a roach, reducing conversation to childish giggling.

As part of my San Francisco experience, he also arranged for us to have tea with Margot Fitzjames, a made-up name if ever there was one. A high-class Madame, she moved in the best circles and was said to be extremely expensive. Our meeting, she had agreed beforehand, was purely for social purposes, not business. When she received us in her large and elegant drawing room, she was wearing only a bath-robe. Most probably she was in her forties. While we were sipping our tea and making small talk, an inner door opened and in came a young man, possibly a teenager. He was fully dressed. Sheepishly, he sidled past without a word and saw himself out. We pretended not to have noticed. Herb reported that in a telephone call the lady had praised our good manners.

The enlisting of writers in a political cause is a feature of twentieth-century literature. Books like Mary McCarthy's *Vietnam* or Salman Rushdie's *The Jaguar Smile*, put together after a three-week whistle-stop tour of Sandinista Nicaragua, are only extended anti-American manifestoes. Herb Gold's *Biafra Goodbye* is a plea to approve what was essentially an act of secession from the state of Nigeria. He took up the Biafran cause, as far as one can see, because these people were being maltreated and it was only human to come to their side. Herb may also have had a sense that the crushing of the Christian Ibos of Biafra by the Hausas and other Muslim tribes was an early portent of the rise of militant Islam.

Over the years we kept up a sporadic correspondence. A letter dated 23 August 1982 enclosed an article he had published a couple of weeks previously in the *Los Angeles Times*. A woman had said to him, "Herb, Have You Heard the Startling News? The Holocaust Never Happened Like They Say." The paper made these words the title of the piece. This woman was university-educated and devoted to the arts, Herb says, and on top of that she'd been the hostess of the party Herb and I walked away from rather than be stupefied with pot.

OLEG GORDIEVSKY
Next Stop Execution
1995

THE DOYEN OF THE post-Communist Russian community in Britain is Oleg Gordievsky. I once likened him to Alexander Herzen, the most brilliant of Russian political exiles in the nineteenth century, whose proposals for liberalizing Czarism in his day might have forestalled the Bolshevik revolution. Gordievsky is not an intellectual, to be sure, but his life is a commentary on the central political drama in the Russia of his day: namely how to become a free individual in a free society. In a KGB career in which he rose to the rank of colonel, he was able to observe from the inside how the Soviet Union rested on terror. Since Communism is an ideology whose end justifies all means of violence and injustice, it was therefore impervious to reform. His decision to work against it, to pass information and Soviet documentation to MI6, or British intelligence, required exceptional courage as well as moral conviction. Promotion to be the KGB Resident in London was an unexpected opportunity to be within easy touch of his handlers.

Those with knowledge of such matters say that he was a classic double agent, in charge of Soviet subversion and espionage in the country while keeping the British completely informed. To the general public nowadays, it seems, the Cold War is the quarrel of a past beyond recall in which defectors on both sides are much of a muchness, engaged in shady business of the same sort. The historic reality is that the likes of Kim Philby had given up freedom in favor of Communism, while Gordievsky gave up Communism in favor of freedom.

With fatal symmetry, two members of the CIA, Robert Hanssen and Aldrich Ames, were double agents, and when they defected in 1985 to Moscow they cast suspicion on Gordievsky though they had no proof he was working for the British. The KGB summoned him back to Moscow and interrogated him under drugs. "I had prepared myself psychologically all the time for this possibility," Gordievsky was to tell me. "I had programmed myself to deny. If I made it difficult for them, I thought I might survive." The most likely outcome was a short spell in one of the underground cells of the Lubyanka, and a bullet in the nape of the neck. Presumably the KGB allowed him to stay out of prison in the hope of catching him doing something that justified the death sentence.

Anticipating just such an emergency, Gordievsky's handlers in MI6 had a pre-arranged plan to smuggle him out of the country secretly in defiance of internationally agreed codes of conduct, a stunt for which exfiltration is the proper term in the idiom of the trade. Quite senior personnel from the British Embassy were to rendezvous with him deep in the Russian countryside, hide him in the boot of their car, cross the Soviet border and drive on into Finland. So far as is known, this incredible adventure is the sole example of successful exfiltration.

Researching my account of the implosion of Soviet Communism, I met Leonid Shebarshin, head of the First Main Directorate of the KGB in the Gorbachev period and therefore harmed by Gordievsky's defection. He said, "The KGB has a long memory, and a long arm, and it doesn't like traitors." Vladimir Putin had come up through the ranks of the KGB to start his first presidency in 2000. Promotion of a secret policeman within the Kremlin inner circle seemed a refutation of everything Gordievsky stood for. Putin is on record with the sinister threat, "Traitors kick the bucket for themselves, believe me." Salman Rushdie is now not the only person living in this country under sentence of death from a foreign power.

Ten years after defecting, Gordievsky published his autobiography, *Next Stop Execution*. It was a sensation. Taking his life in his hands, he had surely contributed to the ultimate defeat of the Soviet Union in the Cold War, perhaps second only to Aleksandr Solzhenitsyn as an individual fighting for freedom. He also exposed a number of Westerners who were Soviet agents. One was a journalist called Richard Gott whom I happened to have met and knew to be a useful idiot of no real interest. A very different agent was Michael Foot, at that time leader of the Labour Party opposition in Parliament to the then Prime Minister Margaret Thatcher. The KGB had given him £37,000, something he claimed he could not remember.

On a winter evening in 2001, Gordievsky came to my house. In accentuated English, the vowels liquid in the Russian style, he liked to continue fighting the good fight. A little earlier in a pub, he said gravely, he had spotted the head of a British trade union whom he himself had recruited as a KGB paid informer. Recognizing that he might be exposed then and there, this man had taken to his heels. Simon Heffer had written in the *Daily Telegraph* that Gordievsky's information that Jack Jones (another trade union leader and very influential) was a Soviet agent "may or may not be true." Gordievsky's rejoinder was deadly: "I was his last case officer, meeting him together with his wife, who had been a Comintern agent since the mid-1930s.... I had the pleasure of reading volumes of his files, which were kept in the British department of the KGB." Or again, A. N. Wilson, an idiomatic master of misrepresentation, in 2004 had written an article in the *Evening Standard* taking the line that the Soviet threat to Britain during the Cold War was "nonsense." Another deadly rejoinder from Gordievsky began with the reprimand, "It was not a very enlightened remark" and went on to enumerate the

Soviet troops and missiles that had been in place to destroy Britain.

The murder in November 2006 of Alexander Litvinenko is a landmark in the annals of crime. An ex-KGB officer, he was a ranking Lieutenant Colonel. His story always was that he had been ordered to kill Boris Berezovsky, an oligarch who had been close to Vladimir Putin but had fallen out with him and settled in exile in London. Instead, Litvinenko befriended Berezovsky and campaigned against Putin; he was also in the habit of dropping in on Gordievsky for a meal or a chat. Flying in from Moscow, two hit-men left a trail of polonium-210, a rare radioactive substance that poisons and kills those who come into contact with it. Litvinenko died rather slowly, and on his deathbed he accused Putin of responsibility for murdering him. Gordievsky has no doubt about it. Discovered dead in his house, Berezovsky was supposed to have put an end to his life, but the KGB has a well-tested saying that any fool can commit a murder but it takes an artist to commit a suicide. Fear for his own security obliges Gordievsky to live under a different name, therefore it is only tradecraft to be sure not to use his real name on an envelope. In a letter to me arranging that this time we'd meet at his house, he refers to "the cannibal Putin." Those cold eyes of his, said Gordievsky, are all anyone needs to know about the man who has built Russia into "a neo-totalitarian country."

Postscript. The Spy and the Traitor, Ben Macintyre's biography of Gordievsky, makes it plain that the exfiltration was a chancy business that very nearly went wrong at several points. Two couples from the Embassy and MI6 went far beyond the call of duty. At a crucial checkpoint on the border, a security guard with a sniffer dog approached. One of the two British women had her baby with her, and with brilliant timing this baby had just filled her nappy. The mother laid her on the boot of the car in which Gordievsky was hiding in order to change the nappy. The dog was put off. Had the British personnel been caught out and detained, the Anglo-Soviet relationship would have been in the balance and we would never have heard the end of it. A Prime Minister less anti-Communist than Mrs. Thatcher might have refused to permit the exfiltration to go ahead, which would have spared Gordievsky the ordeal in the boot but almost certainly cost him his life. Ben honors Gordievsky's profound historical importance and stupendous bravery. Incidentally, Ben is the son of Angus Macintyre, a lifelong friend who sadly was killed in a car accident just after he'd become President of Hertford College, Oxford. Ben's sprawling signature familiarizes my copy of his book.

MICHAEL GRANT

Greeks and Romans

1982

HE INSCRIBED more of his books for me than any other author. They seem to be potboilers only because he had a gift for making scholarship look easy.

ROBERT GRAVES

Collected Poems

1975

A GOOD NUMBER OF PEOPLE know what they know about Roman Emperors only because they are familiar with Robert Graves's *I, Claudius* and *Claudius the God*, which may claim to be the most popular historical novels ever written. They served as parables about power and the moral dissolution of power holders past and present, a central twentieth-century pre-occupation. I also thought that Graves had written *Good-Bye to All That*, his autobiography published in 1929, with such bravura that his wartime experience as a Captain in the Royal Welsh Fusiliers became part of the British national story. Here was a description of how the old, incompetent and heartless as they were, had sacrificed the young on the battlefield, in spite of which here he was recounting the ways and means of coming to terms with the whole ordeal. Every schoolchild is now presented with that version of the First World War and its consequences.

Graves's advice to a young writer is to find a good woman and marry her. He'd had four children with Nancy Nicholson, none with Laura Riding, and lastly four more with Beryl Hodges. As I was making plans to interview him, Beryl reminded me that Robert was eighty-one, hinting that it wasn't really worthwhile to fly out to Majorca.

The village of Deya, then unspoilt, sits on a rocky height above the shore and with a view of the Mediterranean beyond. They lived in a sizable house he'd built there before the Second World War. Graves looked like one of the ancient gods, with a mystique about him. The white curls of his hair and a gladiator's nose broken boxing long ago, suggested an antique bust. On one finger was a scarab and

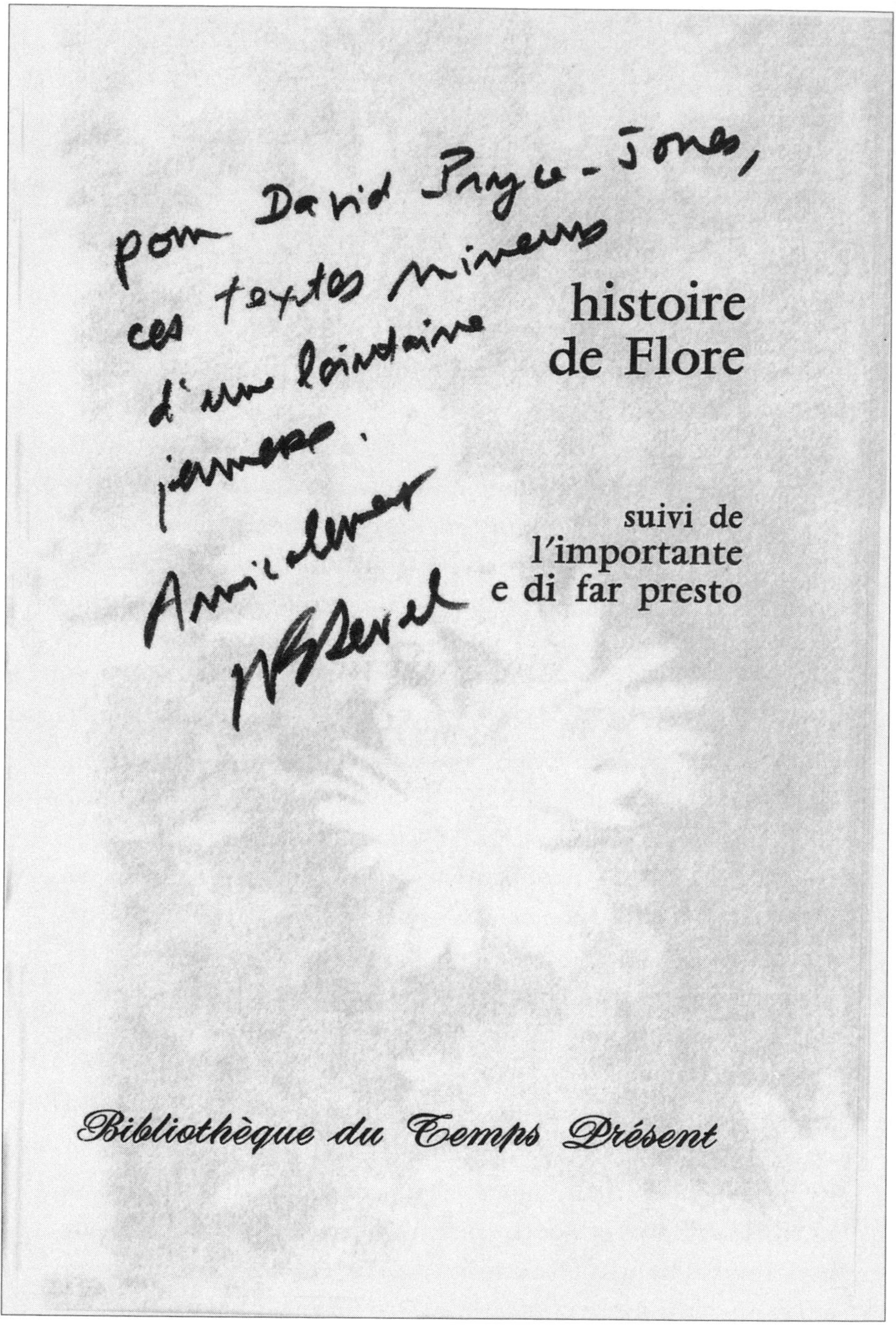

pour David Pryce-Jones,
ces textes mineurs
d'une lointaine
jeunesse.
Amicalement

histoire
de Flore

suivi de
l'importante
e di far presto

Bibliothèque du Temps Présent

on another an Arab amulet and round the neck a Maori talisman of some green stone. He asked me to guess what they were. The persona matched the literary output. Volumes of his poetry, collected essays, novels, histories, more than a hundred titles in all, took over a wall of his study. For some reason, his books did especially well in Communist Poland, he said, and the royalties had piled up but the local currency of zlotys was not convertible, so the money had to be spent in Poland. Beryl and he and one or two of their children were planning to drive out there in a van, buy whatever electrical goods and cameras were available, and sell the lot on returning to Majorca.

A steep descent through trees led to the sea-shore. There was no proper path. Graves and I were slipping and sliding on leaf mould, pebbles, twigs and so on. Having had enough classical education to acquire a sense that knowledge of Latin and Greek is the beginning of wisdom, and I must have been thinking to please Graves when I quoted Virgil, *facilis descensus Averni* (the descent to Avernus is easy). But as I was pronouncing the place name I had a sudden doubt about its case. Could it be Averno? I made a noise that might cover alternatives. Disproving Beryl's fear of his loss of memory, Graves immediately picked up my prevarication. "What was that last word?" Averni, I plunged right in. He growled.

Postscript. In 1968, Graves was awarded the Queen's Gold Medal for poetry. A delighted Peter Levi told me the story of its presentation, and as far as I know it is true. As Poet Laureate, Cecil Day-Lewis had to accompany Graves. On the way to Buckingham Palace, Graves became more and more manic. They stopped at Hawkes, the military outfitters, and bought a regimental tie. To calm him, Day-Lewis kept repeating, "Remember you are Captain Graves of the Royal Welsh Fusiliers." In front of the Queen, Graves said that the two of them had something in common. And what might that be? "Both of us are descendants of the Prophet Muhammad." The Queen made the gesture behind her back that tells attendants she needs rescuing; a box was thrust into Graves's hand, and the mortified Day-Lewis took him home. His wife, the actress Jill Balcon, was waiting on the doorstep to say that they had to return to the Palace urgently and be sure to bring the box. In the panic of the moment, Graves had been given some order or award due to Lord Mansfield. And when Graves once again found himself in the presence of the Queen, he had just time to get out, "As I was explaining about our descent from the Prophet . . ."

JOHN GROSS

Editor of

The New Oxford Book of English Prose

1998

JOHN GROSS WAS an intellectual, even a highbrow, though neither word seems quite right for someone with so much humor in him, such charm, and whose social gifts were always in evidence. Ideal guest that he was, when did he find the time to do all that reading? He appeared to know everybody and to possess some extra-sensory perception of who was in and who was out, with all their pluses and minuses. Hour-long telephone calls with him were as good as a news service.

Every year at the beginning of summer he used to give a party in the Basil Street Hotel in Knightsbridge. He liked to call himself "the Elsa Maxwell *de nos jours.*" His guest list was so comprehensive that people mingled who normally would not have tolerated being together in the same room. It wasn't the occasional flashes of silence that made his conversation perfectly delightful, as Sydney Smith pinned down Macaulay, but the creative flow of it, a name leading to another name, an anecdote to another anecdote, each one a gem of gossip, irony and quirkiness. "Stop me if I've told you this" was one of his leitmotifs, and another was, "Before you go, there's just time for one more story if you can bear it." His memory was flawless, his quotations word-perfect. Most of all, the intention was to laugh, not to hurt.

It is possible, though I think it unlikely, that the story-telling was protective, an appeal for friendship because in his inmost self John was timid, on the *qui vive* for fear that something or somebody nasty might be in the offing, so it was as well to be all things to all men. More probably, he just agreed with Kingsley Amis's password for today that change means worse, therefore it's sensible to make do with whatever raw material is at hand.

Temperament forced him to enlist in the culture wars of the moment. The cause of these wars no doubt lies in unfathomable depths of history, empire, the death of kings, resentment of one's elders and betters, and who knows what besides. The effect is felt continuously in matters great and small. People have to adjust to the political goals on offer, to reinterpretations of the past, to the way reputations are manipulated to rise and fall, to the uses and abuses of language. As the theater critic of the *Sunday Telegraph*, John particularly held out against reading into plays and operas all sorts of moral or political messages at odds with the original work. At one point he asked if I didn't think that pop music was the great cultural divide. Those born in the era of this immense but mindless revolution in taste and manners were condemned never to understand those born before it, as we had been.

John's regular contributions to the *New Criterion* under the rubric "London Journal" were dispatches from the front in the culture wars, and they are every bit as illuminating as George Orwell's similar London letters to *Partisan Review*, written during the real war with the Germans. When Tony Blair had just become Prime Minister, John pointed out that he spoke of "rebranding" Britain as though dealing with a supermarket; the wider conclusion was that this encouraged the nation to wave goodbye to its historic identity, a pointless and unsettling step. The BBC was also coarsening the culture, John believed, in one typical instance concocting the nonsense that Wordsworth knew Coleridge to be a better poet than he and therefore pressed him to continue with drugs in order to destroy him. After 9/11, John was particularly incensed by a BBC television program when Muslim extremists accused the United States of bringing this outrage on itself, and his comment revealed his state of mind. "You start thinking you can't be surprised anymore – not when it comes to left-wing opinion-makers at least – but you end up being surprised nonetheless." Over the last twenty-five years, John would wryly underline, nobody from the BBC had been in touch with him. Culture wars are fought from the trenches, in close combat.

Most of the correspondence from John that I kept simply evokes company and good times. "I do hope that I didn't outstay my welcome the other night; if I did I can only plead it was the pleasure of seeing you that kept me." Writing from a Park Avenue apartment, he hopes we can meet in New York. For five long years, he had the Sisyphean task of reviewing two books every week for the *New York Times*. He seemed to manage this easily, and the goings-on of his colleagues on the paper added to his repertoire of irresistible stories. By this time, he was also a regular contributor to the *New York Review of Books* and to *Commentary* – in other words, he occupied a position in no-man's land.

One postcard asks rather typically if I have read a review by a critic we both held in low esteem, of a new book by a famous novelist we held in even lower esteem. "In a grim way it might amuse you." And here's another dated March 1981 with a portrait of Mao Tsetung gazing with poster-like uplift into the distance. A strip across the bottom of the card reads, "Father's Mind Was Set on a People's Republic." On the reverse are five printed lines all in capitals: "The Youth of Today – Narcissistic – Depraved – Dangerous. All Over the World Right-Thinking Folk Are Crying Out This Thing Has Gone Too Far. Our Young People Are Sick. A New Magazine Chronicles the Terrors of Teen Tyranny. Time Is Running Out — Final Days — Edited by John Stalin." Underneath this inspired but presumably fictitious name, John has simply jotted "T.L.S." and thanks me for a review for him of Saul Friedländer's *When Memory Comes*. Now an eminent historian, Friedländer described unforgettably what he had gone through as a child in the war, and drew the conclusion, equally unforgettable, that Jews "obey the call of some mysterious destiny."

John was only thirty-four when he published *The Rise and Fall of the Man of Letters*, but the book has the scholarship and poise of someone at the close of a long and thoughtful career. It also opened a front in the culture wars. John wrote that some English men of letters had been gifted while others were boring, but all had contributed to a literature that was a national glory. Academics with university salaries, however, had then driven them out. Critics had become either too specialized to be of interest or they were just doormen at the discotheque. Although he was cataloguing men of letters as a more or less extinct species, John chose to become that very thing himself, like a latter-day Eminent Victorian, but one who reserved the right to flick ink from the back of the classroom. At various moments in this role as man of letters, he was literary editor of the *New Statesman* and of Melvin Lasky's *Encounter*, a commissioning editor with the publishers Weidenfeld & Nicolson, and from 1974 to 1981 the editor of the *Times Literary Supplement*.

The official history of the TLS compliments John for maintaining an extremely high standard of reviewing, "helped by the fact that he had no difficulty in discussing almost any subject with his contributors on an equal intellectual footing." Roger Scruton, for one, tells me that he was virtually unknown until John commissioned lengthy articles from him. Another contributor whom he introduced was Alastair Forbes, a member of a well-connected Bostonian family who had made his home in London and Château d'Oex in Switzerland. His know-all name-dropping and a prose style that was a log-jam of sub-clauses gave him a certain cachet. My biography of Unity Mitford was an ideal opportunity for him to show how much more he knew than I did, about Unity, Hitler, the other Mitfords, the whole political and social background of Unity's drama. When he asked to review it, John weighed the pros and cons for several days before accepting the risk, he told me afterwards. In the event, Forbes took the line that my father and I had moral defects that destroyed the right to have opinions. Alan had edited the TLS from 1948 to 1959. An embarrassed John rejected the review, whereupon Forbes re-titled it "The Piece the Jews Rejected" and circulated a hundred or so photocopies around London, including one put into my mail box. The scandal persisted until John eventually published an edited version of the review.

For a writer, as John put it, "the fact of having been born a Jew can mean everything or nothing," or, he adds in a rather characteristic qualification garnished with a bracket, "(more usually) something in between." *Shylock*, published in 1992, was John's first attempt to discover through the medium of print what being Jewish might mean for him. Shakespeare's Jew has long been a stereotype, a villain who has become part of world mythology. The demand for a pound of flesh has provided an enduring foundation for anti-Semitism. Actors have tried to play Shylock as a comic character, or as noble, heroic and ultimately tragic. What's always left, though, in John's conclusion, is "a permanent chill in the air."

John's memoir of his childhood and upbringing, *A Double Thread: Growing Up English and Jewish in London*, addresses his identity as an English Jew more directly. He dedicated the book to his children, Tom and Susanna, of whom he was limitlessly proud. His recommendation was that everyone with these two threads in their identity should feel relaxed about it. John did not enter the sea of the Talmud, as he put it in the words of a religious dictum, but his father, a doctor, and his bookish mother gave him a sense of Judaism, including Hebrew and Yiddish. His experience was very different from Saul Friedländer's, but he too could come to think that Jews obey the call of some mysterious destiny.

John's upbringing was, nevertheless, overwhelmingly ordinary and English, for which he was grateful. During the Second World War, the family moved from the East End of London to Egham — "A Small Town in Surrey" is the title he gives to the relevant chapter. What formed him were boys' comics, the songs of those pre-pop years, period films, teachers in friendly schools who led him to the poetry of Eliot and Auden and the prose of James Joyce, even cricket, and not an anti-Semite or a proper Communist anywhere on the horizon. The path was short and straight to an Oxford scholarship in a college whose Warden, the majestic Maurice Bowra, liked to boom to the attending world, "All my geese are swans."

An innately modest man, John made no claims for himself. A spasm of disavowal would certainly have crossed his face on hearing that he has influenced literary perceptions and taste and will continue to do so. His anthologies — *The Oxford Books of English Prose, of Comic Verse, of Essays, of Literary Anecdotes,* and *The Oxford Book of Parodies,* (which came out just before his last illness when he was still able to take pleasure in the reviews) — are celebrations of the English literary tradition, its range and its civility.

FREDERIC V. GRUNFELD

Berlin

TIME-LIFE BOOKS 1977

S ON RULLAN, Fred Grunfeld's house, was an abandoned monastery in the Majorcan countryside near Deya. The road to it petered out into an improbable dusty track through fields planted up with crops. A good place to get a lot of writing done, and Fred did a lot. Born in Berlin in 1929, he came from a family that owned one of the most elegant stores at the city center. He had experienced the stormtroopers smashing up plate-glass windows. Growing up in New York, Fred answered to Stalin's jibe about "rootless cosmopolitans." *Prophets Without Honour* (1979) is a detailed and moving account of the men and women who had given Europe the cultural life that was destroyed before Fred could take what would have been his rightful place at its forefront. Although written for the mass readership of Time-Life Books, his *Berlin* is a requiem for the by-gone Weimar Republic. Other subjects of his range from a social history of Hitler's Germany, a biography of the sculptor Auguste Rodin, to travel books and studies of Kings and countries, and even games and musical instruments.

We dined in what in the days of the monks must have been the refectory, now all candlelight and shadows. Another guest was Henri-Louis de La Grange, the great authority on Gustav Mahler. When the conversation turned to Mahler's symphonies, Fred could keep up with him. He was only fifty-eight when he had a fatal heart attack.

<hr>

ROMAN HALTER

Roman's Journey

2007

As soon as I could concentrate on the causes and effects of the Second World War, I began to make no allowance for Germans but took against the whole lot of them. Hitler and Nazism had been a blot on humanity, and the German nation was responsible. A Gestapo official with the name of Doctor Six had put together a list of over thirty thousand Britons destined for summary execution in the event of a successful occupation of the country and my father was on it. My mother, Viennese and Jewish, would have been deported and murdered. As I attempted to explain to myself the inexplicable, I found that the German language and the literature, even the poetry, couldn't help but convey an uncritical sense of superiority. In culture as in soldiering, Germans were able to do what other people couldn't or wouldn't.

In one of his several successful but spasmodic incarnations, my old Oxford friend Alasdair Clayre was an architect. Through the Architectural Association he met Roman, an artist and designer especially in the medium of stained glass. Alasdair introduced him here, there and everywhere. Gentle in manner, usually smiling and speaking with the well-controlled bravura of a foreign accent, Roman had the air of a man of destiny. Friends with a house on the Costa Brava invited us at the same time, and there he swam with one or the other of my small daughters on his back. Physically very strong, he lifted a full gas cylinder as though it was a bottle of milk.

Sometimes he'd talk about the European past or the Middle Eastern present, always succinctly as if there was nothing more to be said. He'd send me war-time reminiscences that he'd written up and published and gave me a landscape he'd painted of Jerusalem, quite a miniature but glowing with color.

So I was aware that he had been a teenage slave laborer making Wehrmacht uniforms in the Lodz ghetto at the orders of Albert Speer, Hitler's Minister of Production. So I was aware that in February 1945 he'd been going through Dresden on a Death March from one center of genocide to another when the firestorm bombing of that city started; the SS guards ran away and Roman and others jumped up to their necks into the freezing Elbe and stood cheering the explosions and the flames — I think of those shivering fugitives whenever the firestorm is treated as a war crime. So I was aware that Roman alone of his immediate family had survived Auschwitz. Some 800 Jews had lived in the small Polish town of Chodecz, and Roman was one of only three of them still alive at the end of the war. When he then returned on foot to what had been his family's house, strangers had appropriated it and they shut the door in his face.

Roman had been present the day that Albert Speer had inspected the workshop making Wehrmacht uniforms in the Lodz ghetto. The director, a well-known Jewish industrialist, had seen fit to pin on his striped prisoner clothing the medals he had won in the First World War. Then and there, one of Speer's adjutants had ripped the medals off and knocked the man to the floor. Published in 1995, Gitta Sereny's book about Albert Speer has the telling subtitle "His Battle with Truth." Hard-headed as she was, she came to the conclusion that Speer hadn't been lying at the Nuremberg trial to save himself from the gallows, that he really was a lesser monster than the other defendants. Working on her book, she "grew to like" him, injecting into her account a sentimental tendency to excuse him. Roman knew better. After Speer had served his twenty-year sentence, Roman wrote to him and they met. Speer remembered the incident at Lodz, agreed that he had been content to watch the beating of the director and above all that he was responsible for dispatching the workshop slaves to Auschwitz in the knowledge that they would be murdered. That was enough for Roman. All he wanted was the truth.

Nothing could have prepared him for the unprecedented dreadfulness he experienced on his journey. When he was young, crime had taken the place of law in his life and it would have been only normal if he had expressed himself with rage, hatred and bitterness. In that case, though, this book would have taken its place as one more testimony among the many others already half-neglected on the library shelves. Roman's complete absence of anger and self-pity instead makes for a lasting renewal of humanity.

ALDOUS HUXLEY

Island

1962

I MET ALDOUS HUXLEY in the bleak service flat in Chelsea where
he was staying during his visit in 1961. The sitting room was
colorless, the walls beige and bare. On a table was Iris Murdoch's *A
Severed Head*, the novel he happened to be reading. He was the first
literary figure that I interviewed and I was not properly prepared for
it. I thought (and still think) that *Brave New World* is one of the twentieth century's masterpieces, on a level with Bulgakov's *The Master
and Margarita* in its power of analysis and its black humor. But intelligence like his could slip into the higher foolishness, for instance
advocating pacifism in the face of Communism and Nazism pre-war,
and experimenting with hallucinatory drugs post-war.

Huxley had a very distinguished appearance. His was the impressive face of someone who followed the advice of Socrates and led an
examined life with whatever degree of resignation. He pitched his
words slowly and carefully in what I imagined was the way intellectual undergraduates had enunciated in the Oxford of his day. He
also had fortitude. Some months previously, a forest fire had burnt
out his house in California and everything in it. Gone was correspondence from friends, for instance D. H. Lawrence, Lady Ottoline
Morrell and Bertrand Russell. There could be no question now of
writing his memoirs. The loss of his past, he said, was "a particularly cruel way of enforcing the teaching of the saints and mystics."
On the other hand, he went on, this was preparation for the greater
loss soon to come. In an act of desperate courage at the last possible
moment, he had risked entering the blazing house in order to rescue the finished manuscript of *Island* that had been lying on his desk

prior to its dispatch to the publishers. When he worked at home, he could write two thousand words on a good day and in the future he would be returning to the United States to build a new home and start all over again.

Island expresses for one final time Huxley's lifelong wish that the world were a better place. It was the writer's business to investigate what had gone wrong, and why. Civilization in its modern form as he saw it imposed alienation. Millions of children had never seen a cow and were upset to discover that milk didn't start in a bottle. Science, manners, even the landscape were all changing for the worse. He had gone for a walk in the Surrey countryside which he had known and loved since boyhood, and where he had set the scene in *Brave New World* of the Savage's heart-stopping revolution to be free even if nobody else was. Now he had found there an arterial road and the roar of "infernal machines." Political power was in the hands of twenty or so men who were as irrational as the next fellow. William James had wanted to find a moral equivalent to war but the only suggestion so far was sport, and that wouldn't do. My impression is that the pacifist in him expected Kennedy and Khrushchev between them to blow up the world. Just before leaving, I asked which of his novels he thought was his best, to which he answered that it was for others to say, and what was my opinion about *Point Counter Point*?

By coincidence, a day or two later I encountered him in the street and then a second time when I got into the lift in Harrods, of all places. On that last occasion his brother Julian was with him, and they were awkwardly silent when I greeted them, most probably wondering what my intentions were and whether I was tracking them.

PAUL IGNOTUS
Political Prisoner
1959

U NCLE PAUL, as he asked Clarissa and me to call him, had inherited the pseudonym Ignotus from his father, who was a journalist as well-known in Hungary as himself. Uncle Paul's manner, his whole demeanor, was wonderfully old-fashioned, not to say courtly. He might come to kitchen supper, or we would have a drink in the bleak flat in Prince of Wales Drive where he lived, a lonely widower and very much an exile. He had no money, but survived somehow. It was rumored that his old friend Arthur Koestler took care of the financial side of things, even though – or perhaps, because – he is on record ascribing to Uncle Paul "the gullibility of a naïve liberal."

60 Andrassy Street in Budapest was the headquarters of the AVH, the secret police of the Communist era. Now a public monument, this building still retains a row of cells, below ground level and therefore windowless and claustrophobic. Attached to the walls of each cell are photographs of those once arrested, detained, interrogated and tortured here. Taken long before I knew him, the photograph of Uncle Paul shows a thoughtful and gentle young man. Twenty-four hours in one of these sinister cells, one could suppose, might have been a death sentence for him.

Political Prisoner is Uncle Paul's testimony. The book will always be a shock because the inhumanity it depicts is so ordinary; just a tale of cruelty and wickedness that has no point. Uncle Paul is speaking for himself, a very credible representative of the millions of men and women whose lives were similarly wrecked as though Communism had been some natural disaster against which nothing could be done, any more than against bad weather. Sentenced on trumped-up charges to fifteen years of forced labor, he took the chance to escape from Hungary in the revolution of 1956. The flight was so stressful that the child his wife had been expecting was still-born. The book's final sentence reads, "That little creature who had never seen the sun paid with her life for ours." I have a letter from him dated November 12, 1973, a fortnight after Clarissa had given birth to Adam. The spirit and the grammar of this invocation to Adam are his: "Welcome in this bloody world! Don't be despaired anyway; with parents such as yours even this world can be quite sweet."

B. S. JOHNSON
Albert Angelo
1964

"ONE OF THE BEST WRITERS we've got," proclaims a strap across the dust jacket of *Trawl*, the novel B.S. (Bryan Stanley) Johnson published in 1966. The words are not attributed to anyone and it may very well be that he wrote them himself. He lived in a handsome square not far from the City with a favorite restaurant at one corner. After a meal he'd go to some bookshop alone and once or twice with me. If he found one of his own novels, he made sure to prop it up conspicuously, in the window most likely or on top of a pile. If the shop had no copies, he'd rebuke the assistant along the lines of "You do realize, don't you, that the *Sunday Times* calls this author clever and funny and likens him to Rabelais?" He carried on even after one assistant said, "There, there, Mr. Johnson, it's quite all right." Oh how desperately he wanted to be famous.

I was the *Sunday Times* reviewer who had praised his first novel, *Travelling People*, published in 1963. Maurie Bunde, one of its characters, is the victim of a heart attack and normally the pun on the name would have stopped me from reading any further. But here is an experimental search for new forms in fiction. The standard he-said she-said narrative has been exhausted, worked to death. In this novel, wavy black lines on three quarters of a page replace conventional story telling. Death is represented by two and a half black pages. These experiments come thick and fast. "It requires no small talent," I wrote a bit heavily, "to make an engaging subject-matter out of style." The letter thanking me for my review was an appeal for friendship.

Bryan gave off unhappiness like a scent. Born in 1933, he had some bad experience as a child evacuated in the war. *Clay*, a poem of his, has two final lines that may hold the key: "Doing the best thing for me to their mind:/ war or parents: which did more to destroy?" He'd left his secondary modern school early and only the public library had made him a widely read and cultured man. I see him as he was in that local restaurant, hungrily eating, his face overweight with melancholy.

The poet Paul Engle had set up and still ran the Writers' Workshop at the University of Iowa. I recommended Bryan to him. "Engle seems to have misunderstood," Bryan wrote to me, adding, "I did not want to go this year." Besides, he'd met someone just leaving for Iowa, who was "generally not looking forward to it."

In 1969, Bryan published *The Unfortunates*, a novel of loose sheets with no pagination, supposedly to be read whimsically in any order. The author was therefore offering to share creativity with the reader. The French were doing that kind of thing. Bryan might have had all the fame he'd ever wanted as a homegrown Robbe-Grillet. The next thing I knew was that he'd got away, taking his own life and leaving something of a cult.

DAVID JONES
The Anathemata
1955

I N THE LATE 1950S, towards the end of his editorship of the *Times Literary Supplement*, my father took me to meet David Jones. A poet, he said. I had never heard of him. Since my mother's death, my father had me on his hands and did his best to fit me into his life. I must have been at a loose end that day. It is just possible that this was his way of engaging me in serious things like religion and art that he didn't care to discuss, most probably on the grounds that I ought to be able to think it all through for myself.

David Jones lived in Harrow and Alan drove there in the rather grand Bentley that satisfied one side of his character. With us was Father Illtyd Evans, an intellectual Dominican. Some local nuns were supposed to look after David but there was no sign of that. The room in which he slept was also the studio where he worked. A large picture window made the room seem more spacious and better lit than it was. Paper, old letters especially, painting materials, books, odds and ends, turned every surface into a clutter of heaped untidiness. Drawing pins in the four corners attached the picture he was working on to an easel. Nobody had yet mentioned to me that he was an artist as well as a poet. With great ceremony, he gave each of us a cup of tea and a Bath Oliver biscuit.

Born in 1895, David Jones was only some twelve or so years older than Alan. Their backgrounds were very different. David's father was a printer, Alan's father was a Guards officer, but both families had a sense of Wales and Welsh identity. One of David's constant regrets was that he knew so little of the language. A time was to come when Alan and I bought Teach Yourself Welsh books, but we soon caved in.

Under the influence of the Jesuit Father Martin D'Arcy, famous for his social and his proselytizing skills, Alan and David Jones were among the many who at that moment had converted to Catholicism. *Twenty Seven Poems* is the self-explanatory and none too imaginative title of the slim volume that Alan published in 1935. Try as I might, I have been unable to get much out of these poems; they seem devoid of emotion and coldly superior in tone, like exercises to provide evidence of talent on the part of an up-and-coming young writer. David Jones's *In Parenthesis*, a prose poem published in 1937 almost coincidentally with Alan's *27*, is very different, not an exercise at all but a statement from the heart. Vaguely suggesting something that has been excluded when it ought to have been said, the title is too distant, too clumsy to do justice to this astonishing epic of the First World War. Enlisted in the South Wales Borderers, David had spent weeks in the front-line trenches at Mametz Wood and then been wounded in the Battle of the Somme. In some 200 pages of text and more than thirty of notes, he dramatizes the experience of soldiering and the phenomenon of Britishness down the centuries. A range of classical allusions, references and quotations, not to mention barrack-room slang, transforms the war into a mythology that is first of all personal, then national, and finally universal.

The preface is supposed to be helpful, so a paragraph chosen at random from it will give an idea of what David expected from the reader. "Every man's speech and habit of mind were a perpetual showing: now of Napier's expedition, now of the Legions at the Wall, now of 'train-band captain', now of Jack Cade, of John Ball, of the commons in arms. Now of *High Germany*, of *Dolly Gray*, of Bull-calf, Wart and Poins; of Jingo largenesses, of things as small as the Kingdom of Elmet; of Wellington's raw shire recruits, of ancient border antipathies, of our contemporary, less intimate, larger unities, of *John Barleycorn*, of 'sweet Sally Frampton'. Now of Coel Hên – of the Celtic cycle that lies, a subterranean influence as a deep water troubling, under every tump in this Island, like Merlin complaining under his big rock." An awestruck Kathleen Raine, herself not the most accessible of poets, was to make the point that very few of us possess David's "wide knowledge of history, of etymology, of the Christian liturgy, of many crafts and ways of making and doing, not to mention those Welsh sources which for most are the worst stumbling block of all."

Since death consummates his vision of battle, David Jones has generally been praised as a pacifist ranking with Wilfred Owen and Siegfried Sassoon. But on several occasions I heard him speak about the First War, and Mametz Wood in particular, with something close to nostalgia and certainly showing that he wouldn't have wanted anything to be other than it was. There was about him some intimation of inner purpose, a spiritual calling, no less.

I think that a Bath Oliver and tea in a bone china cup formed so definitive an image of him because he saw the ways of the world as wicked. Real artists had no business entering the market place. True, he published in prestigious international journals like *Botteghe Oscuro* in Italy or *Art and Literature* in Paris and they were glad to put his name on the cover. The award of the well-endowed Bollingen Prize for poetry should have made him rich. However, the Inspector of Taxes in Harrow treated the prize as taxable income. Auden, T.S. Eliot, Henry Moore and Igor Stravinsky spoke for David at a tribunal but by the time the Inspector finally won his case all the prize money had to go in taxation and lawyers' fees. Refusing to sell his paintings, he kept a pile under his bed and left them in his will to the National Museum of Wales. In 1959 a selection of his essays was published under the title *Epoch and Artist*. It is further evidence of his unworldliness that he dedicated the book to Saunders Lewis, a prominent writer in the Welsh language but a home-grown fascist who founded Plaid Cymru, the Welsh nationalist movement. On the eve of the war against Nazism, Lewis attacked and badly damaged a Royal Air Force facility and was sent to prison for it.

David Jones had a fundamental unifying creed that in my view goes something like this: God created all things; when Man creates something he is paying homage to God; art is therefore by its nature sacramental; its beauty lies in the fact that it is a form of prayer. In an earlier period, a man so worshipful and artistic would indeed have become a monk. In the modern age, he had found refuge in this one-room monastery of his own, living exclusively for his art. In the mid-1930s, a rich well-wisher had paid for him to travel to Jerusalem. Rumor had it that the stigmata of Christ had then appeared on him. What he actually had was a recurrent psychosomatic rash, according to Thomas Dilworth, his latest biographer, who also records the horrors that overtook David when the psychiatrists got their hands on someone the likes of whom they'd never encountered.

Clarissa and I were married in 1959. We visited David now and again. It was a seal of friendship that he reviewed for me as literary editor a book about the Celts and then did the card that marked the ordination of Peter Levi into the Jesuits. Artistic marvels, his inscriptions consist of a brief text composed from biblical or classical sources and recorded on paper or vellum in a pastiche of Greek, Roman or Celtic lettering. One on the wall of my study reads, "Dic nobis Maria quid vidisti in via" (Tell us Mary what you have seen on the way). The royal blue of the lettering is set off by the scarlet of Maria and the edges are embellished by early Christian motifs.

Clarissa was expecting our first child when we received this letter from David, dated October 19, 1961: "It was *very* kind of you to come and see me. I *did* enjoy that. Here are some Welsh Christian names that I said I'd send to you. Girls first: Angharad, Eurfron (pronounced ire-vron meaning golden bosomed), Essyllt, Eurolwyn, Indeg, Teleri, Nest, Creiddylad (Cordelia) Morfudd (pronounced mor-vith, 'th' as in 'then'), Modlen (Magdalen), Rhiannon (Great Queen), Modron (Matroa), Gwenfrewi (Winifred), Lowri (Laura), Sibli (Sybil), Mabli (Mabel), Marged (Margarite), Gwladys, Arianrhod, Creirwy, Bronwen (white bosomed), Gwenllian, Olwen, Megan, Blodwen, Gwenfron, Gwenhwyfar (Gwenever), Goewin (pronounced goy [to rhyme with boy] – win), Elen (Helen), Sîan (Jane), Sioned (Janet), Mair (Mary), Rhonwen (Rowena), Mallt (Matilda), Hunedd, Efa (Eve) pronounced a-vah, Generis, Hawais, Gwanwyn (primavera)

Moli (Molly) — sorry, dears, it's pretty hopeless because all these bloody names, lovely as they are, depend upon the Welsh pronunciation. There are thousands more, but I can't think of 'em off hand. Well if it's a boy, apart from the obvious Welsh names such as Owain, Idris, Llywelyn, Caradoc, Rhys, Illtud, it's terribly difficult. Your idea of Caradoc is as good as anything. Any bloody Englishman can say Caradoc, and if you want other names, what about Isambard and David after yourself? I think Caradoc Isambard David Pryce-Jones sounds damn nice."

October 24, 1961 is the date with his signature on the title page of *The Anathemata*. Thomas Dilworth says that this forbidding word is Greek for "things dedicated to the gods" or "significant things," though what these might be I hesitate even to have a shot at. In any case, ten days later, on November 3, 1961, to be exact, our daughter was born and we named her Jessica.

Postscript. No Pryce-Joneses lived in Wales. Great-uncle Victor had sold Dolerw, the family house at Newtown. Though English, Clarissa's family did live in Wales and she had spent much of her childhood with them in the Wye Valley. Taking me back to Wales, she identified with the Welsh as much as I did, and probably more. Welsh nationalists began to set fire to cottages much like ours, belonging to people much like us. By the mid-Sixties, my father had settled in the United States. Out of the blue, he and I simultaneously received anonymous letters that had been typewritten on cheap paper. We were both accused of writing in the language of the English oppressor. This was treason. If we did not mend our ways, we could only expect the fate of traitors.

ERNST JÜNGER

Journal

Volume 1, 1941–1943, and Volume 2, 1943–1945

1951

RESEARCHING FOR MY BOOK *Paris in the Third Reich*, I was just in time to catch some German officials or soldiers who had played a part in the occupation, for instance Dr. Ernst Achenbach of the Embassy and Gerhard Heller, the military censor who controlled French publication. Understandably, they tried to put themselves in the best possible light, claiming to have acted as much in French interests as in German. Ernst Jünger was different. A staff officer, exceptionally intelligent and exceptionally observant, he kept a day-by-day record of his life in Paris, afterwards publishing it with the title *Strahlungen*, and *Journal* in its French translation. Much more than a timely self-portrait, these diaries fix for posterity the historic moment when the long-drawn contest for power in continental Europe appeared to have ended conclusively in German victory and French defeat.

After the war, Jünger was apparently in the habit of staying in Paris with a French lady. We arranged to meet at her address. He opened the front door and in spite of his eighty-seven years led the way up several flights of stairs. Born in 1895, he appeared to be a holdover from the era of Kaiser Wilhelm and Bismarck. His soldiering began with an improbable spell in the French Foreign Legion, on the wrong side, so to speak. A German infantryman, he spent virtually the entire First World War in the trenches on the Western front. Wounded fourteen times, he was the youngest soldier ever to win the Pour le Mérite, the Kaiser's medal for bravery. By the time of his death in 1998, he was the last living holder of that now anachronistic award. *In Stahlgewittern*, published in 1920 and usually translated as *The Storm of Steel*, is a lightly fictionalized account of his First War experience; it made him one of Germany's most celebrated authors. Two years later, *Der Kampf als inneres Erlebnis* (Combat as an Internal Experience) was about the psychological value of warfare. In his view, battle is the proper test of a human being. I asked him how come he had been able actually to enjoy the First War. His answer was simple: "Killing Frenchmen."

Not a Nazi, Jünger was one of the first to ascribe demonic powers to Hitler, referring to him in his diary as Kniébolo (a name of unknown origin). Close enough to the central Nazi tenet that the strong engage in a Darwinian struggle for supremacy and the weak go to the wall, he could nonetheless pass as a fellow traveler of Nazism. A Captain in his late forties, Jünger had rejoined his regiment in time for the blitzkrieg of May and June 1940. An earlier diary, *Gärten und Strassen* (Gardens and Streets), describes a leisurely march through France, more like a parade that comes to the happy ending of luncheon with French friends in a favorite Paris restaurant.

Trying to analyze why France had fallen in 1940, the eminent historian Marc Bloch wrote a book with the self-explanatory title *L'Etrange Défaite* (The Strange Defeat). To Jünger, there was nothing strange about it. The French had shown themselves unwilling to fight and die for their country. The Pétain government's policy of collaboration accepted that Germany had to have its own way.

Civilized, very well read, a linguist, botanist and zoologist, Jünger spent his time in Paris buying prints and books and visiting churches and museums. Recording the regular invitations he received to meet or dine with famous French artists and social celebrities, he passes no outright judgment on their friendliness. He extended the same amoral and apolitical approach to his military colleagues. Returning from the Eastern Front, a Colonel Schaer tells him there will be no more mass shootings; the sentence is completed with the neutral words, "now one has moved on to gas." The most senior of his

German friends was General Hans Speidel, then the Chief of Staff of Field-Marshal Rommel but transformed after the war into the General commanding NATO. As we talked, Jünger kept telling me that on Speidel's orders he had written a paper about the power struggle in France between the Military Governor with the army at his disposal, and the SS. The paper would show the Military Governor in a good light but unfortunately all copies had been lost or destroyed. From the way he spoke, I suspected that snobbery had played a role. SS General Karl Oberg and his deputy SS Standartenführer Helmut Knochen, the real rulers of France, were too uncouth to be invited into Paris drawing rooms.

Occasionally, Jünger's inner self comes through. One summer night in 1942 he dined at the Tour d'Argent. The Seine could be seen from the dining room of this most renowned restaurant and he writes up in beautifully overblown prose the pearly color of the water and the reflection of the weeping willows on the riverbank. Then: "One has the impression that the people seated at tables up there like gargoyles, feeding on soles or the special duck, take devilish pleasure in looking at the grey sea of roofs under which some of the starving eke out their lives. In times like these, eating well and eating a lot induces the feeling of power."

Several pages of even colder brilliance describe the duty Jünger once had of commanding an execution squad. A German non-commissioned officer had deserted to live with a French woman. When he turned to crime and abuse, she denounced him. The man was tied to a tree whose bark had been ripped by previous firing squads, and within the strips bluebottle flies were busy nestling. Twenty-four hours after D-Day, a convoy of heavy armor went by in the street on its way to the front. The sight of the youthful crews prompted a perfect example of the dark romancing common to anyone who believes with Jünger that war is a fine and worthwhile test of a human being. The diary entry reads: "The approach of death glowed outward from them, the glory of hearts that consent to be effaced in fire."

ALFRED KAZIN

A Walker in the City

1951

WE WERE IN the Century Club where Kazin greeted John Hollander, who had Peter Shaffer as a guest – critic, poet and playwright respectively. In conversation, Kazin and I disagreed about most things but on the title page of his book he wrote, "For David Pryce-Jones whom I am glad to know!" Note that exclamation mark. Subsequently he gives his credentials in a letter to me. In 1947 he was in Amalfi, he says, in a hotel where Isaiah Berlin and Maurice Bowra were also staying. Years later, he's at a party in London when Isaiah approaches and says that they had encountered one another in that hotel in Amalfi. This was not a fortuitous recognition, I gathered, but rather confirmation of his own status.

ELIE KEDOURIE

The Chatham House Version

1970

TOWARDS THE END OF the Iran-Iraq war, Clarissa, an experienced tour manager, was offered the job of taking a few determined or possibly foolhardy tourists to sightsee in Iraq. I thought this could be the moment for me to take soundings of Saddam Hussein and his regime. A cautious Elie Kedourie warned that there was no way of knowing Saddam's mind or what his intentions were. He might be thinking that now was the time to pick a quarrel with Britain, in which case I was an appropriate person to be fitted up with a false accusation and a prison sentence of twenty years. (It wasn't long before Farzad Bazoft, a journalist born Iranian but naturalized British, was treated as a spy and executed in Iraq.) Our visas had been granted immediately without demur, suggesting that we were being induced to walk into a trap. So I dropped out of the tour and missed the drama of a missile from Tehran that landed in the center of Baghdad close to the hotel where Clarissa's tourists were the sole guests. Back in London for a post-mortem with the Kedouries, Clarissa described how old Baghdad had disappeared under cement with the exception of a single house in traditional style preserved as a museum. "That's our family house," Elie said.

Elie didn't like to talk about himself. Jews were the largest single group in the Baghdad into which he had been born in 1926 and his family was one of the most distinguished. He was educated in the English and the French language. Originally from Baghdad and then a refugee in Israel along with tens of thousands of Iraqi Jews, Nissim Rejwan told me how as a young man he had been employed at Mackenzie's, the city's English-language bookshop. Only a teenager, Elie was the sole subscriber in Iraq to Cyril Connolly's *Horizon*. When the magazine arrived from London, Nissim would slip it out of its cover, read it through, wrap it up again and deliver it to Elie three days late.

Elie was fifteen in June 1941 when Iraqi officers allied to Nazi Germany seized power. For forty eight hours, British troops did not intervene, and in that time mobs murdered an unknown number of Jews (from 180 to some six hundred, according to varied sources), wounded thousands and destroyed homes and shops. He seemed to have left Iraq for good in 1946 and a few years later to have been elected a senior scholar at St. Antony's College, Oxford. As far as I know, Elie neither wrote nor spoke about what had happened to him or his house during the *farhud*, the Arabic for pogrom. Grievance and self-pity might do for other refugees, but not for him.

To a young and already great writer David Price-Jones with friendship and admiration Isaac B. Singer

Oct 7 1970

A Friend
of Kafka
and
Other
Stories

Isaac

Bashevis

Singer

Farrar, Straus & Giroux
New York

As an undergraduate, I used to go to St. Antony's to be coached by James Joll, a soft-spoken man of great charm, with fair hair and pinkish complexion and a slight splutter in his speech. From him, I first heard of Elie and the doctorate he had presented at Oxford. One examiner was Sir Hamilton Gibb, Professor of Arabic at Oxford and an eminent orientalist, and the other was James, who knew a lot about nineteenth-century politics in Europe but nothing at all about the Middle East. To ask James about the complicit part he had played in rejecting Elie's doctorate was to bring a rosy flush of shame over his face. Gibb took the Arabist establishment view that the downfall of the Ottoman Empire meant that Arab nationalism was now the dominant ideology in the Middle East and support for it would rightly align Arab and British interests. Having lived with Arab nationalism, Elie knew better and events were to prove how right he was. Soon published under the title *England and the Middle East*, the failed doctorate is now required reading. The Introduction to a later edition is a masterly example of how to dismiss an authority like Sir Hamilton Gibb who isn't everything he's cracked up to be.

A mutual friend, the lawyer Lionel Bloch, introduced Clarissa and me to Elie and his wife Sylvia. Austere in appearance and in manner, Elie had a smile that had some sort of finality about it, like a judge passing sentence. I had one or two tutorials in Arabic either with him or the equally quick-witted Sylvia. He was able to quote poems in several languages and he once said to me that you couldn't appreciate the beauty of Arab poetry unless you read al-Ghazzali in the original. Their house in Hampstead was a meeting-place for like-minded academics such as Beverly and Ken Minogue, a colleague of Elie's at the London School of Economics, and Frank Johnson and John O'Sullivan, both Conservative journalists. On one occasion, he volunteered to show us his notes for *In the Anglo-Arab Labyrinth*, a completely definitive book quarried from the archives to resolve once and for all the disputed question of what the British had or had not promised the Arabs in the First World War. A few brown envelopes contained scruffy bits of annotated paper, and that was all. He did me the favor of reading the manuscript of *The Closed Circle*. When we discussed the comments he had penciled in the margins, I found that he hardly needed to check references, his memory was a sort of Private Record Office.

"Never take your eye off the corpses" was his steadfast advice to all and sundry trying to come to terms with the deadly rights and wrongs of the Middle East. A paragraph more or less at random from *The Chatham House Version* will serve to give an idea of his view of the world. Note the classic prose that does such justice to the moral confidence of his judgments. "It is the common fashion today to denounce the imperialism of western powers in Asia and Africa. Charges of economic exploitation are made, and the tyranny and arrogance of the Europeans are arraigned. Yet it is a simple and obvious fact that these areas which are said to suffer from imperialism today have known nothing but alien rule throughout most of their history and that, until the coming of the western powers, their experience of government was the insolence and greed of unchecked arbitrary rule. It is not on these grounds therefore that the appearance of the West in Asia and Africa is to be deplored."

Elie liked to speak of "settled society" as a value so important that it might well be worth paying the price of tyranny to have it. Nationalism has been the agent of destruction, and the paragraph quoted above continues his indictment of it: "A rash, a malady, an infection spreading from western Europe though the Balkans, the Ottoman Empire, India, the Far East and Africa, eating up the fabric of settled society to leave it weakened and defenseless before ignorant and unscrupulous adventurers, for further horror and atrocity: such are the terms to describe what the West has done to the rest of the world, not willfully, not knowingly, but mostly out of excellent intentions and by example of its prestige and prosperity."

Various essays single out some of the public figures whom Elie holds responsible for manufacturing romance out of Arab reality, for instance the politician Richard Crossman, the colonial official Sir Hugh Foot, Lord Mountbatten, above all T. E. Lawrence of Arabia who displays a "demonic quality" in pursuit of his aims for Arabs. Elie is a voice for millions of defenseless people who had no way of knowing that the imperial powers would set them up and then abandon them, closing their eyes to the corpses.

J. B. KELLY
Arabia, the Gulf and the West
1980

THE BRITISH EMPIRE is said to have been acquired in a fit of absentmindedness, and in 1960 the then Prime Minister Harold Macmillan gave a speech that marked its demise in another fit of absentmindedness. He spoke of a wind of change, as though Empire had nothing to do with human choices or politics but was a matter of climate over which no control is possible. What the metaphor conveyed was that the British no longer cared to keep the peace in far-off places as they had done in the past. In those far-off places, nationalist politicians, some of them unscrupulous agitators, well understood that what began as mob violence about some local issue ended in a demand that they should be empowered. It came naturally to the British elite, civil as well as military, to conclude that they had only to hand over power and independence to anyone who wanted it badly enough, and all would be well.

One serious objector was John Kelly, originally from New Zealand and one-time Professor of British Imperial history at the University of Wisconsin. He and Valda, his wife, lived on Primrose Hill in London, and he first contacted me because he thought my book about the Palestinians had been unfairly reviewed in the *Times Literary Supplement*. He took these things to heart. In his view, the British

Empire had been the sole guarantor of law and order in much of the globe. Attacks on the Empire were attacks on civility. Accused of wrongs they had not committed, those in Whitehall and Westminster who had any dealings with Arabs lost self-confidence. Officialdom internalized what in one of his essays he calls "Obsessive pre-occupation with Arab virtue and British wickedness." This is the cause of "pre-emptive cringe," a phrase he coined and which ought to ensure him an entry in any Dictionary of Quotations.

A very determined character, he'd read through all the relevant archives and he had a way with words that crushed anyone trying to argue what to him were apologetics and falsities. A journalist by the name of G. H. Jansen, for example, in his book *Militant Islam* describes Muslim traders in black Africa as "men of extraordinary spiritual power." John jumped in: "What Mr. Jansen somehow fails to indicate . . . is that one of the staples of their trade was slaves, and that this traffic in Africans by Muslim Arabs was only brought to an end by Western Christians. It is difficult to understand how such a devout anti-imperialist as Mr. Jansen could have overlooked such a splendid example of imperialism in action as the destruction of the East African slave trade — a trade in Africans, conducted by Arabs, financed by Indians, and suppressed by the British."

Perhaps nobody but John could have exposed the bad faith of Ali Mazrui, who gave the Reith Lectures in 1980. The BBC sponsors these lectures with the evident intention that they should be one of the intellectual highlights of the year. When Ali Mazrui from Kenya delivered a diatribe against the West for the slave trade, John responded: "There is not a whisper, not a syllable, about the Arab slave trade, which had gone on for centuries before the first Portuguese navigator ever ventured south of the Equator and which has continued up to our day. It is all very strange, especially for a man who bears the same name as the Mazrui of Mombasa who were among the principal slave dealers on the African coast in the nineteenth century."

The course of events in his view demonstrated that the more concessions were made to Arabs the more they would demand. He was the unrivaled authority on the history and politics of the Persian Gulf, with specialist knowledge of the treaties that local leaders had signed with nineteenth-century British governments. The Saudis had seized an oasis belonging by virtue of one of these treaties to neighboring Oman. The Foreign Office was charged to deliver a legally binding judgment about rightful ownership, and the Sultan of Oman had retained John to present what was a clear-cut case. Yet as he entered the room and before a word had been spoken, as John told the story, he knew the Omanis had lost. Defeatism was in the atmosphere. In the imperial past the Foreign Office had served the national interest, but in the present day they had come to the conclusion that the weak had to be sacrificed to the strong. The Saudi record was one of "bloodshed, terrorism and extortion," but rather than confront as would once have been the case, the institutional decision now was to bow to it. The "strange love affair" that the United States conducted with Saudi Arabia was leading to "the slow paralysis of American foreign policy." Western interests were being put at risk for no good reason. In Riyadh he had seen for himself a depot with hundreds of new-model American tanks but there were no fitters to enable them to take to the field. He also doubted the quality of Saudi Intelligence after finding in some official archive a file marked "Freemasonry" containing nothing but photocopies of the pages in Tolstoy's *War and Peace* that describe Masonic ceremony. Years before such threats were realized he foresaw the use of oil as a weapon in Arab hands, Islamic militancy, and the attempt to ban free speech in non-Muslim countries. In a letter to me dated September 1980, he wrote, "If I see Arabian history in unflattering terms, at least I'm in good company. Wasn't it Edmund Burke who categorized it as 'a record of pride, ambition, avarice, revenge, lust, sedition, hypocrisy and ungoverned zeal?'"

When Margaret Thatcher was Prime Minister, some of her advisors recommended a Middle East policy free from pre-emptive cringe and offered to mark up passages in *Arabia, the Gulf and the West* for her to read. She duly asked the Foreign Office to send over a copy of the book, but instead received a note, "In the opinion of the Foreign Office, this man is not sound."

Postscript. John and Valda retired to the Dordogne. Intending to write the definitive history of Saudi Arabia, John took with him a mass of notes and photocopied documents. I was in the habit of urging him to finish what should have been another magnum opus, but he didn't. Saul Kelly, his son and a historian in the same field, has been editing and publishing much of the writing John left behind. Saul gave me a signed copy of *The Hunt for Zerzura*, his book about Count Ladislaus Almasy, a German agent in the Western Desert during World War II. Of all the signatories I have, theirs is the only father-and-son double act.

ARTHUR KOESTLER
The God That Failed
1971

A FEW YEARS AGO, I was in Budapest walking down a slightly dingy street when I caught sight of a tablet at first-floor level on the wall of one of the buildings. The young Arthur Koestler, born in 1905, had lived here in an apartment that he wrote up as a monument to a lost ideal of home, "stuffed with plush curtains, antimacassars, tassels, fringes, lace covers, bronze nymphs, cuspidors, and Meissen stags at bay." From here he set out to go to university in Vienna, and on to Jerusalem, Berlin and Moscow, with interludes in prison and detention camps, condemned to death as a Communist by the Franco regime in Spain and then again by the Communist Party as a renegade.

The world had been bewildered by trials in the Soviet Union in which Stalin's closest colleagues confessed to acts of treason they could never conceivably have committed, in other words consenting to their own judicial murder. Koestler's *Darkness at Noon* offered the insight that these men were persuaded that their death was in the higher interest of the Party and it was doctrine that the Party could not be mistaken. In fact, the self-incriminations were far less cerebral, brought about by threats and beatings, but Koestler's novel led the way to the intellectual discrediting of Communism before Solzhenitsyn began documenting the grim truth. Koestler further summed up his whole experience in *The Invisible Writing*, two volumes of autobiography destined to be read so long as anyone is still interested in right and wrong. That tablet in Budapest recognizes that Koestler singularly influenced the hopes and fears let loose in the contest to take control of the future known as the Cold War.

Once or twice in the early 1960s I wrote to Koestler suggesting that he contribute to the *Spectator*. It was a forlorn hope; he already had more commitments than he could manage. But on Sunday mornings his friends were in the habit of coming round for a drink, and politely he invited me too. He lived in a large house, a mansion really, in Kensington, and I was a short walk away in a street just around the corner. I was apprehensive. After saying that it was an honor to meet him, what small talk could possibly follow? Besides, I'd heard about a lady who was supposed to have approached him at some gathering and said, "Mr. Koestler, I've just been reading *Darkness at Noon*," and was about to add that this was for the seventh time as the book had changed her views about everything, when he cut in, "And about time too."

Koestler's Sunday mornings had the atmosphere of a highbrow salon. Anti-Communism was the agreed ideology of those present. Mel Lasky, editor of *Encounter*, used to praise Koestler to his face. Others there included Iain Hamilton, his first biographer, George Mikes, Michael Polanyi, Denis Gabor, the broadcaster George Urban and perhaps Ed Shils (who coined *gayim* as the collective plural for homosexuals by analogy to goyim, the Jewish collective plural for Gentiles.) One Sunday, I believe in 1963, Goronwy Rees, one of the rare outspoken anti-Communist academics, took the floor to announce that Anthony Blunt had tried before the war to recruit him into the KGB. Next to me was John Mander, then literary editor of *Encounter*. I asked him if he'd just heard what I'd just heard. "Oh, didn't you know, that's Goronwy's party piece." Some fifteen more years had to pass before the country learned what was common knowledge in Koestler's circle.

"We failed to see," Koestler reproaches his generation, "that the age of Reason and Enlightenment was drawing to its close." In one of his essays, "On Disbelieving Atrocities," all the more memorable because it was published in January 1944, Koestler describes himself as a screamer, a Cassandra; she screamed until she was hoarse and the Greeks still entered Troy. A character in one of his novels speaks for Koestler: "Europe is doomed, a chapter in history which is finished." The sense that he'd got away with it so far but wouldn't always be able to do so, infuses pretty well everything he wrote. I imagine that this vulnerability was always working away in him. "England is the best country to sleep in" was a favorite truism of his. "Old Struthians" is the label he attaches to the British after the Latin for ostrich, *struthio* for their similar habit of hiding their eyes from reality. *Suicide of a Nation?* is a collection of essays that he edited in 1971, by which time he thought that the question mark of the title was superfluous. January 14, 1971 happens to be the date he wrote below his signature in my copy of *The God That Failed*, a book that more than any other interpreted belief in Communism as a quasi-religious phenomenon, a superstition.

I could never quite make out why this quintessential central European intellectual tried to pass himself off as an English gentleman, dressing the part. It didn't quite succeed because the handmade clothes were so perfect that they gave away the disguise. The Hungarian accent couldn't be squared either. Cynthia Jefferies, formerly his secretary and then his wife, was some twelve years younger than him and temperamentally incapable of criticizing him. In an incident recorded by George Mikes, the Koestlers were playing Scrabble when Arthur put down "vince." Surprised that Cynthia should question this, he explained to her that it meant flinching slightly with pain. He owned a house in Alpbach in Austria, and drove his car from there to Kensington. Parking, he rammed hard into the car ahead, and then in reverse hard into the pillar-box behind. Intending to be helpful, a policeman who happened to be on the pavement, pointed to the Austrian license plates and suggested that Koestler was not used to driving on the left. "You think I am a bluddy foreigner?" was Arthur's response, and I have it on good authority, "Couldn't you see zee vindscreen vipers voodn't verk."

The English edition of *Darkness at Noon* is a translation from its original German, and it was published shortly after Dunkirk. As if that wasn't handicap enough, most of the edition was destroyed in the blitz. After the war, Calmann-Lévy, most venerable of firms, brought it out in French as *Zéro et l'infini*. François Mauriac wrote a review and by the end of 1946 half a million copies had been sold. Cassandra all over again, Koestler was in the position of an insider privy to secrets that the Party imagined would never be exposed but now gave him authority to go against fellow travelers and the current Left Bank attitudinizing about Stalin and Communism.

At the point in the mid-1960s when I was getting to know Koestler, Alain Oulman telephoned me. I had never heard of Alain – Pitou as he was known – but he contacted me because the Oulmans were on the family tree of my relations, the Fould-Springers. They lived in the Portugal of Antonio Salazar, the most glum of European dictators. Apparently the illicit Communist Party had held a conspiratorial meeting in the Oulman house not far from Lisbon. Pitou said he had known nothing about it but he nevertheless thought it prudent to settle in London and afterwards Paris. The Oulmans had shares in Calmann-Lévy. Two elderly uncles, both of them directors, were retiring and there was nobody but Pitou to run the business. About thirty years old, he had very little or no experience of publishing, but Koestler was obviously an invaluable property and my role was to help cultivate him, mostly by accepting invitations to one or another of the nearby Kensington restaurants. Pitou's wife came from one of the English families in the Portuguese wine trade. Koestler kept on probing whether she, born a Christian, would try to give a Jewish education to the child she was expecting. Better not, in his opinion. When I asked why he did not write a sequel to *Promise and Fulfilment* exploring today's Jewish identity, he answered, "A dog does not return to its vomit."

On another occasion, Clarissa brought up the name of Jenny Trower, at one time her father's social secretary in the Washington embassy and then Koestler's mistress. He denied all knowledge of her. When Clarissa then told him that she'd just heard Jenny had taken her own life, he swung round, "Now you have spoiled my evening."

Koestler happened to be ahead of me as I was boarding the flight to Iceland and so we took seats together. It was the first week of July 1972 and we were off to cover the Spassky-Fischer chess championship, he for *The Sunday Times*, I for *The Sunday Telegraph*. This was widely perceived as a test of strength between the two sides in the Cold War. The awe I had initially felt towards him had long since subsided. To think of him as impatient or intolerant was to fail to perceive that he was governed by deep and admirable rage against the infamy of the times. As soon as we were in the air, a voice on the intercom asked Mr. Arthur Koestler to make himself known. The airline was offering him a courtesy drink. A stewardess arrived with a bottle, a large home brew kind of bottle without a label, and poured a mug for him and one for me. He drained it straight down so the stewardess could pour another. I could not come to terms with a brew like this so early in the morning, so he drank mine too. Soon closing his eyes, he lay back. "But zis iss murder."

Once in Reykjavik, we stepped straight into slapstick. Bobby Fischer had not arrived and might never leave the United States. The opening ceremony was held in a dark half-empty theater without him. According to the grapevine, Spassky was longing to give an interview to Westerners but could not escape the KGB agents escorting him. So we went to his hotel and found him and half a dozen KGB in one of the public rooms on the first floor. He made for the lift and so did we. On the landing, the KGB froze him out, and managed to crowd all non-Russians into the lift and then deposit them on the ground floor.

Could the restaurant where we took our meals really have been called Nausea? The place had its comic turn too. A man alleged to be the Icelandic national poet was lying at the foot of the bar. Every so often he would haul himself up, point a finger and bellow, "I know you! You are Hungarian, yes! But not Koestler – your name is Istvan Szabo!" and then relapse to his position on the floor. A reporter once more, Koestler was in his element. "He sniffs the air with animal awareness," I wrote in my diary. "He makes me think of an otter, trim, the coat in tip-top condition."

Psychologically Fischer had won before he had moved a single piece against Spassky. The attendant grandmasters agreed that Fischer was a genius, and Koestler had a characteristic phrase for it: "He has understood better than anyone else the midfield aura of the queen" (in his pronunciation "ze qveen").

One of Koestler's campaigns was to lift quarantine restrictions on animals brought into the country. In the end, the local butcher, Mr. Major, tied a huge bone to Koestler's front door with the message, "With the Compliments of the dogs of Kensington." To this day, I think of this if I'm ever in Montpelier Square.

At the beginning of 1983, I arranged to call round. It must have been about six in the evening when I got there. Koestler was alone in the sitting room. When he suggested that we have a drink, I stood up; the bottles and glasses were virtually within reach. But no, I was instructed to send for Cynthia in the kitchen downstairs. She would have to stop whatever she was doing, come up the staircase and pour our drinks. She hardly spoke and she did not give herself a drink. I was made to summon her to come up a second time to pour again.

Koestler meanwhile reminisced about his arrival in Britain in May 1940. The authorities informed him that he could take whatever time he needed to see *Darkness at Noon* through the press and enlist only when ready along with other refugee professors and artists in the Pioneer Corps. Very civilized, he said, a contrast to the way he'd been detained and threatened in France. "It wasn't the Home Office that naturalized me, it was Cyril Connolly." Michael Scammell, Koestler's sympathizing biographer, quotes a letter that Connolly wrote to Edmund Wilson at that time, conceding that Koestler was insupportable but "probably one of the most powerful forces for good in the country."

1983 was also when Arthur and Cynthia Koestler ended their lives in a suicide pact carried out in the room where once friends and kindred spirits had gathered on a Sunday morning. In the manner of the ancient Roman falling on his sword, Koestler preferred the dignity of death to the humiliating suffering inflicted on him by incurable disease. Cynthia's decision to die with him, in Scammell's words, is "a mystery the bystander cannot penetrate." But she was only 55, and that silent figure summoned to serve something to drink is disturbingly submissive, caught in the kind of sacrificial rite the Aztecs once practiced in Mexico.

WALTER LAQUEUR
The Missing Years
1980

LIKE MANY PEOPLE with first hand experience of Nazism or Communism, Walter Laqueur had an aura of expectant pessimism as though the repeat of brutality might be around the next corner. Born in Breslau in 1921, Walter retained a sentimental attachment to the Weimar Republic of his youth. On the eve of Kristallnacht, a medieval-style pogrom, he left Germany to go to British Palestine, soon to become Israel. He never saw his parents again; they were deported from Germany and murdered. Walter spent the Second World War in the unlikely collective setting known as a kibbutz, but I have not found in any of his writings anything about how he managed to combine pioneering and scholarship. *A History of Zionism*, published in 1972, is the standard work on the subject, and probably will never be superseded.

His many books form a running commentary on the great political events of the age. By the time I knew him, he had established himself in London as a leading authority on Nazism and Communism. Truth spoke for itself, he believed, and there was no need for adjectives that roused emotion. He and Leo Labedz were a formidable pair co-editing *Survey*, the magazine that described the reality of the Soviet bloc more informatively than any other. As the Germans were invading Poland, Leo had fled to the Soviet Union, from which he eventually escaped as a soldier in General Anders's army. His judgment of Communist sympathizers and fellow travelers was fundamental. The issue of *Survey* devoted to analyzing the Trotskyite political vision spun by Isaac Deutscher in defiance of reality has claims to be the most effective polemic of the period.

And what might Jews like the Laqueur family have done in the face of tyranny? *The Missing Years* puts that question in the form of a novel, evidently based on the actual experience of people Walter must have known or known about. Reviewing the novel for *Encounter*, I pointed out that elements of choice were still possible. The elderly stayed put, conditioned by cast of mind and past experience. The young break out and try to run for their lives. One particularly memorable detail is that those escaping into Switzerland gave themselves away by falling on the suddenly obtainable luxury of chocolate and devouring it in public, whereupon the watchful Swiss police could identify them as illegal refugees and hand them back to the Gestapo. Survival, then, was a matter of luck. The Holocaust was also the end of common humanity.

Walter's later books tend to have titles like *Farewell to Europe* and *A Continent Astray: Europe, 1970–1978*, charting the moral collapse of the continent. The legacy of the totalitarian ideologies is that European nations are now lifeless and their fate is to become museums; their inhabitants will be tourist guides, guardians, even gondoliers he says at one moment. The inscription he wrote for me in this book runs, "For David Pryce-Jones who will read it in Florence – I envy him."

PETER LEVI

The Flutes of Autumn

1983

O CCUPYING THE BEST PART of one of my shelves are twenty-eight books by Peter Levi – by no means his whole output – and a dozen or more of those desirable items described in dealers' catalogues as "v. scarce." Most of them are presentation copies with a quote from the classics bolstering his signature. A good few titles, for instance *Pancakes for the Queen of Babylon*, *A Bottle in the Shade* or *A Head in the Soup* preserve the memory of his special squeaky and skittish laugh. *Comfort at Fifty* has an annotation in his hand, "Five anti-platonic sonnets." Here's an offprint from the *Heythrop Journal* of his article on the Podgoritsa Cup, a clear glass patera apparently of uncertain origin. In a throwaway footnote he likens it to one similar by Acaunissa who "probably worked at Vichy under Hadrian." Another offprint, this time from the *Classical Review*, opens, "If we had Cyriaco of Ancona's full and original journal and drawings, his immense importance as an archaeological traveller would be even more obvious to everybody than it already is." Cyriaco's numerous journeys,

Peter continues in his own manner, "are as hard to unravel as very old cobwebs."

Within a few weeks of arriving at Oxford, I had heard of this astonishing Jesuit from Campion Hall who'd been out walking on a road when an elderly lady ran him over. The mere naming of Father Peter Levi SJ sounded like satire, turning him into a Vile Body along with Evelyn Waugh's Father Rothschild SJ. Painfully witty, my grandfather Eugène Fould used to joke that Jews who become Christian clerics are "deserters in uniform." In plain language, you can always tell a Jew. Word had it that Peter's father Herbert, known as Bert, came from a large Sephardi family with roots in Baghdad and Constantinople. The house where Peter had spent his childhood was in Ruislip, and somewhere there in a field or a wood. Faith had come to him and he qualified it as "axiomatic," whatever that might mean. At any rate, Peter's father, his elder brother Anthony, his sister Gillian and of course he himself, all became Catholic converts. More than that, Anthony joined Peter as a Jesuit and Gillian entered an enclosed nunnery. His mother Mollie, a born Catholic, lived in Eastbourne where she established herself as a character by owning a Rolls-Royce.

Peter was obliged to serve his novitiate at the Jesuit College of Heythrop. He tended to make fun of it, at least to me. One day the Heythrop Hunt met in the park and a jolly huntsman cantered past to call out to Peter, "Just over from Ireland, padre?" The animals of Chipperfield's Circus wintered nearby, and more than once their exercising scattered the meet. After tea on a Sunday, the trainee Jesuits would gather in the hall to say goodbye to visitors, and I do not forget the look on the faces of all within earshot when Peter said, "It's such a relief to be here and discover that theology is a real subject after all."

Where did poetry fit in? His natural gift for language and imagery was the obvious feature in everything he wrote. He never dated his letters but I have kept almost a hundred of them for their literary quality. One in front of me now, at random, says that Shakespeare is "the knot in whom all ropes end." In another of these letters, he expressed very well the abstract character of his poetry that some admire and others find too one-dimensional. He was trying to "live by something which seems to me religious for which the appropriate words are the consecrated ones, to do with darkness, hermit, rocks, springs of water, God, the just man." Nothing concrete there, nothing personal. He translated Yevgeny Yevtushenko, the poet of Nikita Khrushchev's thaw, and he was present when Allen Ginsberg and Gregory Corso, the poets of the Beat Movement, did a reading in praise of the H-bomb to a room full of nuclear disarmers. "My poems are getting worse and worse," Peter wrote to me, "I'm going to become beat for a cure." In a letter from 1965 or thereabouts, he discussed his poetry. "Sometimes I long for it to be like other people's poetry, and my aerial and earth wired in the ordinary human way, as I always believe they so easily could be." This leads to a cri de coeur: "Christianity is not always easy for poets or poems."

There was something spiritual and striking about Peter's appearance, as though he had stepped out of an early Byzantine icon. Almost as striking, not to say exotic, Dominique de Grunne was a Belgian aristocrat and an ex-Benedictine monk as well, now at Oxford working on an interminable doctorate. Sympathizing with Peter's emotional tug-of-war between poetry and faith, he introduced him to the university's Grand Bohème circle. In a letter to me, for example, Peter describes himself browsing over a non-poem "when who should appear but Dominique. He took me out to tea with Iris Murdoch and her husband, both whose devoted fan I immediately became, in life as well as literature I mean – he was digging in a bamboo clump and she was writing very steadily. They talked about a journey to Spain where he kept imagining eagles and there were some Cocteau policemen." Dominique lived in the picturesque Bishop King's Palace and allowed Peter and me to put on a short play we had written. Our next joint venture, *Down, You Mad Creature* (according to John Fuller the best play title since *The Magnetick Lady*) was a loose fantasy in verse based on the adventures of Ulysses. In

Oxford to receive an honorary degree, Dmitri Shostakovich came to the performance, only to be hurried away by his KGB minders who suspected that the high number of Russian speakers in the audience could only mean a set-up.

From Campion Hall, Peter was sent to teach classics at Stony-hurst, unlikely as it was that he would fit into a traditional Catholic school. "This damp and dismal place," he wrote to me, "I get woken up by birds and the boys talk longingly about summer and about what the Greeks ate and what it looks like when a car smashes into an ice lorry." He once took a troop of Boy Scouts from Stonyhurst to the Auvergne, and sent me a postcard with the news that he had led them to taunt an obstreperous station master by singing out of the train window at some station the old favorite that is almost a folk song, "Il est cocu, le chef de gare" (the station master is a cuckold). Another postcard has a five-word question and nothing else. "Who invented the soutien-gorge?"

Arriving at the Vatican for a stay of two months, he was handed a piece of wood. A colleague explained that this was a chastity stick, which served to tuck in clothing without touching any untoward part of the body. Peter's future came under discussion when he was on holiday with others (but not me) in the house of Dominique de Grunne at Retournac, near Le Puy. Those present pressed him not to take his final vows as a Jesuit, holding so forceful an inquisition that he ended up crouching under a table, so it was reported.

My copy of *The Gravel Ponds*, published in 1960 and his first slim volume, has the enigmatic inscription, " . . . as if the thing in doing were more dear than being done." My first novel *Owls and Satyrs* was published more or less at the same time. Peter was generosity itself. "Your novel is *really* a marvelous piece of work, deeply fresh and orig-inal, painful I thought but in just the right way, very surprising all the time." He kept this up. "I *really* believe you have really got the enormous palpable, growing promise one used to believe all one's friends might have when one was fifteen."

From time to time, he stayed with us in London. Dated January

2, 1963, a diary entry of mine comments, "Everything about Peter is of a piece. There are no corners in which you feel that he has hidden those parts of himself which he doesn't want to show." That Saturday evening we went to a wild party. "Peter said that he wanted to earn the approval of poets and writers, and that anyhow he liked the company of bohemians." At one point in his novitiate, he was told to go to one of the central London railway stations to meet a young Spanish girl and accompany her to Campion Hall where she was due to take up a job as a maid. She had never before been abroad and spoke no English. That day, he and his bohemian friends had too long a lunch and by the time he got to the station no Spanish maid was to be seen. Wondering what on earth to do, he wandered up to St Paul's cathedral and there she was with her suitcase sitting at the base of the statue of Queen Anne. In all innocence she told Peter that she knew this statue of the Virgin Mary would keep her safe.

Almost certainly, the Jesuits took fright at the realization that Peter was a law unto himself and this could well turn into scandal. "Here is a sad little letter," he wrote to me. "They have put off my ordination for a year. An ambiguous purple and pink cloud hangs overhead and the first heavy drops are falling with a musical sound. It means I shan't be spending next winter in Italy." In another letter he dug himself in. "If there were to be changes of deep-level personality or any of that jazz, I should be off my ecclesiastical launching-pad before one could count down to zero . . . but they're amiable animals, and I can't take seriously these resentful-sounding growlings." David Jones nevertheless designed an ordination card. It is one of his finest works of lettering. The name Melchisedek in Greek capitals colored an unimaginable flamingo pink stretches right across the center and at the very bottom the dedication reads, but in Welsh, "from David the painter to Peter the poet." The ordination duly took place in Eastbourne, with Peter face down and arms extended to form a cross on the floor of the church, under the genial gaze of an overweight cardinal and the scowl of thin atheist poets straight from bingeing in Soho.

A Hellenist through and through, he made friends with Greeks who mattered like Seferis or Nikos Gatsos;, he translated Pausanias and wrote his own books about the country. "Everything too good to write about – Parthenon in dark misty moonlight of an eclipse, huge lemon and black butterflies, an owl toowhitting [sic] across the Plaka, rich rich [sic] costume dances (I was so drunk with it I fell asleep and had to have ouzo to get sober) and Oh the sky." Some of his postcards carry Afghan stamps, relics of a ride in the company of Bruce Chatwin just before that country became a battlefield. He gave me a rather bitter description of his opposition to the colonels who took power in a coup in Greece. "Trying to negotiate relief for the families of people in prison or deprived of work, and when people are tortured not pretending it hasn't happened. Not very glorious, is it? Perhaps you fear I am doing something more active. Well, I'm not." He believed that British and American agents – he called them spies – were investigating him. A letter written in this authoritarian period shows dissatisfaction with the demands he was making on himself. "How come I have never been to prison in my life? Arrested yes, in Foustat (Cairo) on the steps of the Cathedral (Benghazi), held (Corfu and Athens), deported, summonsed (as a boy with an air-gun in the woods) and arrested at sea by Admiralty Marshals (Cowes 1973) but never once in jug."

His superiors made sure that in England he saw a very different side of life. "I've just been in Manchester in a hostel for destitute men, meths drinkers and very young and illiterate gypsies and industrial accidents and mild psychotics, a world like the seeds of our own world come true, nearly everyone alcoholic, destitute, ragged, all marriages broken, all jobs lost. There was one night on a brick croft (a sort of bomb site) in the snow, with one or two despairing and unrelievable men staring at the ashes of a grand piano, no more fuel, snow thickening, six hours to daylight."

Peter left the Society of Jesus and the Catholic priesthood to marry Deirdre Connolly. Theirs was love at first sight, though the distracted Cyril Connolly made a characteristic quip, "I don't know what she sees in this Peter rabbi." They lived in a country cottage, appropriate for a story with a happy ending. *Shade Those Laurels* was a comic novel that Cyril had begun and Peter was to complete and publish. Like Cyril, he developed a taste for good food and champagne and the wanderer from the mountain-tops bloomed into a family man. Writing with a fountain pen, he made extraordinarily few corrections on the pages of thick notebooks and that suggests enjoyment. From the cottage streamed poems, reviews, scholarly articles and biographies of Horace and Virgil, Shakespeare and Milton, Tennyson, Lear, Pasternak and others. He seemed the last true man of letters.

Postscript. Caryl Brahms did not share the good looks of her cousin Peter. She was dumpy and her wobbly eye did not help. She lived in one of the Regent's Park terraces, collected glass walking sticks and was inseparable from Ned Sherrin, who was clever and amusing and evidently indifferent to female looks. The two of them knew everything there was to know about the theater and television. They contributed to *That Was the Week That Was*, one of the first programs to conflate satire and rudeness. "Be happy in your stint in America," Caryl wrote on the title page of *No Castanets*, one of her many novels, this one set in nineteenth-century Brazil. She added to the air of improbability that accompanied Peter everywhere.

BERNARD LEVIN

Taking Sides

1979

COMING DOWN FROM OXFORD, I became a feature writer at the *Financial Times* as well as the paper's deputy theater critic, reviewing plays that Cuthbert Worsley, the leading critic, thought not worth his while. The moment the performance was over, those of us with a piece to write in time for the first edition had to rush out and find a taxi to drop us at offices in Fleet Street or nearby. So I got to know Robert Muller, Herb Kretzmar, Milton Shulman and Bernard, the kosher butchers as they were known in the trade.

For fear of being accused of conspiring, it was a matter of etiquette never to speak about what we had just seen on stage. Bernard knew his Shakespeare by heart, always had an apt quotation from the plays, and was often critical of performances at Stratford. One evening there, during the interval he happened to go to the WC and so did I. Two unlikely young roughs were already in the place, and one of them said, "That's Bernard Levin." Bernard disliked it when strangers recognized him, for fear of what he might hear and the conversation that would ensue. The other rough type responded, "Yeh, ain't 'e got small feet."

A fussy dresser, a man making the most of himself, there was an element of caricature about Bernard. Invited by the publisher George Weidenfeld to a small lunch supposedly prepared for shop-talk, Bernard took one look at the main course of sheep brains and fainted dead away, falling off his chair. Quite a time passed before he could tackle the scrambled eggs especially served to him.

Under the by-line Taper in the *Spectator*, nominally the voice of the Establishment, he became an immediate celebrity as a scourge of politicians, daring to say out loud what others kept to themselves. When he joined the *Times*, the paper described him on its front page as "savage, clever, cunning, witty and brilliant," adjectives that any of his columns — sometimes twice a week and sometimes three times — could easily prove. His style could be mannered or direct and even colloquial as needs be. Posterity will be able to smile at Sir Bullying Manner and Sir Shortly Floorcross, wordplay on the names of the cabinet ministers Manningham-Buller and Hartley Shawcross. Once and possibly twice, he corrected the Latin of John Sparrow, the punctilious Warden of All Souls College, Oxford. It was a public service that he took apart so memorably the defects and lies of malefactors of the day like Eric Hobsbawm, Gore Vidal or David Irving, at the same time publicizing the persecution and deportation to the Gulag of Soviet dissidents and refuseniks. Perhaps he had in mind the symmetrical date of the French Revolution but even so it was some years before 1989 that he predicted the coming collapse of the Soviet Union. Nobody could take the place of George Orwell as a commentator on present rights and wrongs, but Bernard came closer to it than all the others.

My biography of Unity Mitford raised the sort of historical, legal and moral questions that usually drew the best out of Bernard. Shortly before publication in the autumn of 1976, Sir Oswald and Lady Mosley, Unity's elder sister, tried to have the book banned, or failing that, discredited. In their view, it was unjust that Unity or anyone else should have to pay a price for admiring Hitler and Nazism. As the Mosley campaign was getting under way, Bernard rang me up for an interview. On two consecutive days he came to the house and went away with pages noting what had been said. On the third day he rang again to say he was sorry but the article for some unfathomable reason didn't work and he was scrapping it. I suspect that the anti-Semitism of the Mosleys and Mitfords and their friends was too emotional a subject for him to squeeze into fifteen hundred words. He never explained his dissatisfaction, but it speaks well of him that he maintained his standards by giving way to it.

At about the same time, he brought me into a row of his making. The London Freelance Branch of the National Union of Journalists was in the hands of the hard Left. Some thirty of them invariably attended every meeting, intimidated the rare moderates who had bothered to turn up, and passed resolutions in favor of Che Guevara, say, or the Frelimo in Mozambique. Bernard persuaded enough of us to join the Union in order to vote the hard Left out and put a stop to political gesturing. John Vaizey, the economist and on this occasion willing lobby fodder, was sitting next to me. When I asked him how many Soviet agents were in the hall, he stood up, pointed his finger at them and counted, "Seven." Bernard's motion for democratic reform of the union passed, and then he and his girlfriend at the time, the statuesque Arianna Stassinopoulos, took a few steps towards the door. The hard Left squad broke up. One of them lifted a chair high into the air and went for Bernard seemingly intending to smash it on his head. Some of them then began shouting anti-Semitic insults at Bernard. We summoned the police who arrived almost immediately and cleared the hall. My impression is that for Bernard this was all in a day's work, once again.

BERNARD LEWIS
Faith and Power
Religion and Politics in the Middle East

2010

IN THE LATTER PART of his life, Bernard Lewis may well have been the most influential intellectual in the world. He was on terms with Presidents and Popes, and his books, sold in huge numbers, told the public what to think about Islam. It was a historic fluke that the man and the moment matched so well.

Having lost the struggle for supremacy with the West, Islam had nevertheless been surviving and even strengthening underground. The Cold War in the Middle East was effectively the take-over of the whole region by non-Muslim powers, and as soon as it was over, Islam was free to burst into the open. Ayatollah Ruhollah Khomeini's revolution in Iran and Osama bin Laden's attack against the United States in September 2001 are classic expressions of Muslim empire-building. The West, Christendom, has been here before, its rulers obliged to turn back invasions that might have left the continent of Europe in Muslim possession. Now, in what seems as sudden as a flash of lightning, the general public has to confront the world of Sunni and Shia, jihad and sharia, all terms unfamiliar hitherto and whose significance is therefore primarily in the hands of experts, most of whom are academics. An interview with a Dutch journalist left Bernard the memory of an exchange that was a shocking illustration of ignorance. Rotterdam will soon be a Muslim-majority city, said Bernard. "So what?" said the Dutchman. So you'll have sharia, Bernard said, and the Dutchman repeated, "So what?"

To some extent, I suppose, my view of Bernard has been shaped by his generosity to me. In 1972, I published *The Face of Defeat*, a book about the Palestinians after the Six Day War. Bernard, then a professor at the School of Oriental and African Studies, wrote to me out of the blue to say that it had been his "unhappy fate, or rather duty, to read many books on the Arab-Israeli conflict" but he couldn't recall "any that conveyed the sights and sounds and feelings and realities of the situation with such power, understanding and compassion." And much more in this vein. Those who take up the issue of Palestine and make a cause of it are urging young men to risk their lives in acts of violence that they themselves steer well clear of, and Bernard even gave the page reference where I point out this moral humbug.

Before the war, Bernard studied with Sir Hamilton Gibb, Professor of Arabic at Oxford and an advocate of the nationalism that in fact has brought harm rather than relief to the Arabs. Another of his eminent teachers was Louis Massignon, a leading scholar of Islam at the Sorbonne. Much of Bernard's work has been technical, to do with definition, language and linguistics, ethnicity and identity, issues of gender and race and slavery specific to Islam. I once received an original lecture when I asked him to explain how it came about that an Arab nominative often bears the Greek suffix of –id, as in Fatimid or Abbasid. As well as Arabic, Turkish, Farsi and Hebrew, he knew the major European languages. I once heard him discuss whether or not to deliver a lecture at Siena University in Italian. He traveled extensively in the Middle East and even had a tale to tell about how he had surreptitiously set foot in Saudi Arabia. In the Intelligence Service during the war, he had given propaganda broadcasts to the Arabs. At one point he was responsible for a hundred or so who spoke only Greek, most of them Cypriot waiters. If the officer in the field shows himself to be a coward or a traitor, one of them asked, is it all right to shoot him or is permission required?

A Zionist, every January Bernard liked to hold a seminar in Tel Aviv University. He had strong opinions and saw no reason to keep them to himself. He was the first to be able to say with authority that the old absolutism of the Islamic order is bankrupt and constitutional societies are not replacing it. The enforced imposition of European ideas and values has not put Muslims and non-Muslims on an equal footing but creates conditions for a clash of civilizations. Not a pacifist, he more than once in my hearing summarized current confusion in the Middle East with a good example of his slightly mischievous humor: "We should have dealt with Iraq and Iran in alphabetical order." What was happening in the Gulf, he was highly pleased to say, was Kuweitus interruptus.

In September 2004, I was invited to a think tank in Washington, as my diary records: "Breakfast with Bernard Lewis in his hotel, the Jefferson. He's aged but his head is very dignified, even noble. In 1940, he says, he and everyone he knew, was certain we would win the war. Today he feels anxiety, despair. People have not realised our predicament. The choice he foresees is between a Muslim Europe and fascism. Harold Rhode [a Pentagon specialist who habitually refers and defers to "Uncle Bernard"] arrives and brings along Qulat Talabani, son of Jalal Talabani [President of post-Saddam Hussein Iraq 2005–2014], a very young man who puts the secular and Kurdish case with just the right emphasis. He fears that Iraq is heading for a Shia Islamist regime, and the U.S. isn't doing much to stop it."

In 2006, Bernard went on one of the cruises that *National Review* organizes so that readers of the magazine have the opportunity to meet its writers and a celebrity or two thrown in to enliven proceedings. We set off from San Diego past Mazatlan and Cabo San Lucas down the west coast of Mexico. My diary again: "We also spent a lot of time with Bernard Lewis. He's very mellow now in his nineties, and much cared for by Buntzie Churchill – a very cheerful lady, well informed too. He quotes a recent article by Sadiq al-Azm [Marxist philosopher from a leading Syrian family] to the effect that either Islam is Europeanised or else Europe will be Islamised. The latter seems the more likely. He also believes that Ahmadinejad [President of Iran 2005–2013] will succumb to messianic end-of-days theology, and cannot be trusted to act rationally. Everyone seems to agree that in the hour Iran finally gets the nuclear weapon it will use it on Israel."

Mongols, Ottoman Turks, the British or the French are often held responsible by Arabs and Muslims for the tragic disintegration into violence and war of Islamic civilization, once so great. In the light of his learning, Bernard took the view that the social structure of Islam had not allowed for change, preventing Muslims from finding their place in today's world, or to put it another way, they had brought their fate upon themselves. Edward Said, a Palestinian American and a Professor of literature at Columbia University, had the intelligence and the authority to analyze how the Arabs have come to their present pass and what to do about it, in short to be the Edmund Burke of Islam. Instead he published *Orientalism* in 1978, a polemic fantasizing that Western contacts with Muslims were not what they might seem but the continuation of centuries of struggle for supremacy. He took every opportunity to accuse Bernard of bad faith. This slander has encouraged the anti-Western animus of enough academics and journalists in the next generation to ensure that ancient bigotry still makes a virtue out of war and violence. One of the last acts of Said's career was to have himself photographed throwing a stone at the fence separating Israel from Lebanon. *Corruptio optimi pessima* — the corruption of the best is the worst of all. Bernard was at first taken by surprise that his scholarship should be so insulted, then shocked and finally angered. For him, there was such a thing as truth, and he took his stand on it.

ROSE MACAULAY

Going Abroad

1934

ROSE MACAULAY'S NOVEL *The Towers of Trebizond* had just been published in 1956 and was receiving rave reviews when Alan invited her to dinner. Plain, skeleton-boned, she was dressed as though on her way to an Edwardian feminist rally. Foolishly, I said how much I'd enjoyed her latest novel. Cross-questioning me, she soon saw I hadn't read it, and the look on her face has been quite enough to save me from ever repeating a false claim like that. Full disclosure: *Going Abroad* is signed by her but out of guilt I bought it from a dealer.

KANAN MAKIYA

Republic of Fear

1989

K ANAN MAKIYA published *Republic of Fear* under the pseudonym
Samir al-Khalil. It was a wise precaution for a native Iraqi who
was informing the wide world about the tyranny that was destroying the life of the country. Why was there so much violence in Iraq,
he asks, and why did the intelligentsia collaborate so willingly in
silencing themselves, and also where were dissenters? The book came
out in the brief interlude between the end of Saddam Hussein's
eight-year war with Iran and his follow-on invasion of Kuwait, in
other words, when Saddam Hussein was proving that violence was
the medium in which he operated naturally. Shi'ite, but secular and
worldly-wise, intellectual by inclination, Makiya first studied architecture at MIT. Saddam had erected in central Baghdad the so-called
Victory Gate, actually casts of his forearms some forty yards high
in the air and holding swords that cross 130 feet up in the air. Still
under his pseudonym, Makiya published *The Monument*, a discussion
of the relationship between art and politics in the mind of a dictator. He then lectured on contemporary issues at Brandeis, a university with Jewish associations. His mother was English, daughter of a
schoolmaster, which explains his soft-spoken Oxford accent.

The cover of the pseudonym was soon blown. Here was an Iraqi
with the courage to stand up to Saddam and to look to the United
States to liberate Iraq. This was altogether too much for Edward Said,
the American–Palestinian academic who accused Makiya on the basis
of the printed word of being an agent of Mossad, the Israeli intelligence
service. Said was not in the least troubled that this outburst placed
him in the unwelcome position of defending Saddam and tyranny.

Shortly before the campaign in 1991 to reverse the invasion of Kuwait, I had an exchange with Douglas Hurd, then the British Foreign Secretary. Arabs, I said, well understand overthrowing and then hanging an oppressor like Saddam. It has been almost customary that the one taking power in Iraq makes sure to kill the one losing it. Grimacing, Hurd replied, "There is no question of that." Then call the whole thing off right now, I went on, because Saddam's survival would be seen as evidence of a conspiracy so deep-laid that ordinary people are unable to fathom it and so are left resenting the British and the West even more bitterly than before. I parodied the hymn of the old-time Church Militant:

Backward Christian soldiers
Slinking from the war,
So that the great tyrant
May slay thousands more.

In the event, the Allied coalition took no special steps to lay hands on Saddam and bring him to justice. Their policy was instead to encourage Shi'ites and Kurds to rise in rebellion. These two communities amounted to approximately three-quarters of the population. A minority but accustomed to power, Saddam and his fellow Sunnis subjected the whole country to terror, torture, the use of poison gas and mass murder. Mass graves are still being discovered. Anfal is the Arabic term for this atrocious campaign akin to civil war and Makiya documented it in another book, *Cruelty and Silence*, published in 1993 under his own name. He familiarized Anfal the way that Solzhenitsyn had familiarized the Gulag.

Operating mostly in exile, the formal opposition to Saddam was Ahmad Chalabi and his Iraqi National Congress. He came from a prominent Shi'ite family, some of whom had held high office under the old Iraqi monarchy. Articulate and very well informed, he was a skillful political operator. Too skilful in the eyes of the State Department where they thought Chalabi was bouncing the United States into a war the Department didn't want to fight. Washington floated rumors about supposed misdeeds of his, especially concerning a small bank in Jordan that his private money had launched. The rights and wrongs of it are obscure, but when we met I questioned him and ended up believing his side of the story. It has been a lasting pity that he was denied the role of a de Gaulle in the liberation of his country.

In 2003 the Allies (with the exception of France) were determined to overthrow and capture Saddam. Combat in this case was more like tourism. Instead of Iraqis, American officials were appointed to administer the country although they had little or no relevant experience or knowledge, not even of the language. Chalabi had called on Makiya to draft a constitution with the clear goal of sharing power equitably between Shi'ites, Kurds and Sunnis. Instead, one Shi'ite strongman after another has kept hold of power at the expense of everyone else. The United States lost out completely in Iraq, Chalabi was thwarted and Makiya became one of the best Prime Ministers that poor country never had.

OLIVIA MANNING

The Great Fortune

1960

O LIVIA MANNING lived in a hard-core circle of writers and actors, editors, critics and reviewers and BBC producers, up-to-the-minute in artistic matters, assiduously keeping their names before the public and fretting about royalties and contracts. She rather encouraged all such folk to drop in for a drink in the evening, and it was as well to be sure whom you were talking to. Her husband, Reggie Smith, all over the place physically as well as intellectually,

For David
with fondest love
from Muriel.
Chiesa di S. Giovanni - Oliveto.
Sept. '92.

was often away. Guy and Harriet Pringle, the protagonists in Olivia's sequence of six novels set in the war, are plainly and even comically drawn from married life as Olivia lived it. On one level, she was pleased that Reggie's career with the British Council had brought her to the edge of events that were to settle the destiny of nations, and on another level she had a grudge that the world had treated her unfairly. Guy's part is more reportage than fiction, and Harriet's part is more autobiography than fiction.

First in the sequence of six, *The Great Fortune* is set in Romania where Reggie was posted and amid much circumstantial detail of Bucharest is Dragomir's food store, "where a gentleman might sample cheese unchallenged and steal a biscuit or two." Lionel Bloch, my lawyer and a forceful character, had been born and brought up in Bucharest, and Olivia took it amiss when he teased her with not understanding how the unaffordable luxury of Dragomir's had impressed a child like him. At one dinner in our house, Clarissa accidently spilled some water in Olivia's lap, and she got up at once and left without a word.

In October 1940 the Germans occupied Romania. Reggie and Olivia fled to Athens, "just one step ahead of the Nazis," as Neville and Jane Braybrooke put it in their biography of Olivia. Clarissa, then a two-year-old, was in Athens because her father Harold Caccia was at the British Legation. In April 1941 it was the turn of Greece to be occupied by the Germans. The official boat taking off from the Piraeus was too small to accommodate more than some of the Legation staff, a party of commandos under Peter Fleming and the Caccia family including Clarissa. According to the Braybrookes, Reggie and Olivia left on the *Erebus* "which had been commandeered for the British" including the rest of the Legation staff. Lord Granard is said to have rescued all the remaining British on his yacht, but the Braybrookes don't say if *Erebus* was that yacht. At any rate, Olivia felt that through their British Council connection she and Reggie should have had a place on the Legation boat. The implication was that Harold — and Clarissa by association — had been prepared on behalf of officialdom to leave her and Reggie to the Germans. As it turned out, the Legation boat was dive-bombed and sank with some loss of life, and survivors remained on an uninhabited island in the Aegean until another boat rescued them. Olivia reached safety faster and in less danger than Clarissa.

When she was awarded the CBE, I played on her sense that she had not been properly recognized by writing her a letter to say that the initials stood for a cultural policy of Cash Benefits Excluded. Her lengthy and spirited answer showed that I had touched a soft spot. On the flyleaf of *The Great Fortune* and several of its successors she wrote in a big generous hand, "To David and Clarissa, with love from Olivia."

W. SOMERSET MAUGHAM

Don Fernando

COLLECTED EDITION, 1950

As a boy, I was under the impression that Maugham was the greatest living writer, and if not the greatest, surely the most famous. An appreciative public fostered an image of him as the ultimate cosmopolitan, living the stories he was writing up. Somehow he'd been caught up in the Russian Revolution, and that was glamorous. Somehow he'd collected the best modern art and quarreled over ownership with his daughter, an only child, and that was sensational. Besides, members of my family basked in the reflected glory of knowing him. Known either as Mitzi or Mary, to Maugham she was uniquely Maria. I found a letter he'd written from the Hotel Vendôme in Paris that shows how he could trifle with her. "Dear sweet good and kind Maria, You asked me what I wanted for a birthday present and I told you a handkerchief and you have given me a number. I shall think of you every time I put one in my pocket and how can one think of you without loving you?"

Early in his own literary career, my father had got to know him and in 1953 took me to stay with Maugham at Cap Ferrat in the South of France. I was impressed. You went into what appeared an endless vista of black and white flags on the floor. Then there was a very large drawing room. Martinis were mixed at half past twelve; there were two or three before lunch and the same again at six o'clock. I was very conscious of the Master upstairs in his study, at work. He would come down for a walk and this would be the central part of the day. I was taken around the garden by him, very slowly, with Alan Searle, who'd been his secretary before becoming his partner. Maugham was particularly friendly to me and anxious to know if I'd read his books and what the young thought of them. The movements of his mouth as he overcame his stammering gave him the look of a Galapagos tortoise. It was night and I was in my room about to go to sleep when he came in and sat on the bed. I was slightly apprehensive, but all he did was to give me this copy of *Don Fernando* carefully inscribed, "For David, when he goes to Spain from his ancient friend W. Somerset Maugham."

JESSICA MITFORD
A Fine Old Conflict
1977

"To David Pryce-Jones, Pillar of the Industry (Mitford, that is) with love, Decca." My engagement in this industry was entirely accidental. On the grapevine I heard that Decca and her husband, Bob Treuhaft, were coming to London and were looking for somewhere to live. Their dates corresponded exactly to the date of the semester I would be teaching at Berkeley. For the summer of 1972, we swapped my house in Kensington for Decca's house in Oakland, California, a very short drive from the university. They had left their Communist Party membership cards on a table in the hall where I was bound to see them. In the garage was a new Mercedes-Benz, far more classy than the old Morris we'd left for them in London. Clarissa discovered in Decca's library the stack of books in which her sister Unity had penciled her name and made marginal annotations. A reference to the Polish Corridor, for instance, had prompted her to jot beside it, What's he supposed to do with it, run up and down? Decca was to give me nine of Unity's letters from her Nazi period in the Thirties, and I thought I had the material for an essay reconstructing the mind-set of a fanatic. Decca encouraged this project and we stayed in touch. She introduced me to friends and relations who had known Unity. Something in the loud crisp pitch of her voice indicated that she thought well of herself, expecting to have her own way and to be applauded for it. Slang in her vocabulary helped to narrow the line between her inherited persona as a bright young aristocrat of the Thirties and her adopted persona as a progressive rebel who had thrown privilege away far behind her. Much practiced in the United States and Britain, this posturing was the basis of Communist identification wherever there was no real punishment for disobeying the line of the Soviet Party. Decca's letters, published in a volume of hundreds of pages, document the unworthiness of her praise and blame. I understood she wouldn't approve of the argument in my book that her Communism and the Nazism of Unity were two sides of the same coin, not rival ideologies but interchangeable. As I was completing the book, she told me that if I'd lived through the Thirties, I too would have been a Communist. No, I answered, I'd have been a democrat. Her riposte put an end to our collaboration: "How wet!"

Postscript. In a paperback of *Hons and Rebels*, much the worse for wear, she wrote our names and below them, "house-swappers par excellence." "Chacun son bum deal" were the words that Herb Caen, the local gossip writer, hit on for the swap.

NANCY MITFORD

The Water Beetle

1969

HER INSCRIPTION IS, "David Pryce-Jones after two very enjoyable days, from Nancy Mitford, 15 May 1970." Those two days were indeed very enjoyable for me but hardly so for her, because cancer of the spine was giving her such pain that she could hardly sit still. A famous Paris neurologist, she wrote to me just before we met, told her she had "one of the very most painful things you can have, and there is no cure. Delightful outlook!" She had made her life in France, it was common knowledge, because the love of her life was Gaston Palewski, French of Polish extraction, a soldier and politician loyal to General de Gaulle, and sadly for Nancy the husband of another woman.

According to Evelyn Waugh, her literary model, Nancy was a "nice cheap girl to take out for the evening. Costs you only eighteen and six for an orangeade at a night-club." She had about three hundred letters from Waugh, which she had given to his son Auberon and was "much put out" to learn that he'd sold them. "I couldn't have imagined that Auberon could do such a thing."

London literary gossip was what she wanted from me: Who had reviewed whom, and what was the reading public's response? Who was up, who was down? In return, she told stories about her siblings. Here I learned that at the outbreak of war she had hit on the nickname of Sir Oswald and Lady Quisling for her Nazified sister Diana and brother-in-law Mosley. We Mitfords have our opinions injected from below, she said, a vulgar expression so out of character that when I reported it to whoever knew her, I was accused of invention.

DOM MORAES

Beldam Etcetera

1966

"I INTENDED TO BE like Rimbaud, *maudit*, at the age of twenty giving it all up," Dom Moraes says of himself in his autobiography, *My Son's Father*. Up at Oxford at the same time as me, he was another young poet turning himself into myth. Away in London a great deal, he acquired a reputation without trying for it. His poems were simple and beautiful, an odd mixture of engagement and detachment as though he was leading a secret life. Standing unbidden at the back of a literary cocktail party or a dinner with a glass in his hand, he had the looks of a debauched cherub. He spoke so little and so softly that he might as well have stayed silent. Marriage to Henrietta Bowler took him into the stricken world of Francis Bacon, Lucian Freud and their friends and hangers-on, a good few of whom inflicted fates upon themselves more disastrous than Rimbaud's. Now and again I would receive in the mail a new book with a squiggled ungrammatical inscription: "David love Dom." At the first international literary festival in India, held in 2002 at Neemrana, I was a guest and there was Dom, still the debauched cherub but now with white hair.

LAURENT MURAWIEC
La Guerre d'après
2002

L AURENT MURAWIEC sought me out because his view of the Arab
condition coincided with mine. I had recently published *The
Closed Circle*, which is about one of the enigmas of the present age,
namely why have the Arabs made such a frightful mess of things.
They are heirs to a civilization of their own making. Since the end of
the British and French empires, they have been their own masters,
free to choose how to govern themselves to best advantage. New
nation-states were supposed to replace the tribalism of the past.
Some sort of modernization has occurred in forms such as urban-
ization or transport but little or nothing in spirit. On the contrary,
for well over half a century now the Arab experience has been regres-
sive: multiple wars and cross-border invasions, civil wars, military or
political coups, assassinations of heads of state and other public figures, judicial murder, government by the will of an individual, not
by law. Unable to end in definitive victory or defeat, these kinds of
exercises in raw power are bound to be self-repeating, a perpetual
treadmill of violence. In the circumstances there are no universities
worth the name, no arts or sciences, no Nobel prizes for physics or
chemistry, no advances in medicine. Arabs of course understand that
they do themselves grave injuries. In their code of behavior, success
brings honor and failure brings shame. Perhaps it is only human to
shift their sense of shame on to someone or something else – the
West, the United States, the Great Powers, Imperialists, democrats,
oil companies, Christendom, Zionism or whatever. Through no fault
of their own, in other words, history has come out badly for the

Arabs and it will have to be reversed. Those who treat Islam as a fresh start outnumber those for whom it is a fossil.

The Closed Circle was banned in the Arab world but nonetheless I have anecdotal evidence of support. The lady in charge of the obvious bookshop in Cairo showed me a pile of copies hidden in a backroom. In London, the Egyptian Ambassador bought two copies. An influential Iraqi told Weidenfeld, my publisher, that I was hard on the Arabs but recognizably writing as a friend not a foe. A friend of mine happened to be present when a Saudi Prince told his wife she couldn't have my book until he'd finished reading it.

When Laurent came to the house he was in the midst of one of the media tornadoes that can, and do, scatter bits of debris in Washington. His natural habitat was a high-powered think tank, first the RAND Corporation, then the Hudson Institute. The 9/11 terrorism had occurred some ten months previously and Osama bin Laden was a household name. A paper Laurent had written for the Defence Policy Board at the Pentagon maintained that the entire chain of terror, from planners to financiers and activists and propagandists, were Saudis. Spreading their version of Islam by these means, they could no longer be allies. The time has come, he thought, to take the Saudi out of Arabia. His book *La Guerre d'après* is a blueprint for this reversal of American policy in the Middle East. The scandal was less than it might have been because Laurent, originally French, wrote this book in his mother tongue.

The great and the good on the world stage habitually play down the conviction of Islamist terrorists that they have Qur'anic sanction for their acts. In the immediate aftermath of 9/11 President George W. Bush saw fit to declare, "Islam means peace." Politicians, commentators and churchmen everywhere have followed this lead and repeat that Islamist terrorists are misrepresenting or perverting their religion. Apologias vary. Some Islamist terrorists are supposedly motivated by poverty; others suffer some psychological derangement and should be hospitalized rather than face justice.

Euphemisms like activist, extremist and radical serve the purpose of obscuring reality.

Laurent was not having it. *The Mind of Jihad*, published in 2008, makes it very clear that what is atrocity to the infidel victim is devotion to the faithful perpetrator. Contemporary Arab-Islamic terrorism, he writes, is "the idolization of blood, the veneration of savagery, the cult of killing, the worship of death ... exemplary actions pleasing to Allah and opening the gates of Paradise. In short, they are sanctioned by the highest religious authorities, they are condoned if not approved and organized by government authorities, they are praised by the intelligentsia and the media."

Laurent was a master of controversy in his day.

V. S. NAIPAUL

Among the Believers

1982

A S A MAN AND as a writer, Vidia Naipaul was a free spirit. There is nobody that I can think of to compare him to. One component of that free spirit is of course his use of the English language. Among many passages that have a place in any anthology of English prose is one in *An Area of Darkness* that likens the Taj Mahal to the Duke of Marlborough's Blenheim Palace. Another is in *Beyond Belief* where a beautiful landscape is revealed to be the approach to Tehran's Evin prison in which the Iranian regime does its torturing and judicial murdering. "Hate oppression; fear the oppressed," is global advice from *The Mimic Men*. East of Suez, he observed, "all men are not brothers and luggage is not safe."

Anyone who supposes Vidia to have been an unrelieved pessimist should read his early writings and particularly "The Night Watchman's Occurrence Book," one of the short stories in *A Flag on the Island*, a comedy that is also a perfect work of art.

But being a free spirit had more to it than that. Vidia was born in Trinidad in 1932, outwardly one of the hundreds of millions destined to leave no trace that they had ever existed on this earth. I wonder what would have happened to Vidia if there had been no world war to turn the world upside down. Perhaps he would have been another Mr. Biswas immersed in day-to-day details, possibly a local journalist in the footsteps of his father. But Vidia had his chance and took it.

Arrival in the England of the 1950s to take up a scholarship to Oxford was a hard test of character. In the years at the university he first began to be anxious that he might not succeed as a writer. Not long ago, his college wanted to hang a portrait of him that the artist had donated but Vidia refused permission, as much as to say that he would not return to the halls of unhappiness. If he could have been born with a private fortune, he liked to fantasize, he'd have been a businessman. A sure way to catch his attention was to talk about exchange rates or the Dow Jones. Meanwhile he drove himself to write.

The novelist Anthony Powell was a self-appointed but influential keeper of literary reputations and by 1962 he was recognizing Vidia as "this country's most talented and promising younger writer." At the time I was literary editor of the *Spectator* and I invited Vidia to review for us. On a summer afternoon, he came to the office and we then went to have tea in a hotel nearby. On the way, we passed some workmen on a scaffold. We spoke about the British work ethic until Vidia drew the line, "I'm glad you said that. If you'd said anything else, I would not have seen you again." I never got a review out of him.

My wife and I made friends with Vidia and his wife Pat. Devoted to Vidia, protective and always on the alert to check that he was receiving his due deserts, Pat fell into the exclusive classification of Great Man's Wife. Her face grey-white and tense, she was secretary, copy editor, publicist and slave, saving him from himself with frequent interruptions to conversations, "You *can't* say that, Vidia."

My diary records a telephone call that illustrates how changeable the everyday drama of his life was:

"How are you, Vidia?"

"Very low, I want to die."

"I'm sorry to find you in this mood. I can't think of anybody who has more to live for."

"There's nothing I want to do, it's the realization I'm no longer young, it afflicts all men."

"Well perhaps it's not the moment to invite you to a party for my Cyril Connolly book, but that's what I'm proposing."

"Oh how nice, I shall come, or if I don't I'll find a way of telling you."

Then I rang Pat, who explained, "He's gone over the top" because the noise of builders in the house was getting in the way of the novel he was working on. Vidia came to that book launch and I told him I knew that noisy builders were upsetting him. He gave what my diary calls "a deep throaty laugh."

In 1979, I did an interview with Vidia and I have looked it up. At one point he says, "I hope I am recording and chronicling this extraordinary period of ours." Then he continues, "I know that Trinidad, like India, the other ancestral strand, is a place without any possibility. If a place has some positive element you like to feel for it, it gives you a little hope. There is intellectual nullity there nowadays. No mind at all."

The Middle Passage and *The Loss of El Dorado* show that he knew very well how cruel and unjust some of the colonial past had been. There were sound reasons for the British to feel guilty and Vidia — the grandson of indentured laborers brought over from Uttar Pradesh — was in a strong position to add to them. Contemporary cause-mongers manufacture scandal by passing value judgments on the past in the light of the present, but he was not prepared to falsify reality in this fashion. Instead he put his mind to assessing the colonial past in the light of itself. The British had created a civilization that is open and available to everyone. On his travels, he found it was no coincidence that countries where mind operates were civilized, and those where it did not were uncivilized. Like Socrates, he thought that the unexamined life is not worth living. Vidia's brilliantly emblematic phrase "The world is what it is" captures the view of history and human nature that mind had given him. Those who think that tinkering with reform or resort to political persuasion and revolutionary force is going to change the world into what they would like it to be are displaying a failure of mind. Fictional characters who illustrate the point are disturbers of the peace and destroyers of themselves and others. *Guerrillas* takes the real-life story of one Michael de Freitas, a Trinidadian like Vidia, and creates a frightening modern fable out of it. Imitating the American racist Malcolm X, Freitas raised money from gullible donors to start a Black Power movement in Britain. Believing that he was reshaping the world as he wished it to be, he took his white girlfriend to Trinidad and murdered her there. His illusion finished on the gallows.

Unexpectedly, then, Vidia was conservative in the best sense, on the watch for causes and consequences. Critics of Western mind – of whom there are plenty – could hardly believe that someone from his background had drawn conclusions quite the opposite of theirs. In the eyes of some Indians he was a traitor to his race, and I once heard a Jamaican professor dismiss him as "too brown." The West Indian poet Derek Walcott lampooned him as V. S. Nightfall, though he later apologized for it. A Marxist academic had the jargon for him as "a despicable lackey of neo-colonialism and imperialism."

The humbug of the anti-Western stance is thoroughly exposed in passages like this one from *Among the Believers*. "The West, or the universal civilization it leads, is emotionally rejected. It undermines, it threatens. But at the same time it is needed, for its machines, goods, medicines, warplanes, the remittances from the emigrants, the hospitals that might have a cure for calcium deficiency, the universities that will provide master's degrees in mass media. All the rejection of the West is contained within the assumption that there will always exist out there a living, creative civilization, oddly neutral, open to all to appeal. Rejection is therefore not absolute rejection. It is also, for the community as a whole, a way of ceasing to strive intellectually."

After Pat's untimely death from cancer, Vidia married Nadira Khannum Alvi, from Pakistan. Introducing her, he said to me, "She will bring a rare new fragrance to your social bouquet." It fell to her to deal with the years of his fame. I am of the opinion that he did not care a damn what anyone thought of him. People were free to write books about his supposed bad behavior, his rudeness and intolerance. When it came to his conduct, he did what he did and people said about it whatever they said. On platforms he sometimes asked Nadira to answer questions addressed to him as though they were too boring for words. He also had some view of the continuity of literary life. Great men had engaged in controversies that are the stuff of history, and so should we. Liberal noses are there to be rubbed in the mess of liberalism. He rubbished Iris Murdoch for using the cliché "caring and compassionate." Seated next to someone who described herself as a social anthropologist, he asked, "What is the word social doing here?" He told Michael Astor that a rich man like him ought to set an example and go to prison rather than submit to socialist taxation, for which the proper term is confiscation.

Every writer should have a good row, I heard him say more than once. Besides, he knew he was in the right. The star guest at a literary conference in India, he simply shouted down a speaker inveighing against the former British imperial rule. The next day, the wife of the American ambassador was due to give a large formal dinner in his honor. But she took the view that terrorists and suchlike were following custom, and therefore were not at fault for what they had done. In a fury, Vidia refused to attend the dinner and persuaded many of the guests to stay away too.

With someone of like mind, he let himself go and could even sound diffident. "Tell me" was the signal that he was ready to listen and learn. We went together to a conference in Baku, capital of post-Soviet Azerbaijan. I had an introduction to Khadija, a journalist opposed to Ilham Aliyev, the President and hereditary dictator of Azerbaijan. She arranged for three dissident Azeri writers to come to dinner. Other guests were Tony Adams and his wife Poppy, daughter of old friends of mine. They were living in Baku because Tony, late of Arsenal and captain of the English national football team, was on contract to coach an Azeri team. "Tell me," Vidia insisted to Tony Adams. The two of them had nothing in common, but their cross-questioning was so serious that the dissident writers never got a word in.

While Mrs. Thatcher was Prime Minister, she invited a dozen supposedly well-informed intellectuals to dine in Downing Street and discuss the difficulty of getting it across to the public that they knew better how to spend their money than the government that took it from their pockets. Vidia was on Mrs. Thatcher's left and I was on his other side. As they sat down, Mrs. Thatcher asked what he thought of the Prime Minister of Trinidad. "A gangster and a murderer," said Vidia, to which she replied, "Quite."

On the morning when it was announced that he had won the Nobel Prize, I rang up to congratulate him. "Oh, so you've heard of my little stroke of luck, have you?" he said. He and Nadira invited Clarissa and me to accompany them to Stockholm. At the ceremony, a white-tie affair, Vidia had to step up to a podium and speak for three or four minutes, not more. In the event, he held up his wrist-watch that had broken in the journey and picked out of the classics the story of the Emperor Julian, who, while training with his soldiers, had the "wicker part of his shield" snapped off, to leave him gripping only the handle. With the watch in front of him, Vidia completed a perfect parable about failure and success by quoting what the Emperor had made of his plight, "What I have I hold."

HUGH NISSENSON
The Tree Of Life
1985

H UGH AND MARILYN NISSENSON were members of the network
known as the Friends of Amos Elon (already alluded to in
Amos's chapter). Introduced by Amos, we met in Florence. I took
them out of the city on a summer's day to Ugolino, a country club
with a swimming pool; on another occasion Hugh invited us to lunch
at the exclusive Villa Medici, an architectural monument upgraded
to five-star hotel. Hugh took trouble about his appearance and in
my hearing once described himself as "spiffy." Staying with us in
London, he bought a sword-stick, and walked the streets with this
innocent-looking object which is potentially lethal on account of
the blade hidden in the handle. In their New York apartment was a
foul-mouthed green parrot that Hugh wooed with the words "Give
us a French kiss." The parrot would oblige. Beneath its cage lay the
immense white and fluffy Old English Shepherd Dog whose need
for exercise regulated much of the day's time-table. The Nissensons
also owned a house in France, in the small town of Pontlevoy not
far south of Blois. Hugh handed to Marilyn all responsibility for the
French language. Having supper at the opera and seeing that Kurt
Waldheim, the compromised Secretary General of the United Nations,
was at the adjoining table, Hugh called out "Nazi bastard" loudly
enough to be sure of being overheard.

This apparent gentleman of leisure was a dedicated artist. Consisting of half a dozen novels, some short stories and essays, his collected works pay homage to the power of story telling. In his view,
literature deals with the whole human experience; nothing is so delicate or so brutal that it can't be written about. From Homer and

Virgil to James Joyce and Primo Levi, the greatest artists have told stories – mythologies, if you prefer – that explain to people how they come to be who they are. Put another way, culture is really the stories about themselves and their nation that people believe to be true, whether or not they are. Hugh lived and loved the stories that Americans tell themselves. For one of his novels, he taught himself to use an eighteenth-century musket. A novel purporting to be the diary of an early Puritan settler in the New World necessitated a trip to Britain and close study of the language of the period. A perfectionist, he kept on re-writing until the narrative does what he wants it to do. He consulted Marilyn, herself an author, and he treated films and television serials as primary sources. It was thrilling (his favorite superlative) when experience confirmed what was going on in his head.

Over the years, reviewers and academics have been writing the obituary of fiction on the grounds that everything that could be done in a novel has been done. Hugh believed in the classic art form and gave it a modern lease of life. In an interview that I filed for reference, he made a declaration of faith: "I really feel compelled to make beautiful things, beautiful artifacts, out of my words." In a passage with a weird and wonderful imagery that celebrates the telling of stories, Vladimir Nabokov is speaking of Gogol but he might just as well be speaking of Hugh's novels. "At this super-high level of art, literature is of course not concerned with pitying the underdog or cursing the upper-dog. It appeals to that secret depth of the human soul where the shadows of other worlds pass like the shadows of nameless and soundless ships."

Below his inscription on the flyleaf of *The Tree of Life* Hugh wrote some lines of Swinburne's which Marilyn tells me that he particularly liked to quote.

"Yea, is not even Apollo with hair and harpstring of gold,
   A bitter God to follow, a beautiful God to behold?"

EDNA O'BRIEN

A Pagan Place

1970

C OVERING THE YOM KIPPUR WAR of 1973 for the *Daily Telegraph*, I found myself once again trying to understand the ways of the Middle East. After the fighting was over, an Egyptian army corps was encircled, and Henry Kissinger and General Saad el-Shazly, the Egyptian Chief of Staff, were closeted in a tent in the Sinai desert deciding how to proceed. If Egyptian defeat could be presented to the watching world as victory, honor would be satisfied and a peace treaty might follow – a few years later, Menachem Begin and Anwar Sadat were to prove the point. Back in London, I suggested to George Weidenfeld, my publisher, that I add another chapter to *The Face of Defeat*, my 1972 book about the Palestinians, a party at the mercy of an eventual peace treaty. George had just invited the well-named Aldine Honey to accompany him to Israel. Edna O'Brien made up the party. *The Country Girls* had established that the Irish literary tradition was safe in her hands, but it was said that she wanted to escape from the Ireland that is the backdrop of her novels. For some obscure reason I had the impression that she wanted to write something other than fiction and was thinking of a travel book for George to publish.

This unlikely quartet was staying at the King David Hotel in Jerusalem. We went our separate ways but a day came when we all met up in the lobby. It was one o'clock, we were ready for the Coffee Room with the view from its big window. Always thinking ahead, George suddenly said that the war was over, people like us should show every sign of goodwill to the Arabs and we would have a proper lunch at the main hotel on the Palestinian side of Jerusalem.

At about half past one, the four of us entered that hotel's dining room. Immediate hush. The atmosphere hardened. Elderly notables dressed in formal suits and ties occupied every table and every chair. They stared. Edna and Aldine were the only women present. We stood about. The headwaiter's facial expression spoke more than any words. At last he seated us at the one and only table on a platform running along one of the walls – away from everyone else, yet in full view. Some time after two o'clock, unwillingly, the headwaiter at last placed before us a saucer with some olives. Holding one of these olives between pursed lips, Aldine invited George to take it. When he leaned forward to do so, he appeared to be kissing her. Horrified effendis had had quite enough. The room seemed to shudder. If peace brought scenes like the one they had just witnessed, these men preferred war.

Half an hour later we had still not been able to order a meal. George was determined to stick it out; I proposed instead that we cut our losses and go sightseeing. Under a clear blue sky, Edna and I made our way past the shops on Salah-ad-din Street going towards the Old City. The noises and colorfulness of Arab life were new to Edna and fired her imagination. The Church of the Holy Sepulchre is at the center of historic Christendom and the closer Edna came to it the more the afternoon had the feel of a pilgrimage. Oh, she turned to me to say, if only the Mother Superior of her school back in Ireland or the Father who had taught the Catechism could see her now, what would they think!

Architecturally, the Church is fortress-like; on almost every day of the year, to enter is to pass from brilliant sunshine into the slightly mysterious gloom of the cavernous interior. Across the threshold, Edna prostrated herself without warning on the flagstones of the nave. As with the effendis earlier in the hotel dining room, there was a mass reaction. It was as if clerics and monks and acolytes in attendance, guardians of the shrine, tourist guides, had been waiting for this opportunity. Briefly the patter of footsteps hurrying from all directions, then the dog-pile with a storm of broken English that

BEYOND BELIEF

Islamic Excursions Among
the Converted Peoples

V. S. Naipaul

For Clarissa & David
at the end of our
fabulous five days at
San Martino 29 July 98

LITTLE, BROWN AND COMPANY

went something like this: Missie Missie, what are you, you Catholic, you Protestant, hundred shekels I show you everything, for you Missie special eighty shekels, you Armenian, you Orthodox, what are you? Then I could hear Edna saying, "David, get me out of here!"

Back in the King David, Edna gave me a Penguin paperback of what was then her latest novel. The cover shows a naked female form so artfully photographed and reproduced that there's no telling what's what. Edna's inscription is, "David — in Jerusalem with love. Sorry about the cover!"

STANLEY OLSON
Elinor Wylie
1978

WHEN STANLEY OLSON came to live in England early in 1969, he was 22. His ostensible purpose was to write something about Leonard and Virginia Woolf and their publishing venture, the Hogarth Press. One obvious person to interview on the subject was Frances Partridge. I had heard all about her from her son Burgo when both of us were employed by the magazine *Time and Tide* and before the heart attack that killed him prematurely. From his account, I had her logged as a bad mother, a self-satisfied Bloomsbury snob, amoral, and to top it all off, a pacifist in 1940 of all years. Stanley's friendship with her for a while gave me reservations about him.

Quite soon he knew his way around literary London. He fitted in. In appearance and in manner he seemed older than his years, mysteriously middle-aged. A perfectionist in matters great and small, he also couldn't help cutting a dash. There was nothing bohemian about him. It was his style to exaggerate praise and blame, to speak comically about what was serious and seriously about what was comic. I once wrote about him: "Moan, whine, impossible, ignorance, awfulness, boredom, were favourite words in his vocabulary. In every sphere nothing but the best would do." Tish Lampert, a sometime girlfriend of his, was American but nothing in Stanley's accent or clothing or habits gave away his nationality. I knew there were Midwesterners of Swedish origins and vaguely assumed he was one of them. The London literati couldn't help thinking of him as a Henry Jamesian character at home in books and conversation.

He lived in a pretty mews at the back of an exclusive Georgian square in the West End. I first met Sybille Bedford there. She and Stanley had a lengthy discussion about the apparently inadequate facilities for storage of several leading wine merchants. Once or twice, I caught sight of him pedaling through the traffic on a tricycle. Attached to it was an open trailer in which he conveyed Wuzzo, a particularly playful cocker spaniel in need of exercise in one of the parks. Lunching at Claridge's, he would leave with sheets of the hotel's headed writing paper, giving the impression of being at home there. An invitation from the Duke and Duchess of Devonshire to spend the week-end at Chatsworth was a passport to the higher social reaches. For fear that a servant might unpack his suitcase, Stanley bought a roll of tissue paper to spread between his clothes to make-believe that he had a servant at home.

Most of his friends assumed that Stanley must have private money. The country might be experiencing economic crisis but his extravagance ran unchecked. As far as I was aware, he made no effort to find regular work; he did a little freelance journalism and book reviewing, not enough to pay the bills. Years in the writing, his first book, *Elinor Wylie*, the biography of a Twenties poet now read mostly by academics, came out in 1979. I was sent a proof copy whose cover and title page misprinted the author's name as Stanley Owen, an unprecedented error but a good example of serendipity. The inscription reads, "To David, with great pleasure from Stanley Olson OWEN." A graphologist would be in his element analyzing

Stanley's handwriting, the letters so identical and minute that the words can hardly be read even with a magnifying glass. It looks as if he was making sure not to give anything away. Here is a sentence I have deciphered. "I absolutely detest Jacques-Emile Blanche: such a painful snob and such a *poseur*." Or another, "How I agree with you about the complete awfulness of Graham Greene; never liked him, never felt any desire to try to like him and never understood why people go weak at the knee over him: nausea?"

Stanley's second book, *John Singer Sargent: His Portrait*, was published in 1986, receiving a cloudburst of critical approval. He wrote to me, "I can never quite grasp why people had it in for Sargent because he paints Jews. Jealousy; they couldn't get a commission? The Wertheimers were delightful people — even if the next generation has gone to seed rather.... But then I cannot understand anti-Semitism. It is a tiresome prejudice and worse, downright evil. But I could go on for pages. Thank God Sargent was a cut above those morons who looked at his subjects and sneered."

The next project, a biography of Rebecca West, was making heavy weather. Stanley was becoming more than usually histrionic about the business of writing and more than usually spendthrift about the business of living. In July 1986 he had a stroke. I visited him in hospital and found that he could understand conversation but could only express himself involuntarily and exclusively in four-letter words. Three years later a second stroke was fatal.

His cousin and literary executor and now biographer as well, Phyllis Hatfield, was writing to me in 1991 with questions. In the opening pages of *Pencil Me In*, her book about Stanley, she describes dancing with him at his bar mitzvah. This came with the force of a secret suddenly exploding. His Russian-Jewish grandfather, an immigrant who could hardly speak English, had changed the family name of Olshanitsky to Olson because it sounded American. His father had made a huge fortune providing spare parts for electronics. Living in Akron, Ohio, the parents had thought it in Stanley's interest to send him to a military academy on the East Coast. They could never have understood their son but they always paid his allowance and more besides, so they must have been proud of him. Phyllis Hatfield does her heroic best to present Stanley as a gifted young writer who had "an uncanny sense of how to be amusing" and viewed the ups and downs of life with "ironic detachment." But that can't be all there is to it. Instinct gives me the feeling that something very different, some element of fear too deep to bring into the open — the comic masking the tragic — must have driven him into exile and impersonation of an English dilettante.

IRIS ORIGO
War in Val d'Orcia
1947

"PORTRAIT OF A LADY" is the title of the profile that I wrote of Iris Origo, a borrowing from Henry James that is rather obvious but nonetheless fitting. The ladies in that great man's life and in his novels were like Iris, connected to British peers and American millionaires. Highly cultivated, she was an old-fashioned bluestocking engaged in matters of the mind. Edith Wharton and Virginia Woolf both helped to start her literary career. Newly married, she and Antonio Origo, a Marchese, bought La Foce, a large house with an estate of 3,500 acres in Val d'Orcia, an unspoilt out-of-the-way valley south of Siena. Caroline Moorhead's biography of Iris describes with the lightest of touches how between the wars Antonio was a Blackshirt and friend of Mussolini while Iris was presenting critics of Mussolini as heroic.

War in Val d'Orcia takes the form of a diary that reaches a climax in June 1944 when artillery starts to shell La Foce, partisans take up positions and German soldiers move into the house under the shadow of death and destruction. It falls to Iris as the Marchesa to take responsibility for the children of local villages, and she does so naturally, *noblesse oblige* as the French say. She and the children might well have been killed in the fighting. Danger did not bring fear with it and the happy ending, one feels, is well deserved. As the front line at last rolls on, a British Major is at the door asking, "Are you Marchesa Origo? The whole Eighth Army has been looking for you." He brings the news that her cousin Ulick Verney of the Scots Guards is at GHQ only a few miles away. One sentence in particular shows how she has remained herself through the experience of war. "I wish very much that I had a clean frock to put on."

More than reportage, this book is a lasting testimonial. When I asked her to sign *War in Val d'Orcia*, she did not hesitate. "To David Pryce-Jones who, unlike the author, possesses a copy of this book."

J. B. PRIESTLEY

Margin Released

A Writer's Reminiscences and Reflections

1962

I TOOK IT FOR GRANTED that Priestley and I might not get on too well and it is safe to assume that he must have thought the same about me. Class-conscious monotonous pipe-smoking old bore from provincial Bradford meets sheltered young aesthete from smarty-boots London who is sneering only because he could never be anything like so popular. Characters in the novels Priestley wrote between the wars have names like Jess Oakroyd, Welkinghurst and

Ormenroyd, they live in Coketown and Bruddersford and Brock-shire. He could speak of himself as Young Jack P. and talk about lads, or in pseudo-patois "t'folk back o' t'mill." He must be the last writer to sprinkle the page with expressions like "Bah!" or "Heigh-ho!" and mean them sincerely.

Socialism was buried in that vision of the country and of course it has shrunk to folksiness if it still exists at all. Its moment came in 1940 when a German invasion was a real possibility and the British nation was going to have to decide what was to be done about that. A traitor, William Joyce, was broadcasting from the Ministry of Josef Goebbels in Berlin that Nazi victory and British defeat were now imminent. Familiarized by the pitch of his voice as Lord Haw-Haw, Joyce made headway that rattled the government. Someone had to broadcast that we were all in it together. The moment called for sentimentality and sharing and Priestley was just the man for it. His war-time broadcasts on the BBC established him as a popular writer, perhaps the most popular in the country.

What worked for the British, in his view, works for everybody. The Soviet Union, he thought after a trip there in 1945, "shows a wisdom in dealing with its own peoples . . . the wide Soviet land glitters and hums with their dance and song." He dismissed George Orwell as "a bit of a misery." Reviewing *The Ordeal of Gilbert Pinfold* in the *New Statesman*, he speculated that Evelyn Waugh was so pretentious that he had to be on the way to a mental breakdown from which he wouldn't recover.

Priestley and his wife, the archaeologist Jacquetta Hawkes, lived in a very desirable eighteenth-century manor a mile away from Shakespeare's Stratford-on-Avon. Socialism had not lowered their life-style. We walked up and down the carefully mown lawn and it was rather endearing to hear him say that his floppy black hat made him look like a Chinese executioner. He thought he had "a rather special public which belongs chiefly to the professional middle class. Fashionable types don't bother with me, but because I've never been in fashion I've never been out of fashion. There's a kind of contempt for writers, isn't there?" Avant-garde was not a term of praise. Our pastors and masters, humbugs the whole lot of them, were imposing themselves in the name of the State or the Good Life. The letters he received, he growled, were all from the Inland Revenue. "Just because I think the lot of them have gone barmy doesn't mean I've become a Tory. Soaking the rich, indeed! The only thing they'll soak in are the waters of the Caribbean." Harrumphing midway between boasting and complaining, he was the last man of letters with a Leftist patent of about 1910. And by the way, Phoenix, Arizona, was where he and his wife liked to spend the winter; the dry climate suited them very nicely.

GWYNEDD RAE

Mary Plain in War-Time

1942

THIS WAS THE FIRST BOOK inscribed by its author that I received. Gwynedd Rae had a vivid imagination and used it to invent stories for children about Mary Plain, an endearing and frisky little bear from the zoo in Berne. It has always seemed to me that Paddington Bear has to be a close relation of Mary Plain and lawyers might be able to make something of that.

Gwynedd Rae became a neighbor when my parents' house in London was bombed and they moved to Kent. I was six years old, and due to the accidents of war I had been in the hands of relations in France, Spain and then Morocco. I spoke English with a French accent. On a Sunday we would walk from our Castle Hill Farm through woods to reach Knowles Bank in time for tea. Old Mrs. Rae ruled this unpretentious and attractive eighteenth-century house in brick. What with shawls, lace, a scarf, some sort of cap, she might have sat for Whistler's Mother. Both of us determined to win, we played drafts, halma, spillikins, snap and Snakes and Ladders.

Kenneth Rae, her son, had published my father's books and after the war devoted his time and money to creating the National Theatre. Known as the Owl Man on account of his thick spectacles, he featured in the Mary Plain books as the person who allows Mary to live more as a human being than a bear. Neither he nor Gwynedd had married. Tall and strong-boned, she looked rather masculine. Years later, I found that in the war she had written letters to my father urging Christianity. This Mary Plain book brings me into the story. Among the illustrations is a drawing of me, a very good likeness too and surely destiny for a six-year-old.

JEAN-FRANÇOIS REVEL
La Tentation Totalitaire
1977

THE *NEW YORK TIMES* commissioned me in 1977 to write a profile of Jean-François Revel. Having written a column for ten years or so in the weekly magazine *L'Express*, he was a ringleader of French intellectual life, holding the fort with Raymond Aron, his colleague on the magazine. I spoke of "his steady and witty onslaught against humbug in all its forms." He had committed himself to defending one of the simplest and most urgent propositions, that "democracy is diminishing to the point of extinction, and this ought not to pass unchallenged." Now was the time for all good men to come to the aid of freedom and sanity.

La Tentation Totalitaire (translation unnecessary) is a polemic against what he considered a permanent infatuation with Stalinism. Appeasement of Hitler had been a mistake for which Europe had paid a very great price. Appeasement of Soviet Communism was a mistake of the same order and it came in numerous forms, for instance Euro-Communism, Finlandisation and the Campaign for Nuclear Disarmament. The words "Americans Go Home" repeatedly chalked on the walls in French cities or the hundreds of thousands demonstrating against the positioning of cruise missiles in what was then West Germany, made no distinction between fear and hope. Across the continent, the slogan "Better red than dead" became believable and popular because of, or in spite of, the crafty implication that surrender to the Soviet Union was the pathway to survival and peace. For reasons too profound for psychological treatment, Revel warned, free human beings wish, at least with some part of themselves, to be relieved of their freedom, even if they will have to be sorry for it afterwards.

Jean-François inscribed this book, "Pour David Pryce-Jones, en souvenir de nos agréables entretiens à Paris, bien amicalement J-F Revel le 2 Septembre 1977" (translation still unnecessary). He encouraged me to ring him up whenever I was in Paris. He looked for dragons to slay, and he slew them, occasionally taking me as a spectator. At one literary gathering, he did not let the film director Agnès Varda get away with saying that she never read Solzhenitsyn because he was on the Right. One other time, we were at his publishers. In the hall of the building, a writer of some fame greeted him but he did not reply, because as he later explained, the man had been a collaborator in the war. "He has the look of someone who enjoys life too much to want to spend it picking fights," was my way of saying in the profile that he had long since given up bothering about his waistline in favor of good food in good restaurants. The most unlikely of the dozen or so books he signed for me is *Un Festin en Paroles* (Putting banquets into words), published in 1979 and nothing less than a history of gastronomy, or as he expressed it on the title page, "Pour Clarissa et David, cette promenade littéraire à travers l'archéologie de la cuisine." A few days after publication of the profile, I received a telegram. "Merci pour ce magnifique article stop je vous promets de maigrir sans maigrir amitiés Jean-François," which might go into English as "I promise to thin down without thinning down on friendship."

GREGOR VON REZZORI
Memoirs of an Anti-Semite
2007

Y OU HAVE A HOUSE in Florence, an acquaintance of Russian origins by the name of Alexis Gregory said to me, then you must meet Grisha von Rezzori, he's a real cosmopolitan. The Italian surname with its German ennoblement is a hybrid that made him unique. He lived at San Donato in quite a large house hidden in woods so far off the beaten track that it seemed he must have wanted solitude. Not so. He encouraged visitors. There was a guesthouse to which Bruce Chatwin had invited himself for the weekend and stayed eight months finishing a book.

Grisha was well built, rugged, a survivor with a post-Habsburg image and tweed jackets cut for him by the tailor in Principe's, the shop in Florence where the fastidious went for their clothes. His eyes were blue, his voice deep. Beatrice, his wife, stood back as literary life passed over her head. Glossy magazines carried articles about her and the modern art gallery she ran in Milan. On the walls were pictures, experimentally abstract for the most part, and on the side-tables were photographs from the previous century of her Armenian forebears who had lived distinguished lives in Beirut and wore Ottoman uniforms complete with medals and tarboosh.

Czernowicz, or Cernăuți in Romanian, the main city of the Bukovina, was the birthplace of Grisha and coincidentally of a number of Hollywood film producers. Grisha's fiction evokes a place and a time of which nothing is left except stories and memories, some comic and some sad. Commissioned before the war in supposedly the best regiment in the country, Grisha had been one day the officer mounting the guard at the royal palace of Sinaia when orders and drill came out wrong. The memory of that shambles of a parade with soldiers marching out of step in different directions still made him laugh. On the spare front paper of my copy of *Memoirs of an Anti-Semite* he drew a cartoon of an officer in ceremonial order with bear-skin and sword, saluting a lady lying invitingly on a couch. The caption conveys a whole way of life: "An officer of the Unsprezece Rosiori never accepts money from women." According to Grisha, a commission in this cavalry regiment was the social peak of the *beau monde* of Romania.

Stalin took advantage of the pact with Hitler in August 1939 to invade and incorporate the Bukovina among other territories. Living in Berlin in 1940, Grisha asked the Romanian ambassador for advice. If I were you, as Grisha recalls what the ambassador said, I would go underground and get lost. Grisha claims to have spent most of the war in Berlin nightclubs, as described in a novel with the rather labored title *Oedipus siegt bei Stalingrad*. He and his friends were eventually obliged to wear German uniforms, giving the false appearance that they were fighting for the Third Reich rather than using it as a bolt-hole. He spoke freely but I sometimes asked myself if he was also speaking fully.

Queen Helen of Romania, once the monarch, was now a refugee like him. Her house in Florence, the Villa Sparta, was a combination of austere grandeur and discomfort. The windows seemed designed to keep light out. Although Queen Helen had known hardship and dispossession, she had good looks and held herself with an imposingly straight back. Whatever the news, good or bad, she had a habit of limiting her response to "Ach, fancy!" spoken with such an accent that it sounded like German. "Dinner with Queen Helen," an entry in my diary in 1980 reads: "The Villa Sparta is sold. By November she must be out and in a flat in Lausanne. She shows me with her finger on the table how close she will be to the Palace Hotel. Her lawyer has made everything as difficult as possible. She has to justify each possession she takes out. The customs are counting her shoes and dresses.... She is not going to Prince Charles's wedding, she thinks there may be an attempt to spoil the occasion."

A theme of hers was how unjustly the Allies treated her father in 1918. The diary continues, "What was the name of that journalist before the war who knew everybody? Pryce-Jones?"

"Pryce-Jones is me, Ma'am."

"Pryce-something, then."

"Perhaps you mean G. Ward Price, Ma'am."

"Yes, he told me we were entering a new Dark Age. And so we are, he's proved more right every day."

Queen Helen read me a letter written in English from her niece, Queen Sophia of Spain, evoking the recent official visit to Spain of Nicolae Ceaușescu, General Secretary of the Romanian Communist Party, then seeking a role as intermediary in the Cold War. As the parties were making their way through the corridors of the Escorial Palace in Madrid, Ceaușescu stopped and asked for his presents. It is the custom to give suitable gifts to official visitors, he said, and he was surprised to find his Spanish hosts so disobliging. Be quick, King Juan Carlos whispered to Sophia, go to the safe, find a diamond brooch and wrap it up. She did so, but then in a shambles of another order, couldn't find in which of the many Palace reception rooms the Ceaușescus were waiting for their pay-offs.

ERICH SEGAL

Love Story

1970

SOME BRILLIANT PEOPLE, for instance George Steiner, make you feel stupid while others, for instance Erich Segal, make you feel as brilliant as them. I first heard him give a lecture, really a tour de force, on the unlikely subject of Jews in the classical Olympic Games. Slight but evidently athletic, he had been a runner in his time. When I then buttonholed him, it was as if we were the oldest of friends. France had played a large part in his education, as in mine. Presented with the Légion d'Honneur, he asked me to come along to the ceremony. Pinning on the decoration, the French ambassador innocently asked, "Sur quel champs de bataille avez-vous gagné votre médaille?" (On which battlefield did you win your medal?) "Paris," Erich answered, launching into conversation about literature.

His Hebrew was also fluent. I possess a scarlet silk yarmulke that he gave me for Seder one year. He commuted from his home in Hampstead to Wolfson College in Oxford. Thinking that my Latin and Greek must be at a working level, he also gave me volumes he'd edited in a series headed *Oxford Readings* which went from *Greek Tragedy* in 1983, via *Aristophanes* in 1997 to *Menander, Plautus and Terence* in 2001. *The Death of Comedy* is Erich's guided tour through world literature (with a nod in the title to George Steiner's *The Death of Tragedy*).

Anthony Powell in one of his reviews makes the point that self-pity is the necessary ingredient of a bestseller. *Love Story*, I take it, is a drama, even a melodrama, with the requisite element of self-pity. To me, Erich gave no sign of ever being sorry for himself or embittered by experience although universities in the United States refused to grant him tenure; jealous colleagues whispered that a best-selling author like him couldn't be a scholar; and in his thirties, unusually young, he developed Parkinson's disease. He inscribed his books in handwriting whose increasingly unreadable squiggles testify to physical infirmity but also to superior character and courage.

ALAN SILLITOE

Raw Material

1972

NOT MANY NOVELISTS have influenced me, but Alan Sillitoe is one of them. I had been brought up to think of literature as the recording of the human comedy. Some of those who kept the record, I understood, suffered and sacrificed, sometimes to a greater extent than other people. What couldn't be enjoyed could still be understood. Coming up to Oxford as an undergraduate, for the first time I was made to feel that the attitude I had towards literature was selfish, that only the rich and the spoiled could afford to reduce a major art form to entertainment. The human comedy was a figment, then, a delusion. Writers knew, or ought to know, that in reality they were engaged in class warfare. According to Stalin, writers were "engineers of the soul," which in practice meant that they were state officials dictating the beliefs and practices that would propel the working class towards its pre-determined victory over other classes, something many Oxford intellectuals would have considered the approved ending of the Cold War. At a college party, some don asked me what I was doing. Working hard, I said. He took hold of my hand, ran his fingers over it and said, "Not manual, I see."

Saturday Night and Sunday Morning (1958) and its successor *The Loneliness of the Long-Distance Runner* (1959) seemed to be dispatches from the front line of the class war. I had no experience of a character like Arthur in the former novel or of the anonymous Borstal boy in the latter. Conversation in a Sillitoe novel that went, "Well, my old man ain't never got no fags either, but I wun't bother to save 'em for 'im if I found any," sounded fresh and convincing in grammar as well as subject, giving voice to people who had no voice. The dust jacket of *Loneliness* carries the sentence, "His father was a labourer at a bicycle factory in a Nottingham suburb where Mr. Sillitoe grew up." I doubt that my father had ever set foot in a factory or a suburb either, for that matter.

A phenomenon of the class war is the individual who benefits from inherited privileges while denouncing and doing whatever can be done to destroy them. Oxford University in my day turned out such characters in their thousands as if their three years as undergraduates had been a sustained tutorial in how to make feelings of guilt an integral part of their self-satisfaction. I was one such. My early novel *The Sands of Summer* is indebted to early Sillitoe, except that he had lived what he wrote and I had to imagine everything. Put in its real light, he was a genuine protester, I was merely patronizing.

As literary editor of the weekly magazine *Time and Tide*, I asked David Caute, an Oxford contemporary and friend and Marxist too, to review Sillitoe's *Key to the Door*. He spoke for many other critics and most of the literate public when he wrote with approval, "Clearly Sillitoe attaches the highest value to the honest, fearless instinct of a proud working man," and he spoke particularly for me when he went on to pass the exclusive class judgment that Sillitoe "now stands in the forefront as describer and interpreter of working class life." I invited Sillitoe to contribute and he came to the office. Picture my surprise that he wanted to review the new edition of the Baedeker Guide to Spain, and a novel by William Saroyan, master of the sentimental ending.

Raw Material is a last word, an adieu to the hard and fast subject matter of class that had hitherto singled him out. Success is good for some people. Through his own efforts, the bitter young rebel from

Nottingham evolved into a bohemian living in a house like a barn in a fashionable district of London, happy to entertain, to travel and even to write poems.

ISAAC BASHEVIS SINGER

A Friend of Kafka

1970

I INTERVIEWED ISAAC SINGER IN 1970. He lived on the Upper West Side of New York in an apartment block that enclosed a courtyard. Scrubby trees and bushes planted at its center gave the whole building a dark and foreign air. On the mailboxes, the polysyllabic names from Eastern Europe were like a transplant from Krochmalna Street, a setting in which the mythical Jews of Singer's fiction had lived their mythical lives in a mythical Warsaw. He gave me *A Friend of Kafka*, another collection of his short stories that had just been published. On the title page he calls me "a young and already great writer," but weakens the compliment by misspelling my surname. At the same time, he presented my daughters with a copy of *Zlateh the Goat*, one of his several books for children, inscribed, "To Jessica and Candida and to their charming parents with love."

Generosity to those he thought well of came naturally to him and the other side of the coin was readiness to call writers he didn't think well of charlatans or hoodlums. I sent him my book about the Palestinians, *The Face of Defeat*, published in 1972, and he endorsed it: "It is really a book which everyone should read. The truth is that the Arabs did not have to be defeated. They could have stayed in their homes in Israel and lived a better life than in exile. The main thing is that you are an excellent writer and the facts speak for themselves."

Fame had already caught up with him. On the floor of the room in which he worked were a number of mail-bags which did not look as though they had been opened, or ever would be. "They're always writing to me," he said of his readers. "I can't get away with anything." He had a way of cocking his head to one side as if listening and learning, and immediate facial movements gave away his thoughts. "You aren't a radical?" he asked, suddenly stricken with anxiety by something out of place that I must have said. There was a mischievous humor in him but my impression was that the fate he had managed to escape in Europe had given his inner self its special poignancy.

Unusually in a contemporary writer, Singer let the doings and sayings of his characters speak for themselves rather than be a medium for the author's voice. When I taught creative writing for an academic year at the University of Iowa, I tried to get it across that plain statement makes any and every character and context believable, even the most unfamiliar. By way of illustrating the point, we read in class some of the sketches in Singer's memoir of his Polish-Jewish childhood, *In My Father's Court*. One member of the class drew attention to himself by wearing a heavy tweed suit and a felt hat, a turnout not much seen in Iowa. He sat at the back of the room and never spoke. A day came when I spotted him in the university library laughing at what he was reading, which I saw was the score of orchestral music by Anton Webern. He was to tell me that he had once played the tuba in a band that had toured Batista's Cuba. It was almost midnight a few days later when he rang the doorbell and handed me the manuscript of a novel with the title *Bodkin*. Barton Midwood had come into my life.

Bodkin imagines a world in which all human endeavor is mere disturbance. The mysteriously silent individual at the back of the room had done consummate work. I sent the manuscript to my publisher, Arthur Cohen, the editorial director of Holt Rinehart and a man of exceptional intelligence. Thanks to Arthur, *Bodkin* was published by Random House in 1967. A review in the *New Statesman* of the English edition spoke of it with awe as "a literary discovery." Francis King found it "weird and troubling." Bart inscribed a copy for me. "I hope you enjoy this book. It is the best I have in me. If I had never met you, I should probably never have written it. If the author of *The Stranger's View* [my novel of 1967] likes it, that will please me more than the Nobel Prize, the Pulitzer Prize, the National Book Award or even an angry letter from the Pope." *Esquire*, the *Paris Review* and other prestigious magazines published short stories of Bart's that were collected in *Phantoms* (1970), his second book.

Isaac Singer liked *Bodkin*. He said that Bart reminded him of Bruno Schulz, who was shot dead by a Gestapo man in the streets of his native town of Drohobycz in 1942 before he had had time fully to use his literary gift. My father was living in New York, and in the course of a visit to him I took the opportunity to introduce Bart to Isaac Singer. I was sure they'd get on. Unexpectedly Bart turned up in London, met Antonia, Clarissa's younger sister, and was married to her for about a year or so before he returned alone to New York. A worried Isaac wrote to tell me that he had tried and failed to stop Bart calling round so often. Bart, he went on, was completely *meshuggah*, he had taken to coming up to knock on the door and then to lurking for long periods in the scrubby trees of the courtyard. Real life was taking the shape of one of Singer's mystifying stories. As a precaution, he felt compelled to go with his wife and live in their apartment in Miami.

MURIEL SPARK

A Far Cry from Kensington

1998

THE FLIGHT PATH OF Muriel Spark is a wonder to behold. Her conviction was that the purpose of writing is to give pleasure, and in all her books she paid attention only to the innermost self that was her exclusive guide to that end. She had a poet's instinct for the right form and a colloquial style all her own that allowed her to range the whole way from the comedy of manners up to the great unanswerable questions of the human condition. In an age when writers expect to be judged primarily by their sexual, social and political commitments and are therefore encouraged to be one more shocking than the other, Muriel's wit and independent mind set were conservative as well as revolutionary, that strange combination that surfaces when things go wrong. Since she was speaking for lots of people with hopes and fears like hers, she was successful and deserved to be.

Born in Edinburgh in 1918, Muriel identified herself as a Scot. "All my ways of thinking are Scottish," she liked to emphasize, explaining that this meant "being rather precise." A faint Scottish accent sometimes crept into her speech. *The Prime of Miss Jean Brodie* is an ode to Edinburgh as Muriel remembered it from her youth: the haunted November twilight coming in across the Dean Bridge, Holyrood Palace where Mary Queen of Scots had once slept, the churches in frighteningly dark stone, "sober churchgoers and quiet workers," and mothers who call their children "dear" when English mothers say "darling." Like many others in the late Thirties, Miss Brodie thought Mussolini one of the greatest men in the world and she said as much as she set about shaping the personalities of teenage girls who were her pupils in the Marcia Blaine School. Famous Scots like Hume, Boswell and Robert Burns also have to be kept in mind.

Close and mostly unexpected observation of detail gives Muriel's prose its personal touch. An aside on the part of one of the several fictional writers in her novels notes how "A chance descriptive detail in the right place" brings a scene to life. A striking example occurs in *Curriculum Vitae*, her autobiography, where in the sentence that first introduces her father Bernard Camberg (known as Barney) she makes the major point that he was Jewish and the minor point that he wore the same clothes as other fathers and spoke as they did too. Employed by a rubber company as a fitter and mechanical engineer, he appears to be someone about whom there is nothing of great significance to say. According to Muriel, her mother Sarah (known as Cissy) Uezzell had "a rather rare old English name." In spite of this surname, or perhaps because of it, Cissy was wholly or partly Jewish, a mixed heredity for which Muriel coined the phrase "Gentile Jewess" and used it in the plural as the title of one of her earliest stories. Granted her acceptance of Jewish as well as Scottish identity, Muriel belonged to a minority of a minority.

Sydney Oswald Spark (known as Solly and later by his initials SOS, the Morse code signal to summon help) put in a truncated appearance in her life. Born in Lithuania like Barney's parents, he had emigrated with his mother to Edinburgh. Thirteen years older than Muriel, he had a contract to teach mathematics in Southern Rhodesia, nowadays Zimbabwe, and in 1937 at the age of nineteen Muriel joined him out there. "Why I married this man," she gives way to a rare burst of self-reproach in her autobiography, "I will probably never know. It was a disastrous choice." A son, Robin, was born. Muriel did not care for the colonial company that was on offer socially; she never met Doris Lessing, a Rhodesian by birth, a future novelist and the same age as her. Moreover, Solly became alarmingly violent, showing more and more signs of a nervous disorder that was probably genetic and in any case condemned him to be a permanent hospital patient. Muriel saw no irony in retaining his surname on the grounds that Spark has "some ingredient of life and of fun" missing in Camberg.

Escaping, Muriel spent the last year of the war in Britain. Fortunate at last, she was taken into the Political Warfare Executive, a covert operation that under the auspices of the BBC and the Foreign Office was broadcasting to Germans what now is designated as fake news. One aspect of her job was to take afternoon walks with selected high-ranking prisoners of war and as prettily as possible extract stories from them that PWE could exploit. Muriel's life at that point was imitating Muriel's art.

"Long ago in 1945 all the nice people in England were poor, allowing for exceptions," is the opening sentence of *The Girls Of Slender Means*, published in 1963, by which time nasty people were rich, allowing for exceptions, or in the final words of that same opening paragraph, "the best of the rich being poor in spirit." Muriel's over-riding aim at the time was to establish herself as a writer. The ruthlessness with which she did so is recorded by her biographer Martin Stannard, though he calls it dynamism. A single page of his lengthy book covers the period when Muriel decided to make whatever sacrifices were necessary in order to write full-time. This involved a parting of the ways with lifelong consequences. First of all, she consciously cut loose from family life by dispatching Robin to be brought up by his grandparents in Edinburgh. She adopted a solitary life in a London boarding house with no way of anticipating that it would inspire fiction. Finally, she joined the staff of the Poetry Society, a marginal and even moribund organization that was a blind alley as far as literary careers were concerned. Stannard smoothes over all this by showering her with select adjectives that have nothing to do with the turmoil of that moment, for instance witty, irreverent, beautiful, placable [sic], capable, courteous, teasing and even sexy.

She had a particular passion for the poems of John Masefield, the poet laureate, so old-school that he had been consigned to oblivion in his lifetime – which did not prevent Muriel from conducting an uncritical interview and writing a book about him. The poets and publishers who Stannard picks out as Muriel's colleagues or acquaintances were part of the crowd shuffling in virtual anonymity along Grub Street with nowhere else to go. The one exception was Derek Stanford, more a scribbler than a journalist, and he too would have been forgotten except that he had had an affair with Muriel during the years of her self-discovery and wrote a book about her as well as his memoirs. There is evidence that people who ran into her felt pity for a young woman so dogged and so forlorn. The word went around Grub Street, "Please be kind to Muriel."

The public at large first heard of Muriel in 1951 when the *Observer*, an established Sunday newspaper owned by David Astor and required reading for liberals, held a competition for a Christmas short story. The prize was £250, a large sum at the time, large enough to attract some seven thousand entries. Philip Toynbee, the paper's lead reviewer and the most influential of the prize's three judges, later claimed to have "the slightly satanic feeling" that he had called Muriel into being.

"The Seraph and the Zambesi," Muriel's winning story, is a surreal tour de force as astounding now as it then was. The protagonist, Samuel Cramer, a pseudonym Baudelaire had invented for himself, was said to be going strong in Paris early in the nineteenth century and is still going strong in 1946. Half poet and half journalist, he is occupied keeping a petrol pump four miles south of Victoria Falls in the Southern Rhodesia that Muriel had experienced. The voice of Muriel can be heard directly when Cramer says, "The greatest literature is the occasional kind, a mere afterthought." Appearing in a draught of scorching air, the Seraph sets a destructive fire. Cramer's initial friendliness turns into a hostile chase and the Seraph is last seen hurrying away "at about seventy miles an hour and skimming the tarmac strips with two of his six wings in swift motion, two folded over his face, and two covering his feet."

The Seraph, then, is both real and visionary, a mysterious conjuncture that Muriel is exploring for the first time. Religious belief in invisible divinity is an act of imagination and it seems probable

LE CRÈVE-CŒUR
ET
LES YEUX D'ELSA

These two books were first published
separately under the imprint:
Horizon / France Libre.

Other books published (in French) by
Horizon were:

  Michaux. Aux Pays de la Magie
  Sartre. Huis Clos.
  Apollinaire. selected by Chr Brown.
  Sartre. Baudelaire (in English)

in English: Toyota. Tea with Mrs goodman
  Masson (with Trois colours)
  tr. by Douglas Cooper.
  The hanged gran by
  Paterson.
  goya. Malraux (with Trois
        colours) —

all published in one co?.

Cyril Connolly

that she deliberately left readers to discover meanings for themselves: Perhaps this is an allegory about God and Man, a projection of hellfire, even a fairy tale told for the sake of its beauty. Discussing Muriel's religious disposition, Stannard has this to say: "The will of God and human will were at odds," and he immediately elaborates, "It was, she believed, the will of God that she should be a Christian and a writer."

In 1954 Muriel converted to Catholicism. It so happened that the two outstanding British writers of that moment, Evelyn Waugh and Graham Greene, were Catholics: the former supported her first by expressing in private letters his admiration for her fiction and then reviewing her exuberantly in *The Spectator*; and the latter organized a fund large enough for her to live on. However, Catholicism came between her and Derek Stanford. Increasingly critical of him, Muriel found refuge with the Carmelites at Aylesford Priory, a retreat for troubled Catholics. Perhaps she was not all that troubled, as she is quoted complaining of others there, "All these people hanging about, waiting for miracles." The affair with Stanford came to an end in 1958, after which he came to represent in her mind the bad side of human nature. The iron entered into her soul when he sold to a university the letters she had written to him, and their lost intimacy was in the public domain. It is common knowledge that Hector Bartlett, scorned in *A Far Cry from Kensington* as a treacherous blackmailer and virtually cursed in dubious but memorable French as a *pisseur de copie*, is closely modeled on him.

Memento Mori, published in 1959, questions reality altogether. Various elderly and distinguished people answer telephone calls, only to hear a disembodied voice that tells them, "Remember you must die," the very words a handpicked slave had to whisper in the ear of a Roman emperor in the hour of his triumphal procession through the city. This parable, if parable it is, is left up in the air. The unidentifiable caller may be a villain or he may be God, and if the latter either benevolent or threatening.

The Ballad of Peckham Rye, published the following year, is an equally brilliant existential parable, again if parable it is. Dixie and Humphrey are in church to be married. In accordance with the conventional ceremony, the vicar asks Humphrey if he will have Dixie for his wedded wife. No, says Humphrey, "to be quite frank I won't," and he drives away on his own. Responsibility for this scandalous conduct is laid on Dougal Douglas, a friend and neighbor. Though he could be innocent, the two bumps on his scalp where a plastic surgeon took away two horns are compromising. He says of himself lightly, "I'm to be one of the wicked spirits that wander through the world for the ruin of souls." In short, human happiness is at the mercy of evil.

Blackmail, betrayal and violence in these novels are merely the ways of the world. A good example is the incident that moves *Memento Mori* to its close. "The man by the dressing-table hesitated nervily [sic] for a moment, then swiftly he was by Lettie's side. She opened wide her mouth and her yellow and brown eyes. He wrenched the stick from the old woman's hand and, with the blunt end of it, battered her to death. It was her eighty-first year." Even brutal murder is matter-of-fact. In contrast to the run of contemporary novelists, she is out neither to shock nor to moralize, only to record what confronts her. Muriel spent a month of 1961 traveling in Israel and researching for *The Mandelbaum Gate*. Like Muriel, its protagonist Barbara Vaughan is a Gentile Jewess and she intends to sort out some final truth about herself and the country where religious revelation originated. Instead, two symbolic characters, Abdul the Arab and Mendel the Jew, reduce everything to nonsense: "My father, blah, blah. Long live Ben Gurion! Long live Nasser! Long live Islam! Long live all fat men! Israel! My mother goes quack-quack all day!" Barbara disappears in a cloud of unknowing.

Early in the summer of 1980, I was asked to interview Muriel. By then, she was either recognized and admired in literary pages as an original writer, or else held up in gossip columns as a paid-up member of the jet set. For several years she had lived and worked in New York, then in Rome and now in Tuscany. A narrow dusty track snaked through olive orchards to the house, actually a *casa canonica* complete with a dilapidated chapel, that Muriel shared with its owner, Penelope Jardine (known as Penny), an artist in her own right. As luck would have it, my father, Alan Pryce-Jones, was one of those who had been kind to Muriel. Editor of the *Times Literary Supplement*, he had commissioned a lead essay from her. Known in the trade as a "Middle." It was unsigned, but over the years she kept repeating how this piece had boosted her.

Like most writers, Muriel had various fetishes about pens and notebooks. She wrote in a quite readable longhand in ink with very few corrections and never a second draft. She had an expression about being "on the production side" but believed in inspiration. Penny then typed, also taking care of correspondence with publishers, film producers, agents and accountants. An extravagance was that Muriel had shared ownership of a racehorse with Alan Maclean, brother of the Foreign Office traitor Donald Maclean and her editor at Macmillan's.

For six days of the week Muriel would sit at her desk and write. The seventh day, not necessarily Sunday, was always set aside for relaxing. Italy was good enough for Byron and Shelley, she liked to say, so it's good enough for me. Muriel had bought a BMW, and Penny drove the two of them in it to lunch, usually in a restaurant in some isolated beauty spot, and on occasion to Florence, to Harold Acton or John Pope-Hennessy or us, last representatives of the British who in previous centuries used to settle in the city for the sake of its culture. Penny refused to fly, so they embarked on immense drives across Europe, often to accept some invitation. In 1998, Muriel did a reading at the annual literary festival in Hay-on-Wye, near my home. Afterwards she came to lunch bringing Doris Lessing, a friend of long standing and more than that, an alter ego. They reminisced – the one certain that human agency is decisive in this world, the other certain that it is not the whole story. Asking about a novel I was writing, Muriel borrowed from Shakespeare to hope it would be "something rich and strange."

Muriel and Penny often came to our family home in Florence as well. She relished stories, especially one with Italian politics and a conspiracy theory in it. One day I told Muriel how in the lobby of the venerable Winter Palace Hotel at Aswan on the Nile I had observed a respectable Scottish lady pick up a westernized Saudi wearing shorts and a baseball cap the wrong way round, boisterously telling one and all to call him Al. Here was raw material for the imagination. Muriel then sketched out the character and motivation of this unlikely pair, their past and present histories and where this encounter would leave them. Another unwritten novel crystallized around an Italian aristocrat who died of AIDS without an heir, leaving immense properties to his faithful old cook, a woman who could neither read nor write.

Aiding and Abetting is based on Lord Lucan who murdered the nanny of his children by mistake and then vanished without trace. The novel centers on the improbability of this humdrum character, a British Earl what's more, behaving as he did. I had done my military service in the same battalion of the Coldstream Guards and knew him reasonably well. Muriel quizzed me endlessly about correct details, only to invent a second Lord Lucan, false yet indistinguishable from the first, illustrating the mystery of the human condition.

Her son Robin felt that his mother loved writing more than she loved him. The sacrificial element in their relationship was never resolved. The two rarely met as Robin made his life in Edinburgh. The final break between them turned rather mystifyingly on a question of Jewish identity and Jewish law. Expressed simply, Robin, an Orthodox Jew, believed that Muriel had not done right by her Jewish heritage.

Equally disturbing was the question of her biography. Martin Stannard, a university professor, had written a biography of Evelyn Waugh, and initially she approved of him. Reading an early draft, she was dismayed, then obsessively angry at his alleged misrepresentations. She need not have worried. A great deal of research has gone into the biography and with it a great deal of admiration. A sentence in the final paragraph is a summary of his viewpoint: "Her proper habitat, her art, lay in the age of the Holy Ghost. And there she remained, a ghost-writer for God, whoever He may be." Going over to see her a day or two before she died, I found her saying, "I'm a soldier wounded on the battlefield." And then some last words that are pure Sparkite, "I must remember to tell Doris that when one comes to die, one doesn't give a damn."

ALBERT SPEER
Inside the Third Reich
1970

A HUNDRED YEARS FROM NOW, Speer's autobiography, *Inside the Third Reich*, is likely to be the one indispensable source for anyone seeking information about Hitler and Nazism, in the way that Talleyrand's memoirs still influence what people know and think about the France of his day. With the possible exception of Goebbels, Speer was the most intelligent member of Hitler's inner circle and he came from a secure background as well. A shared interest in monumental architecture and huge-scale town planning, we are to believe, led him to see Hitler as a creative force. He had shone, he wrote in his book, in the reflected glory of Hitler's power, striving "to gather some of his popularity, his glory, his greatness, around myself."

Joachim Fest in his authoritative book *Speer: The Final Verdict* quotes Hitler saying to Speer, "I'll sign anything that comes from you," a carte blanche he gave to nobody else. Fest gives credit to the idea that Hitler and Speer saw in one another the fulfillment of their most profound aspirations. They were two of a kind in their lack of ordinary human responses. Only a Shakespeare could do justice to the drama of the final days of the war when Speer ran the risk of dropping in on Hitler in the Berlin bunker and even offered to stay with him to the very end. Whatever mutual deceptions were involved, tears came into the eyes of both men. The German people had let Hitler down and he instructed Speer to give them the scorched-earth policy he now thought they deserved. So much for creative force.

A couple of years after this book came out, I began to research for the biography I would write of Unity Mitford. The same question had to be asked of her as of Speer: how much of her motivation was ideology and how much was opportunity? I had been in Vienna on Unity's trail. After she shot herself and had been sent home to England, her friend and admirer, also a Nazi, Count Janos Almasy took possession of her papers. He had denounced his sister and brother-in-law to the Gestapo and they had hoped to get even one day by purloining or copying some of these papers. Their son, a priest, had kept them stored in a trunk in the attic of the Sacré Cœur. Up in that dusty half-lit setting he handed me the evidence of a dark past and I had it all safe in my briefcase when I caught the train from Vienna to Heidelberg where Speer lived.

Speer's house had the feel of a sepulcher, the windows apparently designed to keep the daylight out. The carved wood furniture, heavy and stained, was redolent of the Germany of Kaiser Wilhelm. Speer was tall and thin, rather elegant in a well-cut grey suit. His eyes were lackluster and his manner was burnt-out. He began by saying that there wasn't the documentation for a book about Unity, so it couldn't be done. I opened my briefcase. "Ihr Buch ist gemacht," he said, Your book is made. In common with all Hitler's cronies, his adjutants and his staff, he was so impressed by the British peerage that he could not find the way through its class distinctions, referring to Lady Unity or sometimes Lady Mitford. As we went over details in her diaries, he became a different person. In his book he records that in Hitler's company she alone was permitted to break a tacit agreement not to speak about politics, and now he remembered who had been present when and where, what had been said to Hitler and what he had replied. His astonishing recall seemed to re-kindle life in him.

For my part, I repeated to Speer what my friend Roman Halter had told me about the time he had inspected the workshop in the Lodz ghetto making Wehrmacht uniforms and did nothing when one of his men brutalized the Jewish director. Yes, he knew who Roman was, and yes, he had had the power of life and death over those Jews. Gitta Sereny put her finger on his evasive technique of generalizing about specifics "admitting a little to deny a great deal" as she summarized it. He knew he had spent his whole life in the shadows and couldn't say why.

JOHN STEWART
To the River Kwai
1988

"For David Pryce-Jones who dislodged a small stone that became a small stream – this memoir – Gratefully." Before John Stewart inscribed his book with this compliment, all I knew of him was that he lived in Paris and was a photographer whose work was widely published and exhibited. At a chance meeting for drinks in the house of a mutual friend, he told me that he was writing a book and asked if I would read what he'd done so far and tell him why he was stuck. With a sense of shock, I learned from his unfinished manuscript that he had been captured in the war by the Japanese and sent as a slave laborer to the infamous Burma railway. He described the ordeal with astonishing objectivity, but he had refrained from letting the reader know how he came to be so abstract, in short who he was. What should have been autobiographical was historical. What he had to do was give the reader reason to trust him.

He saw the point at once. It was simple. Stewart was an adopted name that hid the fact that he belonged to a very well-known Jewish family and he couldn't build a convincing memoir without revealing his real identity. His cosmopolitan background, his education in France, his open-mindedness, even his father's Rolls-Royce, all fell into place and explained who he was in the face of a life-and-death ordeal.

Enrolled in the Intelligence Corps, he arrived in Singapore in January 1942, disastrously timed for the Japanese to take him prisoner. He had learned enough of the language to be an interpreter. "Navigating through the labyrinthine Japanese mind," he writes, "was, after food, everyone's favourite intellectual occupation." In Changi he had an inconceivably far-fetched encounter with Foujita, the well-known painter and a friend in Paris days but now an Official War Artist, who greeted him, "Mon pauvre ami, je ne vous demande pas ce que vous faites ici." (My poor friend, I don't ask you what you are doing here.) Sadism and sentimentality were an incomprehensible combination.

The collision of cultures is recorded in a passage that deserves a place in any anthology to do with human nature and its extremes. Speaking to a cadet, John resorted to a Japanese word meaning "bad, inadequate." Like someone possessed, the cadet reacted with a rant, frothing at the mouth, sending for his sword and preparing to behead the kneeling prisoner who had given such offense. John in fact saved himself by knowing and reciting what the victim is supposed to say ritually before the sword ends his life. The cadet dropped his sword, burst into tears and invited John to have some cake and a cup of tea, the one and only time when the slave laborer was treated as a guest. John's misuse of language was wiped away because he had proved his respect for the whole culture.

MARK STRAND

Selected Poems

1980

A<small>T THE END OF THEIR EDUCATION</small> many of my contemporaries contrived to visit the United States exactly as fortunate young gentlemen would have gone on the Grand Tour in the eighteenth century. This was how to discover what was happening out in the wider world. The mail one day brought a book of his poems from Paul Engle and with it a letter that was more a command than an invitation. On the strength of my early novels and the book I had written about Graham Greene, Paul Engle was giving me the chance to teach creative writing for the academic year 1964 – 65 at the Writers Workshop of the University of Iowa. I was 27, husband of Clarissa, father of Jessica and Candida, and chances like this might not come again. We consulted the atlas in order to be able to locate Iowa. Creative writing would have to take care of itself.

Making conversation at the first faculty meeting, I said to one Professor that scholarship now meant collating James Joyce's laundry bills. He drew himself up and said that he had been doing just that these past thirty years. The native Iowan novelist R.V. (Ronald Verlin) Cassill was the Workshop's brooding spirit. He believed in conspiracy. Obscure technical factors convinced him that the real murderers of President Kennedy had not been identified. The supposed power of Jews obsessed him. His one disciple was Richard Yates, author of the cult novel *Revolutionary Road*, but given over in the Workshop to unhappiness, to judge by his hang-dog appearance.

Mark Strand was immediately recognizable as a talent of another order. Good-looking and fit, he had presence and a quick and self-deprecating humor. His laugh came with a slight squeal in it.

Mark's poems had already appeared in literary magazines, and Kim Merker, a fine-arts printer in Iowa City, was just publishing the first collection, *Sleeping With One Eye Open*, a beautifully produced book in a limited edition of 250 copies. "Nothing but the best" was Mark's ambition, and he would achieve it without fuss in his poetry and in his career. A true artist and perfectionist, he was on a life-long journey to discover the inner self. In comparison, many contemporary poets are mere journalists. He found inventive language for anything beautiful or wonderful and could even make whimsy sound normal. "The future isn't what it used to be" is, I believe, a quip of his that has become universal. From him I learned about Jorge Guillén, Carducci, Rafael Alberti and Elizabeth Bishop, a particular favorite. He might have got on well with the young Wordsworth or William Blake.

Mark and his wife Antonia lived a five-minute walk away from us. Through the grim winter evenings we played Crazy Bridge, picquet and bezique. We ate, we talked, we read. Antonia told stories, for instance how her mother had seized hold of the exhibited part of a flasher in the New York subway and dragged him protesting to the cops. Mark also told stories, notably about his father, a figure enshrined in heroic fantasy who may have served a prison sentence in Mexico City. Mark had bought superb pencil drawings by Bill Bailey, then unknown but an Old Master in the making. He introduced Clarissa and me to Daniel Lang, another classical artist.

Mark and Antonia went their separate ways, he marrying Jules and having a child with her, she marrying a psychiatrist on the West Coast. As poets do, Mark circulated after leaving Iowa City, writing to me from universities or institutions that paid him to take up residence, the Committee on Social Thought at the University of Chicago, the University of Utah, the American Academy in Rome, and so on. He sent me nearly all his books except those he wrote for children. Prestigious prizes and awards, the title of Poet Laureate Consultant in Poetry to the Library of Congress, did not affect what I can only call the innocence of his vision. The inscription of his *New Selected Poems* (published in 2009) is, "For David and Clarissa, for old times sake and with love." At each meeting we took up where we had left off. Staying with me in Florence, he wanted to buy a leather jacket, so I took him to Bemporad, the obvious shop. After trying on jackets interminably, he suddenly walked out empty-handed. Staying with me in London, he arrived with two bottles of vintage Château Siran. Nothing but the best.

Here is a postcard from his New York address, not dated but probably 1978. "Our lunch in New York was too brief — in an effort to make up for it I shall visit London for a day or two in April. I am finally turning to prose. (Discount *The Monument*.) I just sold a humorous piece to the *New Yorker* and may become a regular food columnist for another magazine. I've written very few poems since *The Late Hour* — Did you like it? I met V. S. Naipaul at a party, one of the smartest people I've ever met, you can tell in 30 seconds. He's your friend, isn't he? How did your interview with Derek Walcott go?"

Or this letter from Salt Lake City, also not dated (possibly 1985 — the book he refers to is *Mr. and Mrs. Baby*), in answer to one of mine. "That was the nicest, sweetest letter anybody ever got about a book. It cannot be topped. No one need try. So, amigo, thank you. Thank you. Not that it is of astonishing interest, but the book was attacked twice in that paper fit only for a gorilla's anus, *The New York Times*. First in the daily by an uncomprehending Japanese-American with no sense of humour, then in the Sunday by another idiot. Fortunately, good reviews are coming in. I mention this only to dispel your high opinion of literary opinion this side of the Atlantic. But the English . . . well, we can only wait and see. Chatto & Windus is bringing it out next year and they have a very high opinion of the book. Apparently their readers' reports were amazing; I say 'apparently' because I haven't read them. Having dipped my toes in the chilly sea of fiction, I am back to skinny-dipping in the warm pond of poesy."

Postscript. Mark was so annoyed by the attitude to his work of *The New York Times* that he made sure his publishers did not send review copies of his books to the paper.

AMIR TAHERI
The Persian Night
2009

P olitique internationale, a heavyweight journal published
in Paris, put me in touch with Amir Taheri. An Iranian journalist in exile, he had one foot in Paris and the other in London. He
made no great claims for himself, but his articles in the English-
language press or in Arabic outlets like the Saudi newspaper *Sharq
al-Awsat* are vivid and informative insights into whatever is going on
in the palaces, the mosques, the barracks and prisons of the Middle East. He was among the first to understand that Ayatollah Khomeini's seizure of power in 1979 is as definitive an episode in world
history as Lenin's coup in 1917. Islamism is an ideology of military
conquest, but the mullahs run a regime so corrupt, contradictory
and self-serving that in the end they are bound to be their own
undoing. Optimist and humanist, Amir is a steadfast dissident.

"Once again I meet Amir Taheri for tea at Richoux's in Piccadilly,"
I read in my diary. "He's exactly punctual. Charming, soft-spoken,
extraordinarily well informed, he carries the entire recent history
of the Middle East in his head. I quiz him about the period that Ayatollah Khomeini spent in France at Neauphle-le-Château, courtesy
of the stricken shah of Iran: names, dates, sequence of events, all are
in place as if he'd prepared for a viva. If there were a hundred of him,
al-Qaeda and jihadis would be perceived as public enemies with no
future prospects."

In September 2008, Alexandra and Roger Kimball came to stay
because Roger had organized a conference in London on soft jihad.
Besides Amir, among the usual suspects attending was Ayaan Hirsi
Ali, an exile from her native Somalia and a root-and-branch critic

of the Islam of her upbringing. Previously in a review of *Infidel*, her autobiography, I'd written, "If there's hope for reform in Islam, it lies in the example she sets." Again from my diary, "So graceful a figure to be so steely." Also, "Amir Taheri came to lunch, and invited us and the Kimballs to dine in a Persian restaurant near his flat in Marylebone. He's for sanctions and against bombing Iran." Next entry: "Amir Taheri came here from a demonstration at the Iranian embassy. Protesters are going to occupy it next week, he says, half the embassy staff are on their side. He doesn't think there's going to be a massive crack-down … things will turn out all right but it's hard to see quite how the regime might collapse. Amir proposes to write a book on Islam's place in the modern world, what it ought to be. No more biography of Ayatollah Sistani, as previously planned. He was full of information as usual, and I've never seen him laugh so much."

BENJAMIN TAMMUZ

Requiem for Na'aman

1982

AT OUR FIRST MEETING, Benjamin Tammuz asked if Alan Pryce-Jones was any relation. Since my father got around everywhere, this was a question I was used to. Alan's book about Beethoven had been published in 1933 and now I learned that it had been translated into Hebrew. At the time a teenager in British Mandated Palestine, Tammuz had read the Hebrew edition and said that he had been influenced by it. His own novels, *Minotaur* especially, have a resonance all their own. The inscription he wrote in my copy of *Requiem for Na'aman* is in Hebrew and I cannot read it.

A. J. P. TAYLOR

English History, 1914–1945

1965

A TYPICAL INTELLECTUAL of the 1930s, A. J. P. Taylor made sure to enjoy the privileges he was busy criticizing. He was a rich man's son. In 1919 his father sold his share of the family's Lancashire cotton business and received £100,000 for it, or twenty million pounds in 1995 prices, according to Kathleen Burk, Taylor's biographer. As a young man, Taylor joined the Communist Party, and in 1925 he visited the Soviet Union. Guilt may have been motivating him, but more likely at some instinctive level he felt it safe to support a total change of regime precisely because it would not happen. Nominally an agency facilitating foreign visitors, Intourist was actually an important tool of the Communist Party, controlling movement and conducting tourists to make sure that they saw only sites arranged to impress, like so many Potemkin villages. Taylor fell for it. Attending a postwar Party Congress in Communist Poland, he brought himself to say things that were sure to displease the Party, but all his life he remained the daftest sort of fellow traveler. He could write, "In the end, Stalin was a rather endearing character."

The trick that brought him fame as an original historian was to stand received opinion on its head. For him, the British and the Habsburg empires had to be ridiculous while the nationalisms that destroyed them were popular. British statesmen who made peace were incompetent, while Germans who made war, like Bismarck and Hitler, were defensible. In *The Origins of the Second World War*, his most characteristic book, he argued that Hitler was a politician like any other, taking his chances where he found them. Nazism, then, was a set of accidents, not a deliberate program of conquest and mass murder. Not surprisingly, Taylor became the darling of neo-Nazis and Revisionists. It takes a very clever man to be quite such an idiot. When I told him that his depiction of Hitler was contradicted by a lot of documentary evidence, he snapped back, "I trod on their toes this time" as though that were a valid defense.

We ran into one another in the London Library when I was doing research for my book about Unity Mitford. Taylor immediately responded that he dined regularly with Sir Oswald Mosley, Unity's Fascist brother-in-law, and he could take me along with him. I hesitated for a long time but eventually decided that Mosley knowingly or unknowingly might provide some useful leads. Dinner was in the Ritz. Old as he was by then, Mosley still had fantasies that the nation might call on him. When rhetoric wasn't quite enough to make the point, he had a way of protruding his eyes, making his face look like a ridiculous mask. In his element, Taylor fed him political and historical subjects. Love of power was what had drawn this improbable pair together. It was fatal to Taylor the man to have no moral structure, and it was fatal to Taylor the historian to have no sense of truth. In the event that Mosley had become Gauleiter of a Nazi Britain in 1940, Taylor might very well have collaborated. As the meal was coming to an end, Mosley asked me for my opinion. I heard afterwards on the grapevine that my silence had unsettled him.

WILFRED THESIGER

Arabian Sands

1959

MARRAKECH IS ONE of the best-preserved Muslim cities not just in Morocco but anywhere in the world of Islam. Clarissa and I were spellbound by its appearance and its liveliness. In the middle of one night, however, I was woken up by a loud unfamiliar noise which I supposed had something to do with the boiler and hot water. Then I saw the cupboard trundling across the room. The sudden realization that this was an earthquake drove us, and apparently everybody else, hurrying and shouting out into the city's open squares. A storks' nest had been shaken off the ancient fortified wall and two storks were ceaselessly flying from the empty top down to the pile of twigs on the ground and then back up, evidently deciding whether to rebuild here or find some safer place. Later we were advised to give ourselves a treat by going to a French restaurant miles away in the High Atlas Mountains. The place proved nondescript except for a table at which sat two Englishmen. Instantly recognizable, Lord Auchinleck and Wilfred Thesiger looked their part as Field Marshal and explorer respectively. I introduced Clarissa and myself and so we had lunch next to these living legends.

Every spring, Thesiger brought his mother to Morocco and in this year 1979 they were staying in a small hotel in the Kasbah of Marrakech. Mrs. Astley was then nearing ninety. In 1910, already expecting Wilfred, she had made a three-week trek on a mule from a port on the Red Sea up to Addis Ababa, where her then husband, Wilfred's father, was Minister. The British Legation was a mud hut and there were no wheeled vehicles in the whole country.

Arabian Sands is an *Apologia Pro Vita Sua* like no other, and a bravura passage in it conjures up memories from childhood in Ethiopia. "I had watched the priests dancing at Timkat before the Ark of the Covenant to the muffled throbbing of their silver drums; I had watched the hierarchy of the Ethiopian Church, magnificent in their many-coloured vestments, blessing the waters. I had seen the armies going forth to fight in the Great Rebellion of 1916." The family photograph album has snapshots of corpses hanging from trees, of a man lying next to his arm and leg, severed in punishment. Thesiger was ten when his father died, and his mother settled with her four sons in Old Radnor, which consists of a few houses in a lonely part of Wales, country that he revisited to the end of his life.

In London, Thesiger was an attentive son who stayed with his mother. The product of Eton and Oxford (where he got a Blue for boxing), he was the personification of an English gentleman with a bowler hat and rolled umbrella. In the morning I would ring up, Mrs. Astley would mutter into the telephone and then I'd hear her bellowing in a very different tone, "Wilfred, cut along here, it's for you." I found it impossible to reconcile this conventional figure with the man who says of himself in *Arabian Sands*, "I wanted colour and savagery, hardship and adventure." We were in his mother's drawing-room one day when he fetched an envelope containing learned papers and listings of his travels and writings and out fell a passport photograph of a handsome Arab in traditional dress and keffiyeh, with Arab-style moustache and trimmed beard. This other self was unrecognizable, I told him and he gave me the photograph; I have it still. Whenever he came to dinner with us, I made a point of inviting admirers of his. Making no concessions, he spoke exclusively of his wars and travels. Women who had sat next to him used to complain afterwards that he never looked them in the eye. Most probably he was homosexual, but in that case he had repressed it so deeply that the least acknowledgement on his part was out of the question. I wonder how well he knew himself.

At the age of 25, Thesiger was one of the couple of hundred British members of the Sudan Civil Service who kept the peace for the many tribes long accustomed to internecine rivalry. In 1940 he was appointed Orde Wingate's deputy in the campaign to liberate Ethiopia from Italian occupation. *The Life of My Choice*, Thesiger's autobiography, offers contradictory opinions of Wingate. On the one hand he was "inspiring" and had "greatness," while on the other he was "past the stage of rational behaviour." Thesiger was shocked that Wingate summoned officers to his room, where he received them lying naked on his bed. Even worse, he could be seen lowering his trousers and cooling his bottom in waterholes from which others would have to drink.

For the first five years after the war, Thesiger explored Arabia, crossing the desert known as the Empty Quarter by camel. Motorized vehicles were available, but their use would have given the exploit a very different character, modern and out of keeping, whereas the primitive was noble. "All that is best in the Arabs has come to them from the desert" is a grandiose generalization in *Arabian Sands*. Thesiger does not spell out what the best is or was, but the Bedouin who accompanied him are shown practicing age-old virtues of courage and endurance and their exemplary conduct speaks for itself. Actually the crossing served no useful purpose, it was a test of hardship and adventure that he had imposed upon himself, much as someone might climb Mount Everest, say, or row alone across the Atlantic.

I first realized that Thesiger had transposed the myth of the Noble Savage into the Arab context when his brother Roderick told me about an incident in the Libyan desert during the war. Wilfred was with a Long Range Desert Group hundreds of miles behind enemy lines on a mission to sabotage a train bringing up reinforcements for the German army. As soon as the train was blown up and burning, Bedouin appeared from nowhere to loot what they could. Wilfred grabbed one of them, saying that British soldiers had killed those German soldiers because that was their duty, not so that scavengers could pick over the bones of the dead. He hit the man, broke his jaw, and the Bedouin scattered away into the sand dunes from which they had come. The punishment was pointless. The moment the British officers drove away, the Bedouin were free to return for the plundering. Their offense was to show Thesiger that he was romancing reality and what comes out of the desert is not necessarily the best.

An incident that quite unconsciously reveals how easily Thesiger persuaded himself that tribal brutality is heroic is written up in his Introduction to *Bedouin Poetry from Sinai and the Negev* (1991), the work of Clinton Bailey, an American-Israeli with a good claim to be the leading specialist of this academic subject. In the course of one of his travels, Thesiger had a meal with a local Emir and two men from the Yam tribe. One of the latter recounts an ordeal that Thesiger is passing on as evidence of the superiority of the Bedouin way of life. A party of Manahil tribesmen had attacked his encampment, killed his nephew and driven off the camels. He and others went in pursuit and shot dead four Manahil. Another Manahil, bin Duailan by name, remained behind to cover his companions as they escaped with the camels and he shot five of the pursuing party before his rifle jammed. This enabled the narrator to reach him and kill him with a dagger. "By God," he continues, but now in praise of bin Duailan, "he was a man. I thought he would kill us all." This was how he had gained a reputation for all to admire. Within a very short time, according to Thesiger, "bin Duailan's exploit was being declaimed on the far side of Arabia." The poetry may very well be beautiful and popular but it is celebrating lawlessness, raiding, robbery and casual murder.

Postscript. In her eighties, Mrs. Astley was run over by a taxi and her pelvis was only one of her broken bones. Roddy Thesiger told me that her injuries were so severe that the hospital staff agreed she would die in the night and treatment was pointless suffering. I want to see Wilfred, she kept repeating. He's in Kenya, Roddy would answer, and he won't be back for six months. Next morning, she was still asking for Wilfred, they set her broken bones, she lived for several more years and duly saw Wilfred.

GEORGE WEIDENFELD
Remembering My Good Friends
1994

"ＦOR DAVID AND CLARISSA, Intimates of the first hour," is George's
inscription in handwriting so disordered that it suggests this ritual of putting his name in a book is a bore and he's lost patience
for it. When I became a Weidenfeld author, a number of people in
the world of publishing whispered in my ear that George's performance was all smoke and mirrors. There was more than a hint of
Micawber about his finances, the ownership of his business and the
sudden relocations of the offices, while the way he was continually
re-inventing his wives and his editorial directors was the talk of the
town. He disturbed the stagnant pond of literary London by publishing Saul Bellow, Mary McCarthy and Vladimir Nabokov. He kept
Eric Hobsbawm on the list though he disliked the man and everything he stood for. To be rid of enemies, he suggested reversing Noah's
Ark and sending them out to sea, never to return. He was ready to
risk the scandal bound to erupt from publishing Albert Speer's books
or Nigel Nicolson's *Portrait of a Marriage*. With a sort of team spirit, he
supported Michael Grant the classical historian, Paul Johnson, Antonia Fraser and other favorites. (Harold Pinter was known tongue in
cheek as "the Shakespeare of our time" and after he and Antonia
were married George took to referring to them as Goethe and Schil-
ler.) One who blew hot and cold was Isaiah Berlin who nevertheless
published his most celebrated book *The Hedgehog and the Fox* on the
Weidenfeld list. Optimistic by temperament, he divided authors proven
or potential into D and non-D, the initial standing for deliverer.

Friendship mattered to him but it was also tactical. George knew
exactly whom to invite to his lunches and dinners, and how to speak

the few pertinent words that marked the occasion, most likely a book launch. Generosity was instinctive and unfailing but with it came a sense that it might one day be repaid with some timely favor in return. A natural practitioner of *raison d'état*, he would be particularly effusive to anyone he thought disliked or resented him. Lord Goodman, the confidential lawyer to the chosen few, was about the only person George would have nothing to do with, rightly suspecting him of malpractice. The telephone might ring and George would be finding out if I had any information about the newest literary editor or the latest political appointment here or anywhere in the world. Conversations of the kind often ended with a plan, even a date, for kitchen supper in our house. Educated in Vienna, Clarissa spoke German with an Austrian vocabulary and accent, and George could never have enough of this unexpected return to the past. Among those whose delivery he mimicked were Adolf Hitler and Friedich Herr, an eminent professor who comically made learned historical points in the same pidgin German.

A collection of portraits and busts of Cardinals hung in his apartment on Chelsea Embankment. A wide window giving a view on to the Thames added to the formality of the drawing-room. George seemed an impersonation of these powerful single-minded cosmopolitan men and it was in keeping that he was invited to the annual summer conference that the Pope held at Castel Gandolfo. He would go to Bayreuth for the opera, to Jerusalem to sign contracts for the memoirs of Israeli politicians, to New York to be in the swim. When he had a single visitor, he liked to sit and talk in a small inner library room. I was there one afternoon when Kurt Waldheim, the decorated Nazi officer who became President of Austria and Secretary General of the United Nations, telephoned and asked for advice. They had been at school together before the war; George addressed him by a nickname. Then some time later, I was again there when Helmut Kohl, the ex-Chancellor of Germany, rang, also asking for advice. George spoke to them as equals. In September 2009, George's ninetieth birthday was celebrated in a great white tent pitched with flair and ingenuity on a sloping hill that was part of the estate some thirty miles from Geneva belonging to the architect Norman Foster. For the occasion, George had had made a smoking jacket in hunts-man's style, yellow with black trimmings. The fireworks display was visible, we were afterwards to hear, as far away as the center of Geneva. Mark your diaries, George said in a speech, for the same day ten years from now when I shall be a hundred.

The last time I saw him, he showed me his family tree. A forebear in Prague in the sixteenth century had been a famous rabbi, his rep-utation apparently still remembered. George suddenly gave way to self-pity, saying, "What have I achieved by comparison?" And as he asked what ought to have been a merely rhetorical question, tears trickled down his face.

DAME REBECCA WEST
The Meaning of Treason
1949

"MY SALUTATIONS TO David Pryce-Jones," Dame Rebecca has written on the frontispiece of this book, with her signature and the date, 1973. At that time, the attraction of so many British people to Nazism before and even during the war seemed to me a worthwhile subject to write about. I had the example of Unity Mit-ford and her Hitlerite sister Diana Mosley already in mind. *The Mean-ing of Treason* was the obvious trail-blazer. Nothing much could be added to Rebecca West's marvelous portrayal of William Joyce, other-wise Lord Haw-Haw, hanged for broadcasting throughout the war from Berlin. John Amery condemned himself to the gallows by pleading guilty at his trial, and she thought that all along he had "slapped the normal human process in the face." I wondered if so expressive a judgment could be put into biographical form. We corresponded. "I probably know much less about John Amery than you do," she wrote. "I should be so very pleased to see you and to be of any help I can."

It turned out that we had met once before in quite other circumstances. I was born in Meidling, my mother's family house in Vienna. Dame Rebecca's husband Harry Andrews, a banker and German-educated, had been in Vienna in 1936 dealing with the crisis caused by the collapse of the Creditanstalt, one of the factors creating the economic instability giving rise to Nazism. At my father's invitation, the two of them came to Meidling. Dame Rebecca remembered seeing me when I was a few days old.

Since the publication of her first book, a study of Henry James, she had been a singular figure on the English literary scene, unconventional in behavior, in opinion and especially in the vividness of her language. A competitive Virginia Woolf found her "a cross between a charwoman and a gypsy." In her life she had a number of lovers, famous men all, one of them H. G. Wells. After breaking with him, she wrote him a letter that shows her spirit. "I know you are a great humbug. I also know you're a great man." Anthony West, the son she had with Wells, seems never to have got over his illegitimacy. In her biography of Dame Rebecca, Victoria Glendinning surmises that public quarrelling energized the two of them.

To Rebecca West, Communism and Nazism were twin evils and she entered into close combat with apologists for either dogma. She suspected that Yugoslavia was doomed to be a testing ground for these political horrors and as war approached she went there to see for herself. Written in a few weeks, her *Black Lamb and Grey Falcon* in two hefty volumes is as remarkable a travel book as any in the language. She idealized the Serbs of Yugoslavia as magnificently and misleadingly as T. E. Lawrence did with the Sherifian Arabs in *Seven Pillars of Wisdom*. Long after her death and the disappearance of Yugoslavia, her book survives as literature.

for David and

New Selected Poems

—

MARK STRAND

Clarissa
for old times sake
and with love,

Mark

ALFRED A. KNOPF   NEW YORK   2009

Quite rightly, she advised me that she had sounded out relatives of John Amery and "it would not really be a suitable proposition" to write about him. Unity Mitford's Nazism also slapped the normal human process in the face. The concluding sentence of Dame Rebecca's review of my Unity book illustrates the genial way she made her language rise to her subject. "The moral atmosphere in which these events took place is that of a burnt-out fairground."

Now and again I would go and have tea in her spacious apartment with a view out over Hyde Park. At some point she went on a trip to the Middle East. In Jerusalem, Teddy Kollek, then the Mayor, gave a reception for her. Next stop, Beirut. The telephone rang in her hotel room and a voice said, You have been fraternizing with the Zionist enemy and I am from the PLO with orders to shoot you. I cannot be word-perfect but her answer was along the lines that she had lived a full and rewarding life, had only old age to look forward to, the dear boy should be sure to load his gun and come to the right floor, she would leave the door open for him. She heard no more.

I like to think of her as the high priestess of the temple.

MICHAEL WHARTON
The Stretchford Chronicles
1981

OPENING THIS BOOK at random in order to recall the real Michael Wharton hiding under the pseudonym Peter Simple, I hit on this passage: "This is England's End. And it may be right and fitting that modern England should end in a torrent of litter, shouting, iced lollies and mechanical uproar spilling down over the rocks and into the inviolable sea."

Here is a voice like no other. Michael was a heart-felt conservative. The custom of the past had made the country great and valued, only to be replaced by experiments that made the country small and unworthy. Much too clever to indulge in anger about a process of modernizing that he could not prevent, he turned to satire as the highest and most unanswerable form of political and social commentary. Socialists, ecologists, technicians and scientists, all manner of people, were busy creating an absurd and ugly life for everyone, when they ought to know better.

Stretchford is the name that Peter Simple has invented for the kind of town that is a model hell. When he talks about it, his face takes on the hardness and coloring of a Toby jug. From time to time, one of the benighted might unexpectedly agree with some opinion of his, in which case Michael liked to quote a line from Virgil: *nec tali auxilio nec defensoribus istis* (not with such help, nor with such defenders). In other words, he will be responsible for himself.

The Peter Simple column that he wrote for the *Daily Telegraph* made the kind of mark on the conscious public that Gulliver amid the Lilliputians had made. *Peter Simple* is the title of a novel by Frederick Marryat, a long-forgotten Victorian author, and I have no idea why Michael took it over for his purposes. True, he could be hard on himself. His ideal newspaper was *The Feudal Times and Reactionary Herald.* One columnar hero was Colonel Sibthorpe, a Member of Parliament in Victorian days who set his face against every kind of change so singlemindedly that he could not be considered serious and therefore nobody except Michael has ever heard of him.

Memorable caricatures have escaped from the column to become part of the national literary stock. Mrs. Dutt-Pauker, for instance, is the owner of Beria Garth in Dorset, Glyn Stalin in Wales and Marxmount, the Hampstead mansion where she is grandmother to a "four-year-old, bearded, baleful-eyed Maoist demonstrator." Other typecast enemies to be mocked to death are President Ngrafta of Gombola, the "brilliant progressive Tory MP Jeremy Cardhouse," Dr Heinz Kiosk "chief psychiatric adviser to the South-Eastern Gas

Board," and the Earl of Mountwarlock whose major-domo is "one of the few practicing werewolves left in the Midlands." Some thirty years ago, to give one more example of his inventiveness, the column purported to be a letter from Sandra to Clare Howitzer, an agony aunt. "My boyfriend, Jim, is a manic-depressive, one-legged, homosexual dwarf. He wears kinky boots, carries a flick knife, sucks ice-lollies all the time I am talking to him and is very hairy. I am wondering whether my love for him is just a passing teenage infatuation or whether we can establish a normal, adult, satisfying, psychologically complete love-relationship." To which Clare Howitzer replies, "You have got a real winner there." The satirist proves to be a prophet. At one point, I asked him what the effect of his column was. "Absolutely none at all," and he added quickly, "I don't expect to get more than a footnote in the history of literature." Jonathan Swift's Gulliver satire, the greatest in the language, has indispensable insight into human nature and the life of his period, and the same goes for Michael Wharton.

ALEXANDER YAKOVLEV
USSR: The Decisive Years
1991

A SUCCESSFUL POLITICAL CAREER in the Soviet Union depended on being with the winning side in any and every confrontation. This involved a process, largely invisible to outsiders, of allegiance and promises to the powerful, and betrayal of the friendship and principles of those without power. To the winners, rewards, to the losers punishment that ranged from dismissal and ostracism to twenty years of hard labor in the Gulag and judicial murder. Alexander Yakovlev spotted early on that Mikhail Gorbachev was a winner, which committed him to unconditional support for glasnost and perestroika, though whether he really believed in the reforms he was promoting was a constant enigma. In return, Gorbachev appointed him to leading positions including membership of the Politburo. In the final months of the Soviet Union, the head of the KGB and other old-style Communists determined to get rid of Gorbachev, if necessary by force. Defending himself from becoming a loser, Gorbachev saw fit to dismiss Yakovlev. Had the so-called counter-revolutionaries succeeded in their aborted coup of 1991, Yakovlev might well have paid with his life.

Politicians and commentators in the West were mostly disposed to take Gorbachev at his word and give him credit for making the world a better place. Whenever he appeared in some Western city, huge crowds turned out to admire and chant "Gorbi." As reform began to contradict the basic tenets of Communism, however, I expected him to accuse the United States of destabilizing the whole Soviet order and then to declare a nuclear alert, close all borders, impose military rule and have the KGB commit a massacre in some city as an exemplary warning. Repression did occur, notably in the Baltic Republics and Georgia, but on a limited scale and apparently without central organization.

My book, *The War That Never Was* (or *The Strange Death of the Soviet Union* in the American edition) addresses the question why Gorbachev had not tried to save Soviet Communism by resorting to maximum force as Karl Marx, Lenin and every previous General Secretary of the Soviet Communist Party would have advocated without a qualm. Given such an outcome, Gorbachev's successor as General Secretary might still be in the Kremlin.

One possible explanation is that Gorbachev was a man of principle who would not make himself responsible for loss of innocent life. That is the noble image of himself that Gorbachev in his retirement has been doing his best to establish, presumably with an eye on posterity. An alternative explanation is that he really believed his reforms would enable a perfected Communism to deliver on its promises. In which case, he was simply deluded. Having heard him give a lecture and having read his book, I was pretty sure that he would take a line moulded to present himself as a hero of democracy, but all the same I wrote to ask for an interview. On one of my trips to Moscow in the early 1990s, I had an appointment at the imposing offices of the Gorbachev Foundation with Anatoly Chernyayev, a Gorbachev loyalist. Gorbachev was quite willing to talk to me, he said, the fee would be twenty-five thousand dollars.

In the course of other trips in the republics that had comprised the Soviet Union or the satellites of the Soviet bloc, I had the impression from various former First Secretaries and Ideological Secretaries, all of them hardened Communists, that they were wondering why they had so tamely allowed themselves to become losers. Nobody had foreseen that reform would incite subjected people to mobilize on the streets. It was an irresistible matter of identity. Gorbachev did not give orders to open fire at Popular Front demonstrators because that would have been firing at his own program of reform. I was advised to talk to Alexander Yakovlev. Never before had a member of the Politburo come clean and admitted that Communism was a criminal enterprise from first to last, targeting the whole of humanity, not just Russia. He was known to have said that a single live bullet fired by a soldier at a mob was bound to be the end of Soviet power.

Yakovlev was always busy, in the provinces, away from his office, abroad. At one point, though, he had been invited to Israel and I flew there too. Early in the morning when we had arranged to meet, the telephone rang in the room of the hotel in Jerusalem. Announcing himself to be a professor acting for Yakovlev, a disembodied Russian voice said there would be no interview until I had settled the question of an honorarium (pronounced onn-or-rharium). One thousand dollars. I explained that it was not the custom in the West to pay for interviews. After lengthy discussion, we settled on a hundred dollars. Face to face with Yakovlev, I didn't like to raise the subject and it struck me much too late that the professor was onto a scam and Yakovlev may have known nothing about what had been done in his name. Much later still, I came across the observation of Andrei Sakharov, dissident-in-chief, that he sensed in Yakovlev "an indelible residue of Leninist doctrine." If so, it's evidence that the success of nationalism and the failure of Communism were really and truly accidental.

Postscript. Anatoly Lukyanov, a Gorbachev colleague turned opponent and sentenced to prison for his part in the aborted 1991 coup, also asked for a fee when I interviewed him. Fifty dollars.

AFTERWORD

"WHAT IS THE END OF FAME? / 'tis but to fill a certain portion of uncertain paper," said Byron who awoke one morning to find himself famous as well as somewhat tetchy. What he intended to be a wisecrack fits *Signatures* rather well. The motor of fame is fashion, which is uncertain by definition. Here and now, it's still not so difficult to turn notoriety into a synonym for fame by setting out to say or to write something shocking – "pushing back the frontiers" as progressive stars are prone to express it, preferably on television. The fate of novels and histories of serious purpose all too often is to become fodder for doctorates written by one specialist for the benefit of another. The Nobel Prize for Literature is supposedly one of civilization's building blocks but a large number of winners are completely unknown to the general public. I would propose *The Oxford Dictionary of Quotations* as the model for a critical record of fame. A nucleus of writers survives from one edition of the Dictionary to the next, and together they provide evidence of what the nation thinks of itself at any one time. But many writers feature in one edition only to disappear without trace in subsequent editions. Universal genius is a law unto itself and the uncertainty of fashion is always cruel, but the personalities presented in *Signatures* at least deserve to be remembered by generations yet unborn.

INDEX

INDEX

INDEX

DESIGN & COMPOSITION BY CARL W. SCARBROUGH